Katie Baird's moving memoir and the lessons she learned as a Peace Corps Volunteer brought me to tears. It reminded me how much our Peace Corps experiences made us citizens of the world.

> — Donna Shalala, former U.S. Secretary of Health and Human Services, former member of the U.S. House of Representatives, and former Peace Corps Volunteer (Iran 1962-64)

A truly remarkable young American finds herself in the early 1980s living for two years in an Islamic community on the Senegal River in West Africa. She is there to transmit modern rice growing techniques, about which she knows next to nothing. Baird is a spellbinding storyteller about those who she came to love and also about her own poignant, joyful, hilarious, and awkward moments there, and about how she learned more than she taught. Her globalization of the heart is an inspiring antidote to polarization and parochialism.

> — Samuel Bowles, Santa Fe Institute, and author of *The Moral Economy*

Katie Baird's story would have been gripping enough on plot alone, but add to that her lyrical, beautifully-crafted prose and her deeply-attuned ability to report what she learns in a fascinating country, makes *Growing Mangos in the Desert* a memoir not to be missed.

> — Rachael Herron, bestselling memoirist

A West African village gains universal relevance in Katie Baird's moving account. At the heart of this book is the story of an extraordinary collaboration -- one that begins in mutual wariness but develops into a testament to persistence in the face of adversity, and to the power of community organizing. Read it with hope and heartbreak, and finish it with a renewed sense of the possible.

> — Lesley Hazleton, author of *After the Prophet* and *The First Muslim*

A delightfully engaging story of misunderstandings and mishaps, achievements and disappointments, discoveries and connections, in a fascinating country that few English-language readers will know anything about at all.

> — Don Kulick, author of *A Death in the Rainforest: how a language and a way of life came to an end in Papua New Guinea*

Katherine Baird's memoir describes a young woman's adaptation to a completely foreign place, and her commitment to improving the lives of those in a Mauritanian village in the Fuuta. Yet her memoir also attests to the strong friendship that developed between two people separated by age and culture. For both of these reasons it deserves to be read.

> — Adama Gnokane, retired Professor of History, University of Nouakchott

Katie Baird's memoir, *Growing Mangos in the Desert* transports readers to a land few have visited, and to a time and place that no longer exist. With humor and deep respect, she describes the impressions and experiences of an American living in the village of Civé, coming to realize that sometimes 'the helper' has far more to gain than the people being 'helped'. Katie's memoir brings new ideas, new realities, and new ways of understanding to the world around us.

— Nancy Rolock, Henry L. Zucker Professor in Social Work Practice, Case Western Reserve University

Growing Mangos in the Desert by Katie Baird is an amazing first-person account of young Katie's journey to Civé, a small rural village at the very edge of Mauritania.

Katie Baird takes the reader along on her spell-binding journey into a world of abject poverty that slowly reveals the rich depths of tradition and friendships that cross all boundaries of race, religion, gender, and formal education. Neither her Peace Corps training nor the other volunteers prepared her for the realities of being dropped in a society where she was barely able to communicate, and the only source of water was the river that separates Mauritania from Senegal—a river that turned into stagnant pools separated by foul-smelling sludge in the equatorial heat of summer.

Katie's meteoric growth as she assimilates into the village and the mounting tension as she and the village chief navigate the mine fields of politics and the red tape of aid organizations is as exciting as that of a well-planned thriller—and even more heart stopping because it's all real.

— Dixiane Hallaj, author of *Breakfast in Palestine*

Growing Mangos in the Desert

Growing Mangos in the Desert

A Memoir of Life
in a Mauritanian Village

Katherine Baird

Apprentice
House Press
Loyola University Maryland

First Edition

Casebound ISBN: 978-1-62720-361-6
Paperback ISBN: 978-1-62720-362-3
Ebook ISBN: 978-1-62720-363-0

Printed in the United States of America

Design by Maggie Beams
Edited by Katie McDonnell
Promotion Plan by Hannah Aebli
Map by Olivia Snell

Published by Apprentice House Press

Apprentice House Press
Loyola University Maryland
4501 N. Charles Street
Baltimore, MD 21210
410.617.5265
www.ApprenticeHouse.com
info@ApprenticeHouse.com

For Dave, Ben, and James

Contents

Prologue

In 1984, I settled into a small Mauritanian village located along a 300-mile stretch of the Senegal River referred to as the Fuuta Toro—Fuuta for short. As a Peace Corps volunteer, my mission in Civé was to help villagers grow rice in new irrigated perimeters built with foreign dollars. These perimeters represented international communities' help in tackling a two-decade long drought that ravaged the region. Unfortunately, my assignment was not particularly well thought out, as even with a crash course in rice cultivation, I knew desperately little about a livelihood on which so many here depended. As if that wasn't enough, the words and actions of all those in Civé swirled about, leaving me as baffled as did the posse of donkeys that arrived at my gate each morning braying urgent messages my way.

Decades later, I marvel at my pluck, plunging as I did into the unknown, convinced that with good intentions I would make a difference in this suffering land.

And yet, against all odds I did make a difference. Or so at least I thought.

In 1987, I left the village of Civé, happy with my accomplishments as I headed for a master's program in agricultural economics. My plan was to return to Africa, maybe even this exact bend in the river, and continue working to lift poor rural communities like Civé up from poverty.

But like many bright plans of youth, mine were first dimmed by detours, then snuffed out by the passage of time. A few years after I left Mauritania, a violent civil war broke out and my accomplishments there suffered the fate of clothes hanging to dry as the cartwheeling Harmattan winds storm through. Eventually, my master's degree segued into a PhD, then came a wonderful husband, two darling boys, and a coveted faculty position at the University of Washington.

One March day in 2012, I sat in my living room grading papers. The phone rang. Five minutes later, the call ended. My chest ached. News had reached me that my dear friend in Civé, Mamadou Konaté, just died.

For days I silently mourned Mamadou's passage. The fact that he would have no obituary stung. If anyone deserved one, it was Mamadou. So, I began writing a eulogy. I spent days scouring my basement for the tattered spiral notebooks that served as daily companions during my time in Civé. One after another, I read the vivid detail they contained and relived my thirty stressful and emotional months in Civé.

To my surprise, one of the first entries I scribbled made note of some imposing man named Mamadou Konaté who had just visited my hut. His rude manners had irritated me, especially after he announced that I would bring fruit trees to his village. I penned with confidence my determination to resist him, as well as all future demands I was sure would be forthcoming from this arrogant fellow.

In one of my last entries, written after I had worked tirelessly by Mamadou's side to secure Civé's new fruit trees, I recorded a visit to the rocky uprising cradling the village, a place named Dow Hayre. A friend from the regional capital had come to say goodbye, and we were enjoying the sweeping view of Civé below with the flat dusty nation of Senegal spreading to the south. I told him of my intent to write a book about Civé.

"Put a picture of this view on the cover," Hyder advised me as he scooped up a handful of small laterite rocks, and then took a deep breath as he scanned the horizon.

Rarely do any of us from rich countries get to know the poor in poor ones, except maybe to hear that they are trying to infiltrate our (increasingly walled) borders. For most of us, they remain nameless and numerous, often depicted in newspaper articles and donation pitches as victims desperate for change.

I am lucky. When I think of them, I see faces, feel characters, and hear deep peals of laughter. To them, my unexpected appearance amidst them was probably like that of a swaddled infant left by some wayward pelican. I was curious, odd, and brought great hope of new entertainment. What choice did they have but to shrug at my appearance, then make me part of the local scene?

And so, they did.

Decades later, I now awake each morning to Facebook messages from the children and grandchildren of my friends in Civé, asking if I spent the night in peace.

By writing this book, I hope the reader will also come to wonder if those in Civé spent the night in peace. I also hope to convey how the deep inequalities that mark our planet shape both our own privileged lives, as well as the lives of those in places like Civé.

Mostly, though, I hope to have provided Mamadou with the obituary his life deserves.

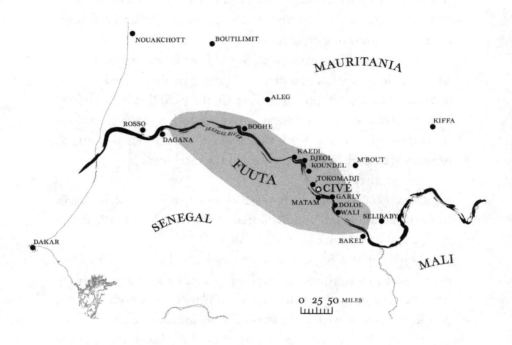

part one
LOWWOL

Chapter 1

Curried Goat

I no longer recall the message Neil bravely delivered to us that hot, muggy South Carolinian afternoon while the lunch in my stomach rumbled.

Then Neil did it: he pinned Macho down, yanked back his head, and deftly slit open his throat. Dark red blood gushed into a carefully placed bucket.

Standing mute, my legs wobbled, time froze, and in wide-eyed horror, I locked eyes with Macho as the goat delivered an unmistakable message: we had betrayed him. Slowly his pupils darkened, his spurting blood gurgled, and his body slackened until mercifully, his eyes spoke no more.

The truth is, though, that we did more than betray Macho that afternoon; we ate him. Or pretended to, at least.

Macho's execution had been our suggestion, us being the young and eager group of Peace Corps trainees standing that day before Neil and his beloved Macho. We'd heard that Neil's goat curry would follow Macho's beheading, but I don't think any of us believed Neil would follow through with our 'turn-Macho-into-stew-meat' suggestion. After all, Macho was Neil's pet, always trotting over whenever Neil silently summoned him. Over the rest of that restless day, I became sure that Neil could never execute Macho.

But alas. He could.

Macho's beheading occurred in the summer of 1984. I had gathered with a dozen other soon-to-be Peace Corps volunteers in

Frogmore, South Carolina. A small corner of American foreign policy, the Peace Corps recruits college graduates for two-year stints in developing countries to provide assistance, and hopefully bolster the image of Americans abroad. These four weeks of stateside training marked the beginning of my three-month preparation for our upcoming positions as agricultural experts in Mauritania.

Over the course of that long-ago July, we suffered bravely through South Carolina's heat and humidity; the locale purposely chosen, we were told, for its similarity with the West African climate to which we were headed. Each morning, we awoke to a full day of long hot farming sessions, each held under sprawling trees or within quaint wood buildings constructed by missionaries a century earlier to educate newly freed slaves.

Applicants to the Peace Corps are asked what 'expertise' they might bring as a volunteer. I probably checked 'none' or 'any,' I don't recall which. Why I was selected for a position in agriculture, I will never know. Maybe it was because of an even more mystifying choice during my junior year of high school, when I joined our school's Future Farmers of America club. My only agricultural experience up to that point took place over a boring weekend when for fifty cents an hour, I pulled up nut grass from a neighbor's weedy yard. Or the time I grew strawberries in our backyard, only to watch them wither and die from my overzealous doses of fertilizer. Whoever said there can never be too much of a good thing didn't know about fertilizer.

Nevertheless, I highlighted my membership in Kailua High School's FFA club on my Peace Corps application, thinking it would look impressive. Yet I omitted the unhappy detail of finishing dead last in our state's annual FFA Soil Judging Contest, as I never could distinguish a silty soil from a clay one. 'Better luck next time,' was all our FFA advisor Mr. Okamoto had said at the time, secretly hoping, I'm sure, that in my case there would be no next time. Little did he know that a few short years hence I would be advising farmers in another country on how to grow their life-sustaining crops.

While I really was not suited for agriculture, I doubt I was better prepared for the other typical professions that volunteers signed up for: health care, fishing, teaching English, or digging wells. Soon I discovered that no one in our tight-knit group at Frogmore knew much more than I did about producing food from anything other than paper bills. At least I was not alone, and we all trained for our agricultural posts from the ground up, planting vegetables in neat rows and watching them sprout, distinguishing the nasty pesticides from the acceptable, and beheading chickens without tools (step on the head and yank the body up, although as I can unfortunately attest, this does not always work). We also studied French in preparation for our upcoming posts in Mauritania.

It was during this training that we witnessed Macho's brutal demise. Macho had become a loyal friend, delighting in any attention we paid him, whether it was scratching his head, thumping his rear end, or simply chasing him around our spacious grounds. Yet, once Neil was pressed on whether he could ever really 'do Macho in,' he probably felt compelled to demonstrate his oft-repeated lesson: Goats are food, not pets.

My role in that muggy South Carolinian afternoon affair, which ended with Macho gently simmering away in a gigantic cast-iron pot amidst an oversized dose of curry paste, was not one I could easily forget. That night at dinner, we awkwardly cleared our throats, shuffled spicy chunks of Macho around our plates, and avoided all eye contact with Neil. While Neil's lesson stuck, that event haunted me. To this day, stored vividly in my brain alongside memories of my first bicycle, and the birth of my two sons, rests Macho's final moments.

Our complicity in that slaying was just one of the experiences we Frogmore trainees bonded over as we battled the heat and oversized mosquitos, grumbled at early morning language classes, and complained when fans in our sultry rooms refused to spin.

After four punishing weeks followed by a brief graduation ceremony, our trainers finally whisked us off in vans to the Savannah Airport to begin our long trip to West Africa. Then they hurried back to welcome the next 'aggie' trainees headed for some other distant African locale in dire need of youthful American expertise.

***

"Where would you like to go?" my Peace Corps adviser had asked me early in the application process. "Africa? South America?"

"Anywhere, really, send me anywhere," I answered, although for reasons I could not articulate, I hoped for a post in Africa.

"Mozambique? Kathmandu?" he challenged.

"Sure. I'll even go to Timbuktu," I returned with a chuckle. In my mind, Timbuktu was some mythical desert oasis, a place existing alongside other legendary locales like Atlantis, El Dorado, or Shangri-La.

Several months later, my acceptance letter arrived bearing news of my posting to Mauritania. At first, I thought I was headed to some remote island known for exotic animals. Lemurs, I imagined, how cool. But then a map tumbled out of the large envelope, outlining an angular country in Africa's northwest corner. Images of lemurs quickly faded, but none replaced them. With furrowed brow, I studied the map, recognizing nothing on it until my eyes, desperate for any familiar marking, wandered beyond Mauritania's eastern border: Timbuktu.

I began reading what I could about Mauritania at our local library. There wasn't much; the one-column description in *Encyclopedia Britannica* noted its physical size and the number of camels, shared detail on its fishing and iron industries, and informed the reader that Arabic was the national language and Islam its religion. Of course, the country's official name, The Islamic Republic of Mauritania, should tip anyone off to that last fact. Since its independence from France in 1960, Mauritania had hitched its identity to the Arab world and largely disassociated itself from its unwelcome colonial master and the large cluster of countries to the east and south which today make up francophone West Africa.

I also learned that Mauritania is a vast country, nearly twice as big as Texas, with three-quarters of its territory located within the rolling dunes, rocky plateaus, and parched scrabble of the Sahara Desert. Here centuries earlier, a nomadic Berber-Arabic population, today called Moors, made its living raising camels and trading over the sinuous trade routes that wound through far-flung oasis towns. The names Moor and Mauritania date back to when the ancient Romans called the Berbers of northern Africa *Mauri*, and the lands they inhabited *Mauretania*. The label Moor eventually came to refer to the Muslim Berber-Arabs then occupying Northern Africa and Spain. Nowadays, 'Moors' refers to those who speak an Arabic dialect called Hassaniya, a group primarily living in the country today known as Mauritania.

Aside from its northern deserts, Mauritania also consists of a southern quarter that forms the western portion of Africa's Sahel, a semi-arid band below the Sahara and above the Sudanian Savannah that stretches from the Atlantic Ocean in the west to the Red Sea in the east. *Sahel* is Arabic for coast. Whoever named it that did so for good reason, as those reaching it after crossing the Sahara must have been as jubilant as long-distance mariners catching their first sight of shore.

I was going to Mauritania as an agricultural expert, which meant the country offered limited opportunities for work. Some rare oases dotted the north. Other than that, Mauritania's arable land is pretty much limited to the floodplains along the Senegal River, which serves as its boundary with its neighbor to the south, Senegal.

It was there in the south where I was to be dispatched to begin a journey and kindle relationships that remain with me to this day.

Chapter 2

Dakar to Nouakchott

I'm not sure why, but during our flight from the U.S. to Dakar, Senegal, memories of my childhood dog Cher flooded my thoughts. I recalled a long-ago summer that dragged on a bit too long. In boredom, I devised a plan to take Cher on daily walks to the backside of our local middle school. There, under a blossoming monkey pod tree, I trotted her up the outdoor stage to begin her training. My goal was to prepare her for entry into an upcoming dog contest, an activity she proved singularly unfit, not to mention unqualified, for.

"Cher is a mutt, not a pure bred," mom gently explained one day after I'd told her about our training sessions.

"But she is all black," I protested.

"Actually, she has a little white spot on her chest," my mom reminded me through a stifled smile.

"But not big enough to notice," I persisted, my voice trailing off.

I had an unnatural attachment to that dog. No one else in my family quite shared this bond, probably because they saw her as the nervous, timid, and dense dog she was. There was, for instance, the time she jumped from my arms and hit the pavement as we drove down our street. Once she hurled herself through our screen door when thunder struck. And whenever we drove through a tunnel, Cher always dove under the front seat and howled.

Finally, I recalled that hot afternoon when I stood in our driveway awaiting my mom's return from the vet. She drove up. My eyes welled. She shut the car door, hugged me, then wordlessly handed me Cher's ratty collar.

***

I wiped Cher's last lick off my cheek as our plane descended then lumbered down Dakar's tarmac to head toward a building resembling a military barrack. Moments later, a blast of hot, musty, and humid air greeted me as I stood at the top of our open plane door. The air was thick with dust and smelled of jet fuel; below men were shouting in some incomprehensible language as they tossed luggage out of our plane's belly. My knees wobbled and stomach growled as I descended, and for some reason my pants and shirt felt two sizes too small. Once in the small, crowded airport, some appointed guide tensely ushered the small group of us outside. Soon we were whisked away to a spacious hotel in Dakar's block-long posh district.

From a very early age Africa had fascinated me. I'm pretty sure this traced back to it being the most exotic of the locales depicted in the *National Geographics* gracing my family's living room table. At the age of ten, our church hosted a visiting pastor from Tanzania, and I recall being mesmerized by his foreign looks and vibrant robes and struck by the contrast between my comfortable life and the impoverished ones he described.

Maybe Africa drew me, too, because I always felt like an outsider in my own surroundings. I grew up in a small town in Hawai'i, arriving at the age of three after my parents, four kids in tow, moved to escape Seattle's cold winter rains. While my red hair and freckles stood out in this tropical paradise, I learned to adjust. I enjoyed a childhood running barefoot outside, with Cher by my side, and swimming in warm waters a short jaunt away.

Still, the world beyond always intrigued me. After high school, I enrolled at UC Berkeley, and soon came to love my economics classes. I took each one on offer covering the challenges in poor countries, and then after graduation arranged an internship with the U.S. Agency for International Development in Washington, D.C., followed by another across town. Yet the problems of poor countries stuck, so at nighttime I took up a letter-writing campaign to convince some overseas organization to hire me. This gained me a desk piled high with kindly-worded rejection letters, but no job. One evening that pile tumbled to the floor, and I dusted off my application to the Peace Corps, filled it out, and mailed it in.

Now, finally, my dream of working overseas had come true.

I had often wondered what it would be like to actually *be* in Africa. Dread and horror were not the reactions I had imagined. During our one evening in Dakar, I joined others in venturing out beyond our gated confines, my body still strangely uncooperative, confined as it was in clothes that no longer felt like mine. Hot sultry air greeted us, smelling of both diesel fuel and rotting pineapples. Discord blared everywhere: urgent car horns, a growing brawl over a dead car blocking traffic, and the machine-gun like fire of a jack hammer, all of which was set to the thumping of countless boom boxes parading the streets. A block on and the smell of rotting pineapples gave way to urine and decaying garbage. We skirted open pools of sewage draining from nearby residences while people of all ages began assailing us. Some were wracked by polio and dragging limp bodies around, rubber slippers on hands as they pleaded in English, French, German, or simply with their eyes for something, anything. Young kids with distended bellies wearing torn and stained clothes clutched ours, their palm up at the slightest indication that we noticed. My thoughts raced everywhere but I could not corral even one into words. How, I wondered, had National Geographic missed this? And why?

It was horrifying to me, both the tragedy of the lives around me, and then the recognition that this fact had to literally stare me in the face for me to realize it. My clothes tugged and the night heat pressed. After consuming a shawarma and lukewarm beer in a dark cafe, I soon joined friends streaming back to the air-conditioned comfort of our hotel.

Early next morning, our trip continued north. Two dozen of us obediently piled into Land Rovers and off we sped on the 250-mile trip north to the Mauritanian capital of Nouakchott.

Mid-day, the sun burned down as the wide, but dirt brown Senegal River flowed steadily before us, bringing with it the smell of mud and a faint but welcome breeze.

Several of us stood taking in the river, our gazes drawn to our new homeland beyond. Beside me, Michelle scanned the activity on the river's banks before plopping a stick of gum in her mouth. Forever cheerful, Michelle had the endearing trait of always speaking her mind.

"Where's the bridge?" she asked, turning to our driver who was now atop our vehicle loosening the net that secured our luggage.

"There's the African Bridge," he replied, pointing to a rickety, jam-packed, raft-like boat just then pulling up to a makeshift dock. He started to toss down pieces of luggage.

"Ha," burst out Michelle. She caught her bag, then waited for the driver to descend so she could hand him a stick of gum. "That's some bridge. Thanks."

Shortly we were cast out onto the river, the air filled with the sputtering engine of our "African Bridge." I listened for signs of the motor's final gasp while watching the river splash at our feet. The sight of Alex, a volunteer from Massachusetts, calmed me as he, nose down, continued to plow through an old geology book on the Sahara Desert that seemed never to leave his side.

Soon enough, we were trudging up Rosso, Mauritania's long, gently sloping mud banks and heading toward a single dirty cement building sporting Mauritania's green flag, with the word '*douane*' (customs) handwritten above its open door. Ten minutes later, our passport stamps were in order.

"Go in peace," a friendly customs agent said before stretching out on a straw mat to sip his tea.

Rosso was a small town with dirty, wide roads filled with huge craters created by the combination of torrential rains and the frequent passage of twenty-ton trucks. This city was essentially the only place in Mauritania where overland shipments could enter the country, and I watched in awe as a steady flow of truck traffic awkwardly swayed northward, each vehicle swollen with rice, wheat, dried milk, cooking oil, cloth, macaroni, barbed wire, potatoes, and bags of cement that, like us, had just perilously crossed the river atop our African Bridge.

Rosso's roads also prominently featured gigantic rubbish piles around which the town's few vehicles had to negotiate. Pawing goats rummaged through each, in competition with skinny boys on the lookout for a tin can or some promising throwaway from which to fashion a toy. Meanwhile, proud residents incongruently graced the streets in their lovely starched white and blue gowns, seemingly oblivious to the stench and poverty all around.

With a look of confusion, I turned to Nancy, an empathetic volunteer from the Midwest who had already become like a personal counselor to one and all. She returned my quizzical look with a nod.

"I think I might like to wear beautiful clothes too, if I had to live in such a place," Nancy pondered aloud. An image arose of my mom carefully choosing her day's outfit before heading off to work.

"Yeah, me too," I responded, and then smiled at an elegantly dressed woman headed our way.

After lunch, new Land Rovers with fresh drivers appeared, and off we headed to Nouakchott. Once on the road, Alex took up instructing us on our surroundings. At a particularly non-descript spot, some rocky outcroppings off in the distance captured his attention.

"That's sedimentation from the Cenozoic period. This whole area was once all underwater. Look at those dolomitic uplifts!" he exclaimed. Probably like everyone else, all I could see was a dry, bleak landscape.

Even in this hostile environment, though, a living room-sized garden occasionally appeared alongside a home fabricated from empty red, white, and blue burlap bags that formerly contained U.S. food aid.

"I think we came to the wrong country," commented Mark, a tall, gangly volunteer from Connecticut, as he began cleaning his glasses. It was hard to disagree, although Janet, who had secured the seat in front of Mark, never let gloom set in for long.

"Heck," she said, hanging over her seat. "It ain't Kansas. And I'm GLAD of that." Janet was happily escaping the conservative confines of the Midwest and had a great knack for knowing when a bit of humor was called for.

Except for such isolated dwellings, not much lay between Rosso and Nouakchott. The paved road pointed due north, crossing over land that was flat as a pancake and unvaried in its orange sand and scraggy shade-less bushes. With each mile, our dusty hard-packed surroundings with its thin layer of sand slowly transformed into mesmerizing rolling dunes: the Sahara.

Like everyone else, I sat glued to my window, in my case alternating between excitement and uncertainty, jumbled together with the discomfort of realizing my gift of being born American. Images of my world, not the one around me, entered awkwardly into my thoughts as we bounded northward. I carefully inspected the strange orange cashew fruits I'd purchased in Rosso, turning one over before pulling the cashew out from its bottom.

Soon dusk arrived and Mauritania's capital approached. Sand slums peppered the roadside, each from afar looking like a junkyard. Yet as we drew near, homes took shape from the agglomeration of sheets, plastic bags, corrugated metal, and tarps. Then you could pick out a goat tethered to a stick, and scrawny boys playing with a piece of cloth wadded into a soccer ball. I picked up my cashew fruit, now missing its cashew, broke it open, and tasted its soft insides.

"La sécheresse," declared our driver.

The Drought. One of the worst in modern history. Now, finally, we were seeing what that meant. I finished my fruit, then unconsciously began another.

Chapter 3

Nouakchott

Our convoy entered Nouakchott's sprawling outskirts as glowing embers of a desert sunset greeted us like a welcoming host. On we drove along sand-covered lanes lined with repetitive sand-colored concrete buildings. Amidst the sky's dwindling light, before us arose a lonely minaret, which gave the city a distinct Arabic aura.

Compared with Dakar, Nouakchott's roads were wide, its trees short and spare, the city spacious, and its streets deserted. The flat city, defenseless against stiff winds that kicked up the flowing robes of the few pedestrians about, was marked by long, moody shadows. With no traffic lights, no stop signs, and no cars to slow us down, we sped onward along a wide boulevard named after some Arabic hero or dictator, I wasn't sure which. The driver turned westward, then carefully maneuvered around a mound of sand.

In low gear we passed a large lot pitched with a low tent, its Moor residents lounging within. Our chauffeur then abruptly turned, stopped, and tapped his horn in front of a huge metal entryway. A minute later, double iron doors creaked open, and into a spacious courtyard we pulled. I blinked at the lush and fragrant trees, bright electricity, and festive music now enveloping us.

"Must have been good," remarked Connie seconds later as she cheerfully grabbed her bag from a rack above me while pointing to the remains of my half dozen cashew fruits.

"I guess," I said with surprise. I gathered up the skins and raw cashews around me and slipped on my backpack.

So began the in-country portion of our training, one led by out-going volunteers who would steer us through lessons on Mauritania's culture, languages, customs, and politics. I and five others shortly learned that we would serve as extension agents with Mauritania's Ministry of Rural Development, an organization known by its French acronym of SONADER. We would help villagers grow a new crop, rice, in newly established irrigated perimeters. We'd heard about this in Frogmore, though I think we also figured someone had mixed up Mauritania with Mauritius or maybe Madagascar. Rice doesn't grow in the desert.

Except that it actually does. At least in Mauritania. And the six of us were destined to help villagers grow it. So twice weekly for three hours, we six attended classes in freshly swept rooms lined with chalkboards, where we crammed in as much information as we could on how to grow rice in the desert.

"At least you grew up in Hawai'i," sighed Jim, a fellow SONADER trainee after one particularly incomprehensible session. "You've seen pineapple and sugar cane fields. Not much tropical grows in Chicago." After a pause, Jim added with a laugh, "Except gigantic cockroaches that is!"

Unfortunately for me, my only proximity to tropical agriculture occurred when friends and I—machete in hand and an idling car nearby—dashed into pineapple fields, then sped off with eyes on the rear-view mirror.

Outside of scheduled class time, our trainers soon began pulling us aside to talk about topics not on our daily agenda. Such as the countless ways that the local Peace Corps staff let down its volunteers. The director, it turned out, was a self-important, self-absorbed man.

Our director also seemed not to notice that we were actually in the Sahara Desert.

"Who the heck wears a three-piece suit and tie when it's 100 degrees out?" asked Jeff while sprawled on his back. "And I bet it's wool!"

There was also the Peace Corps' second-in-command, Stan. While a nice guy, he too was pretty useless. During the first months in my village of Civé, I wrote detailed weekly letters to Stan, asking urgent questions: What is the nutritional value of manioc and how might I get some? Would amaranth grow here? What about leeks? What did he know about improved varieties of corn? Or about making sun-dried tomatoes? How long before soured milk goes bad?

I drew pictures of insects that were devastating the village's cabbage and asked if he knew what they were. I inquired after the pesticide HCH that everyone in Civé used as an all-purpose bug killer, some even dousing their gardens with it the day before carting vegetables off to market. So common was its use that during my first months in Civé, I carefully avoided eating all vegetables that grew above ground.

My steady dispatches to Stan ended once I realized he read not a single one, preoccupied as he was with our director's priorities. Once I found Stan selecting new carpet for the director's office. Another time he was helping him prepare for an upcoming interview with Voice of America. Then there was the day Stan spent scouring Nouakchott's markets for a second lock to his boss' office door.

Volunteers, it appeared, got in the way of the real business of Peace Corps Mauritania.

To be fair, the drama those staff members provided proved wildly entertaining, and in a place where a Kung Fu movie in Arabic with no subtitles constituted entertainment, we were happy to share embellished versions of each encounter.

But once in the village, the Peace Corps' shortcomings no longer amused.

There was the time, for instance, that the director ordered the Peace Corps' chauffeur Demba to retrieve me in my village without telling Demba why.

"Why you here?" I asked with alarm, when a few days later Demba located me out in distant fields.

"Don't know," he responded with a welcoming smile as he pulled candies out of his pocket to distribute to the gathering kids. "Stan only said to bring you back to Nouakchott."

I was soon aboard Demba's truck plowing through sandy roads to Nouakchott. For twenty-four hours I listened to Demba's soothing words and ever-present Baaba Maal cassette, while worrying myself sick about loved ones back home. One-by-one I grieved for each, imagining how they had met their fate. For my younger sister, the answer was simple: She was a health food nut and had overdosed on the brewers yeast she added to every single dish, something I had steadfastly warned her against. And now, she no longer could heed my advice.

Once in Nouakchott, and before Demba had his truck in park, I dashed upstairs to Stan's office.

"Oh. You made it," he chuckled as I breathlessly entered his office. "You're overdue for your typhoid booster."

Intense relief passed over me as images of my loved ones' corpses faded. Noticing my lingering presence, Stan added, "Becky is off today. She'll be in tomorrow. You can come get your shot then."

Rising anger crowded out relief, and in a confused state I turned to leave. Dizzily, I clutched the staircase rail, and saw Demba, prayer beads dangling by his side, looking my way.

"I needed a shot," I told him once I reached the ground floor.

Demba glanced upward, thanked Allah, then gave me one of the few hugs I ever saw a Mauritanian man give a woman in public.

Fortunately, there were numerous bright spots among the Nouakchott crew. Sall, the cook, was everyone's favorite. Whenever he served a meal, Mauritanian food at lunch placed on floor mats and eaten with hands from common bowls, and Western food at dinner dished up on plates bracketed by silverware, he'd circle about to make sure we found his meal delicious. He'd inquire about our favorite dinners back home, and lo and behold, there one would be on the table next evening.

And there was, of course, the chauffeur Demba. Demba was a solidly built man with a broad face, soft eyes, and a ready laugh. He was a bit more reserved than your typical Mauritanian, but once you began learning his native language of Pulaar, Demba quickly revealed his generous, thoughtful, even gregarious side, and would secretly drive us budding Pulaar speakers across town to save us a hot, dusty walk.

For the swearing-in ceremony that converted us from trainees into full-fledged volunteers, I did what many of my compatriots did and dressed in local attire. The ceremony took place on manicured lawns within the lush gardens of the Presidential Palace; once the ceremony was over, we paraded up to the palace for a photo-op with Mauritania's President Mohamed Khouna Ould Haidalla.

"Keyti!" Demba beckoned me over just as I was about to ascend the palace stairs. He ushered me alongside some freshly clipped oleander bushes. "Here," he said as he turned my way, and then to my great surprise, reached over to retie my head scarf—surely the first and only time he had ever helped an adult female with a task akin to tying shoelaces.

"There," he said, smiling as he made the last tuck. "Much better."

That day Demba became my favorite.

Chapter 4

Six Months

In addition to learning details about our upcoming assignment—in my case on growing rice in the desert—we also learned languages. French was followed by one of Mauritania's four local languages. Half of us new recruits began to learn the Arabic dialect spoken by Mauritania's Moors, a language called *Hassaniya*.

Like many in these parts of Africa, Moor society is socially rigid based on birth. It consists of two main social groups: Bidhan Moors and Haratin Moors. *Bidhan*, the so-called "White Moors," are an Arab-Berber people who make up about a third of the country's population. They descended from the indigenous Berbers of the Sahara and the conquering Arabs who arrived around 700 AD. The language Hassaniya is a dialect of Arabic containing remnants of the Berber language once spoken among the people of the northwest Sahara.

Mauritania's Bidhan Moors used to live a nomadic life, eking a living out of the desert. Yet sometimes they captured residents to the south who joined their slave caste. These *Haratin* Moors, commonly called Black Moors, tend to have darker skin. Historically, these Haratin were enslaved and servile members of Moor society. Today, the importance of ancestral lineage remains in Moor society, and the once serf-like status of the Haratin often lingers. Officially, Mauritania has outlawed slavery. Unoffically, up to 10 percent of the population may be in some type of bound servitude. A non-profit monitoring slavery worldwide recently found Mauritania to have the world's highest share of its population enslaved.

Mauritania's three other local languages, Pulaar, Wolof, and Soninke, are spoken by the black Africans occupying the country's southern reaches. Since my posting was to be in the middle portion of the Senegal River valley, I began learning Pulaar. This part of the river valley, which Pulaars call *The Fuuta*, stretches for around 300 miles along both sides of the mid-river valley, from the town of Bakel in the east to Dagana in the west. The Fuuta also extends five to ten miles north and south of the river, its northern border in Mauritania merging into the windswept, semi-arid, and much less fertile Sahel, and beyond that the Sahara.

In Pulaar, the word Fuuta translates into 'country,' a label that vastly understates Pulaars' deep attachment to their Senegal Valley floodplain. The herding ancestors of today's Pulaar residents migrated here from the north a thousand years ago, perhaps crowded out by the southern spread of nomadic Moor tribes. Roving clans of these ancestral herders, called Fulbe, eventually abandoned their semi-nomadic lifestyle to cultivate the river basin's rich alluvial soils. Others among these early inhabitants eventually spread east across the Sahel, and south into present-day Guinea, Mali, Nigeria, Chad, Burkina Faso, Niger, and the Ivory Coast—wherever the dry heat would protect their Zebu cattle from deadly parasites. Descendants of these original herders are today variously referred to as Pulaar, Fula, Fulani, Peuhl, Fulbe, Woodaabe, or Fulfulde, depending on where in the Sahel you are. These groups, many of which today remain semi-nomadic herders, all speak some variant of this language Pulaar.

And then there were the small handful of volunteers who began learning Mauritania's two other local languages. Wolof, a language widely spoken in Senegal, is the main language spoken in Mauritania's southwest corner, while Soninke is spoken along the upper reaches of the Senegal River and into neighboring Mali.

For an English speaker, Pulaar is a complicated language. The adjective 'big' for instance, can be said a dozen different ways, depending on what is being called big. There are twenty-one different classes of nouns, each with its own pronoun. Surprisingly, Pulaars economize on the pronoun for people, as whether the subject is female or male, the pronoun 'o' stands in for both. Recognizing the singular form of a word (*faɗo* for shoe) doesn't mean you'll recognize the plural (*paɗe* for shoes).

Same for verbs, as these change too, depending on if the action is done in the company of someone, didn't occur, is a passive construction, is reciprocal, or if the action involves going someplace—'I buygoing,' for instance, not 'I am going to buy.' Pulaars prize a mastery of their language, probably because doing so is so difficult. All of this was head spinning, but Pulaars proved easy to please: just say 'hello' to one, and often, after a few blinks you will be invited to join them for tea.

***

While it wasn't easy learning Mauritania's languages, our Mauritanian instructors were patient and engaging. And just fun. One evening, our instructors announced they were going to stage a performance for us. After dinner, we gathered in an open courtyard, and after a bit they strolled out, half of them dressed as one of us, the other half as themselves. A tall Pulaar man by the name of Fara Ba was in the former category. He stood before us with hair somehow weirdly colored orange. He carried a cardboard surfboard, had flowers tacked to a shirt, and waved to the audience using the 'hang loose' signal I'd taught him. Another man was dressed in an oversized floppy hat, had large looping earrings, chewed gum, and kept a hand on one hip: Michelle. A tall lanky professor carried a thick book, and wore borrowed shorts, Birkenstocks and fake glasses, an apt rendition of Alex.

After a bit of theatrics, liberally interrupted by tearful laughter on stage, some chairs were produced and the "Americans" before us sat down across from the Mauritanians. Reading from index cards, the Americans began teaching the Mauritanians English.

Gradually the plot unfolded: the setting was America, a place to which these Mauritanians had been sent as volunteers to help 'save' America. The Americans before us were the volunteers' instructors.

What skills were these Mauritanians coming to America to impart? How to pray five times a day; how to make Mauritanian tea; and most importantly, how to just hang out. English lessons began, and soon the Mauritanian volunteers were learning to communicate the essentials: "Time is *not* money," "Take it easy baby," "If God wills it," and "Let it all hang out." Amidst prolonged hysterics on and off stage, in heavily accented English each 'volunteer' sought to master their lessons.

That evening, our sides and cheeks ached. Yet once in bed, I couldn't sleep. Some part of me realized an essential truth in their performance: the humble, hospitable, and easy-going Mauritanians we had come to know probably had more to teach us than we did them.

***

Our instructors taught us more than grammar, common greetings, and the importance of laughter: they also introduced us to other mainstays of a Mauritanian lifestyle, the most important of which is the drinking of tea. Just about everyone in Mauritania drinks tea once a day, and most will drink it as often as possible. One takes a very large dose of black Chinese tea leaves, pouring this into a miniature tea pot full of water to slowly cook over smoldering charcoal. Once the tea boils, you add copious amounts of sugar and, if available, a generous fist full of fresh mint leaves. The tea ritual lasts for three rounds; for each, one repeatedly pours and re-pours the syrup-like drink from as high a height as possible. Done right, the tea tumbles noisily and seductively into shot glasses, a thick yellow head making it appear like miniature glasses of hot amber beer.

The first round is bold and full-bodied, the sugar just cutting the tea's bitterness. Then the teapot is refilled, and the process repeated. Thirty minutes on, a second glass is produced, the black tea's sharpness now tamed by the sugar. By the third and final round, you're drinking a sugary tea-flavored dessert, the perfect cap to the long ritual.

And indeed, a ritual it is. The art of tea brewing entails more than ensuring that each cup is right. You must also achieve the exact progression of flavors from bittersweet to sweet, an accomplishment that requires both skill and judgment, as the temperature must be precise and the timing between rounds exact.

"I married my wife because of her tea," confessed a professor to us one afternoon with a laugh as we lounged on a thin matress called *matlas* between rounds.

"Yep, I would too," piped in Mark, although by now we all knew that despite his assertions to the contrary, Mark would not be taking a female as a life mate. But still, Mark's point was true; for those of us now happily addicted to Mauritanian tea, skill in making it was a very reasonable criteria for choosing one's life partner.

Our professors also instructed us on another vital feature of Mauritanian life: the social graces of communal eating. Mid-day we squatted in small circles around a large bowl. Someone would quietly bless the food, then we would dig into fish-flavored oily rice. With your right hand, you form compact balls of rice mixed with whatever was piled in the bowl's center: fish, cabbage, carrots, goat, or peanut sauce. While eating you engage in steady conversation with those around you, stopping only to quickly plop a well-formed ball into your mouth, or toss a particularly plump morsel on your side of the bowl to someone else. Then you return your hand to the bowl for more rice, all repeated until the bowl runs dry, and someone wanders off to find hot coals for tea.

Both in and out of the classroom, our conversations with professors ranged widely. They stretched from the treatment of

African Americans in the U.S. to dealing with family members you didn't like; from whether one should give money to beggars on Nouakchott's streets to what it is like to be drunk.

After we were sure we could, we inquired into the more personal topics we'd heard much about yet weren't ready to believe—such as whether it was true that young Mauritanian girls had part of their genitalia excised.

"Yes, this is true," said a man by the name of Sow. "We think women are too active if we don't."

"And something grows that shouldn't," added another shaking his head disapprovingly.

At this point, Andy jumped in to ask about slavery. "Are there really slaves here? People owned by others?"

"Yes, unfortunately," replied our dark-skinned Moor instructor Bilal with deep emotion. "My parents were both slaves. Thanks be to Allah, we were able to come to Nouakchott and break our ties with our community. But many remain, mostly deep in desert communities."

Our professors were critical of these practices, but that only made their stubborn persistence harder to swallow.

***

"Do you want breakfast?" My host's voice from the doorway sounded concerned.

"Yes, I coming, thank you," I responded. After 14 hours it was indeed time to get out of bed.

After six weeks in Nouakchott, the dozen of us had returned to the sprawling and depressing border-town of Rosso for a month of field work. Along with the five other volunteers assigned to SONADER, I had finally waded into rice fields the day before. Amidst Rosso's ripe fields we had passed a long day harvesting rice with only a sickle and no gloves. Now my hands harbored huge angry blisters, and my back was so sore that upon returning to my host's home, I had gone straight to bed, skipping dinner.

With bread held by hands that could not close, that morning I drank my coffee while wondering how anyone could do such work, day in and day out? And how exactly was I to instruct those who, in fact, did just that? I could almost see my old high school teacher Mr. Okamoto turn to carefully prune his lanky, forever-blooming orchids, while sadly shaking his head in wonder.

In Rosso, we had each been assigned a local family to live with. I was assigned to the household of Thierno Mamoudou Wane and his family of two wives, a dozen kids, and countless family members. My 'father' was a grand Marabout, a bishop of sorts among the region's numerous imams, or religious leaders. For some reason, this family gave me the name of Fatou Wane, a name that stuck with me throughout my time in Mauritania and marked me as a member of this esteemed Wane clan.

The Wanes were a gracious family, although they probably found me lacking in common sense. Such as sleeping through meals. I also failed to understand that the daily stream of well-dressed, stately older men who came by to pray and recite the Koran with the imam should not be approached by me for greetings. Once with extended hand and a broad smile I drew near to one, only to find my friendly gesture rejected. Instead, this elder man nodded toward me before turning his attention to the string of prayer beads dangling from his palm. Feeling all eyes upon me, I returned to my mat across the courtyard to take self-conscious refuge in my rice manual.

After a couple of weeks in Rosso, we briefly returned to Nouakchott to find our numbers dwindling. One volunteer had fled the country. Another announced that she and her stateside boyfriend were to marry. A third could not get his innards to work, and after umpteen rounds of antibiotics, sadly announced his departure.

Finally, one clear and starry night, our trainers revealed our village assignments by pinning our name to a tiny spot on a hand-drawn map of Mauritania. Over a rare treat of ice cream airlifted from France, we began to calculate how long it would take to visit one another. Half of us were headed north to Moorish desert towns and oases, or east toward the border with Mali and not far from that nation's fabled town of salt and gold, Timbuktu.

The other half of us were scattering among the Mauritanians of African descent along the country's southern border. Of the handful headed to the mid-Senegal River valley where lived Pulaars—a somewhat eclectic ethnic group with a complicated history—I was assigned to the small farming village of Civé. Located on the river's edge to the east, my village was not all that far from where in times long past, a Pulaar royalty had held court. My best friend Julie was a mere day's trip away, close enough so we could spend Thanksgiving together. And then with Christmas, we'd all reunite in Nouakchott for holiday cheer.

The following afternoon found us beneath lush and fragrant Jackalberry trees gracing the capital's presidential grounds, waiting to be sworn in as full-fledged volunteers. Tea, biscuits, and a photo op with Mauritania's President Ould Haidalla followed.

Later that afternoon, I was wandering through tight snaking passageways smelling of incense and tea in Nouakchott's central marketplace. I was on the lookout for a cassette-radio. In one tiny stall filled with various herbs, a large vat of henna, hanging prayer beads, and sticky brown balls piled high on plates, I spotted a small calendar for the year ahead.

"For sale?" I asked in French.

"Here, it is yours," the merchant seemed to say as she eagerly but silently pressed it my way. I handed her a few coins and bid her a day of peace.

That night, I flipped the pages of that calendar ahead six months and circled a date that became my goal; I would commit to this new country of mine for at least this long. Then I zipped it inside my bulging duffle bag and attempted to sleep.

Chapter 5

The Assignment

First thing next morning, three of us sped off with the chauffeur Demba to the dusty regional capital of Kaedi. Located a long day's drive southeast of Nouakchott, Kaedi is situated on the eastern reaches of the Fuuta at a spot where the Senegal River bends sharply right, then right again. At the first bend, a muddy Gorgol River draining a large parched and rocky basin to the northeast flows into the broadening Senegal.

Demba soon had Julie and David settled in distant villages, and my turn had arrived. That morning I awoke and quickly dressed in a T-shirt and *pagne*, which is a sarong-like skirt worn wrapped around one's lower half with a corner tucked into the waist band. Over this I slipped on a flowing outer garment called a *boubou* that reached to the ground.

After breakfast, Demba's muffled horn called to me.

"Did you sleep in peace?" Demba asked in Pulaar when a minute later I climbed aboard his pick-up truck.

"Yes." A white lie. "Are you awake?"

"Yes, yes." Dispensing with further morning greetings, Demba smiled and shifted the truck into gear. He stepped on the gas and, knowing I had about exhausted my Pulaar vocabulary, switched into French. "Let's go."

Off we headed to SONADER, where I was scheduled to meet my new boss, a Pulaar man by the name of Guisse. Guisse supervised SONADER's agents who, like me, worked in the region's villages.

I was nervous but looked forward to our partnership: I'd be in the fields working with farmers, while Guisse would be here in Kaedi, providing me with the oversight I needed and expertise I lacked.

Within minutes Demba pulled up before a plain one-story concrete building with the simple word SONADER painted above an open metal door. I followed Demba through that opening where to my dismay, he straightaway abandoned me to a hard-plastic chair. I sat there fingering the paperwork neatly arranged on my lap while my foot mechanically tapped against the leg chair.

In due time, a man sauntered over, pulled a twig out of his boubou's front pocket, and began using it to scrub his teeth while peering down at me. I smiled awkwardly, wondering who he was.

"Guisse has time for you now," he finally said, then strolled in the direction of my boss' office to prop himself up in its doorway.

I followed behind, swallowing what seemed to be an excess amount of saliva that had annoyingly gathered in my mouth. Then I entered a large room bright with the glare of angled morning sunlight and was soon shaking hands with Guisse. My new boss directed me to sit across from him. For some reason I hesitated, then stumbling for something to say but finding no words, just plopped down across from him. We must have exchanged some pleasantries, although I now have no memory of what those were. I remember being struck by his good looks and perfect teeth and noted the large leather amulet around his neck. I also recall that it slowly became clear to me that Guisse had no knowledge of this new 'partnership' of ours.

"Civé? Ok, Ok. They have two rice cooperatives. And your name is?"

We continued sitting there for what seemed like hours, both of us uncomfortably looking for things to discuss. Meanwhile, the morning light brightened, and the distant recitations of Koranic students known as *talibes*, or *fósinaaji* in Pulaar, drifted in through open louvers. The earthy smell of incense wafted in from the doorway, and I took in the echo of lively but unintelligible conversations from the nearby cinder-block corridors. Behind Guisse, who was likely conveying something to me at this point, I remember inspecting the crooked posters of impossibly perfect Chinese rice fields adorning his pocked walls. Then through a strained smile, I strove to convey to him an abundance of false confidence in broken—or perhaps incomprehensible—French. All the while, my new boss was struggling unsuccessfully to record something on the single sheet of blank paper he had placed before him.

A cogent thought came to me. I mentioned my newest acquisition.

"Peace Corps give me motorbike. I like to go other villages than Civé. Like Tokomadji. And Garly," I sputtered out, mentioning some villages near Civé. I leaned forward to see if Guisse might find that information worth recording.

He didn't. But he did spring to life. Rising, he summoned the man in the threshold still scrubbing his teeth and ordered him to fetch me a can of diesel for my motorbike. As soon as it arrived, Guisse rose to usher me out, shaking my hand with an inattentive 'good luck' while simultaneously shouting a hearty cheer to two acquaintances at the end of the open corridor. Unsure what came next, I felt as aimless as when I arrived. Hesitantly, I headed out, feeling a bit like an old, long forgotten curio, one considered briefly before being casually tossed in the Goodwill box. It would be several more months before I would finally realize that that attitude pretty much summed up my partnership with both Guisse and SONADER.

Hoisting my heavy diesel canister up, I stumbled out of Guisse's office, at the same time becoming uncomfortably aware that my loosening pagne was threatening to slip to the floor. Looking up to see if anyone else realized my predicament, I took in the approach of a towering man headed my way. He was wearing a sky-blue headdress wrapped particularly high, making him appear to me as an eight-foot giant. My can, meanwhile, was pulling me further into the ground.

Trying my best to straighten up, I noticed this man's headdress was accompanied by a matching boubou skillfully embroidered with gold thread, and conspicuously sewn from yards and yards of heavily starched and shimmering Dutch damask. So much stiffening gum had been pressed into his cloth that it hung from his body as if cut from cardboard. It was not just his gigantic stature and his stunning ensemble that drew my attention, but also his mannerisms which were swift and decisive. He was, I noted as I shuffled along lopsidedly, an important, dignified person on urgent business, someone you didn't keep waiting. We exchanged quick perfunctory greetings—May we pass the morning in peace—he looming above me while I fixated on my awkward gait and the pagne now slowly making its way down my legs.

To my great relief, at last I exited SONADER. Stepping out into the dusty lane, I immediately set down my heavy load and hitched up my pagne. Shielding my eyes from the glaring sun, I searched for Demba's white truck. Hardly a second of indecision had passed before I was surrounded by a gang of animated young vendors wearing T-shirts and turbans, each one trying mightily to convince me to buy a solitary Marlboro, a handful of roasted peanuts, or a string of plastic prayer beads.

"Sistah, sistah, you need this, look. Freshly made. Beautiful color. Cheap. The real thing. Like no other. My sistah…."

A stray pair of pink plastic sunglasses on the platter of one caught my eye. As I moved in for a closer look, Demba appeared from nowhere.

"Out, out!" he growled, and an angry swoop of his arm sent the hawkers flying. Scooping up my diesel can, he briskly walked to the waiting truck, his light-yellow boubou fluttering behind in the stiff breeze. I reluctantly glanced over my shoulder at the scattering salesmen before heading to the truck's passenger side. Just as I reached the truck door, Demba inexplicably stopped me.

"We're going back into SONADER," he instructed.

Alarmed, I objected: "But I meet Guisse now!" I had no interest in repeating that awkward ordeal.

"Come meet someone from Civé," he continued, having secured my diesel can in the back of his truck. Reluctantly, I trailed Demba back across the lane, noticing that the hawkers were now waving large clusters of brightly colored sunglasses at me from behind a distant tree.

After re-entering SONADER's courtyard, Demba happily shouted out to that massive man with the sky-blue headdress who across the courtyard was now engaged in an animated conversation with a man sporting an equally tall white headdress. The blue headdress looked up, and with a few long jubilant strides, joined us. He and Demba grasped each other's hand and elbow and began greeting one another in Pulaar.

"Are you awake? … How was your trip? … Have you arrived in peace? … How was the road? … Are your wives in peace? … Thanks be to Allah … How is your comfort?…Praise be to Allah … Your children, they are all in good health?"

And more greetings followed, first one asking and the other answering, then the roles reversed. Meanwhile, the elbow grasps migrated up, the two chests got closer, the greetings quickened in enthusiasm and increased in volume before circling back to start anew. I stood mute, wondering if I might just slip out unnoticed to the relative privacy of the truck's cab.

Perhaps sensing my desire to flee, Demba suddenly turned to introduce me to Mamadou Konaté.

"This is the new Peace Corps volunteer," he said, switching from Pulaar to French. "And Mamadou is the president of Civé's rice cooperative. You'll be working together."

Yikes, I thought, feeling myself shrink as Mamadou's looming presence towered further. I took a step back, then reached up to retie my headscarf, wishing for all the world that I could don that pair of sunglasses.

With Demba's cue, Mamadou reached out his hand. I shook it. We then exchanged subdued, polite greetings. His were cool and professional, containing a note of skepticism as he peered down to size me up. Not surprisingly, he didn't seem all that impressed.

And who could blame him for that? I could just barely get by in French and certainly was no farmer. Beyond ordinary greetings having to do with peace, wakefulness, and Allah, I spoke no Pulaar. My wardrobe was an unconventional, and probably tasteless, American version of the local standard, which I still didn't wear right. At my best, I stood five feet nothing, and this day was far from that. No doubt I failed to instill any confidence at all in whatever limited abilities I might possess.

Mostly, I felt that with one glance Mamadou knew all: that despite my job assignment with SONADER, I knew little about rice, except maybe how to eat it. For sure, I was pretty clueless about growing anything not packaged in a pot and accompanied by instructions, ones ideally containing detailed illustrations and an 800 number. Those requirements pretty much ruled out rice.

In the flash of that handshake, these thoughts and more coursed through me.

Indeed, over the past two weeks, my qualms over this upcoming role of mine had grown by the day. How was I to advise people about growing a crop with the life-or-death consequences that rice had in Mauritania's Senegal River basin? I could warn against letting rice roots mature before they are transplanted; but more than that? Not much, except to be sure to wear gloves while harvesting it. Mamadou's skepticism played into my own insecurity about why exactly I was here, and what I hoped to accomplish. What exactly did Peace Corps volunteers have to offer this suffering county? Weren't we simply Band-Aids, designed not to cure but to make those dispensing the bandages feel better?

Fortunately, Demba and Mamadou fell to discussing something in Pulaar. I listened a bit, hoping to learn a new word. But soon I gave up and instead watched a SONADER worker, who in his red jogging outfit and yellow knit hat seemed exceptionally overdressed for such a warm morning, shoo away a wayward goat from the street.

Finally, still scrubbing his teeth with a now-frayed stick, the man who had fetched my diesel can sauntered over. More drawn-out greetings followed, and then this man slapped Mamadou on the shoulder and said my new boss Guisse awaited him.

Once again Mamadou and Demba resumed their vigorous hand shaking, this time sending the other along with benedictions and final greetings. Mamadou turned to leave, but before entering Guisse's office, he paused.

"We talk soon," he called out to me in broken French. I waved goodbye, then trailing Demba, exited SONADER's building, where I was immediately set upon by the awaiting hawkers, each one quietly but urgently pleading for a quick sale until a final sharp "Out!" from my protector Demba sent them fleeing.

***

Next stop was Kaedi's marketplace. There I completed my final purchases: two four-inch-thick foam mattresses (called a matla); a metal-tipped three-foot long hoe-like agricultural implement (called a *jalo*); a bright baby blue, all-purpose plastic tub; a small midnight blue metal teapot;…and a pair of pink sunglasses.

"Time for lunch!" Demba declared, and from a stall on the edge of town we bought grilled goat meat and soft bread.

Once we'd finished eating, Demba checked his watch. "Wait here while I get gas for the trip," he then instructed. Mounting the white truck, he then sped off, leaning out the window as he did to call out: "Don't forget your water!"

Now alone, I sought out a large bottle of water, enough I figured to last me until my own purification system was up and running, for the murky and at times stagnant Senegal River was the only place in Civé to get water.

I then sat amidst the last of the city's low yellow cement buildings and observed a rock-hard mud field where donkeys roamed aimlessly, and shoeless boys played a spirited game of soccer with imaginary lines and invisible nets. For some reason, I felt a strong desire to join those boys, even though I barely knew the game. Then I considered returning to the shop to spark up a conversation with the merchant who had sold me my water. My thoughts drifted to my boss Guisse, and I reimagined our encounter a few hours earlier, sure now that this was just the start of a meaningful relationship. I even found myself wondering, *is Guisse married?*

Demba's return scattered my thoughts.

"Let's go!" His wide, welcoming smile was beckoning me aboard, as did the rousing lyrics blasting from a newly purchased cassette. A few moments later and the sound of the soccer players' animated shouts and all thoughts of romance receded as we rambled along the last of Kaedi's dirt roads. Soon we merged onto the sandy trail that followed the Senegal River, heading upriver toward Civé.

During that long two-hour drive, my thoughts wandered, and in Demba's fine company, my spirits revived. I considered this upcoming job of mine in Civé, which was more or less clear: I'd be working with the village's two rice cooperatives, and I'd just met the head of one. Packed in my duffle bag was the comfort of three rice manuals and a month's worth of notes on how to grow rice. The fact that the rice campaign had just ended seemed unfortunate, and I was unsure how I'd pass the next eight months until the next one. But, if I hadn't learned much about rice, I could now study those manuals. And for sure I needed to learn Pulaar, as few in Mauritania's rural areas spoke French. And no one spoke English. My thoughts drifted too to the life I was leaving, and to my newly made friends who, like David and Julie, were now settling into distant villages in this adopted land of ours.

Thirty minutes on found us passing through the expansive village of Djeol, a small town abutting a picturesque knoll that oddly enough appeared to me as an arid and miniature version of O'ahu's Diamond Head. The hill jutted up amid the flat landscape, commanding attention and demanding to be this locale's defining feature. As we passed by, I turned to watch as the mount grew distant, surprised by the unusual sense of familiarity it conjured up. Turning forward, I saw a herd of goats clogging the narrowing road. Demba slowed, then leaned out the window and honked, edging forward as he did.

"Tic, tic, tic-tic-tic," he scolded the animals angrily, while revving the engine.

Reluctantly the goats dispersed. A small grey one turned to amble my way. Purposeful in its approach, it looked up at me, then stopped by my door. We locked eyes. I spotted a familiar thin mouth, dark narrow pupils, and two-inch horns. A wave of horror swept over me as my heart leapt to my throat and I grabbed my neck. It was him, haunting me from the beyond: Neil's best pal Macho.

Chapter 6

Home Above the River

By the time the village of Tethiane appeared in the distance, Macho's ghostly appearance had vanished. Our truck plodded onward, following a deeply rutted trail through a handful of similar-looking villages. Approaching the outskirts of each, Demba announced its name, followed by some tidbits on its history, agricultural activities, or the people within.

"Koundel: Diaw, Diop, Sarr," he reported as we approached the village of Koundel, rattling off the last name of its residents. I looked at him blankly. Seeing my face, Demba laughed, then turned down the music blaring from two speakers. "They are fisherman," he declared, a fact I should have remembered since Pulaars' last names signal the owner's caste.

"Seydi Diaw. Seydi Sarr," Demba called out to those within earshot as we moseyed along the dusty lane splitting Koundel in two.

A short while later, we reached the hamlet of Tokomadji. "A Fulbe village," Demba informed me, indicating its residents hailed from Pulaars' elite light-skinned herding caste. *Fulbe* is the name of the herders who a thousand years earlier emerged from a drying north to settle the Fuuta, establishing themselves as the region's aristocratic landowners in the process.

"Next is Civé!" Demba cheerfully announced. Increasingly unnerved, I wondered how we had arrived so quickly.

Beyond Tokomadji's last cluster of huts, the road emerged from the sandy uplands and turned sharply right toward the river. Soon we were surrounded by thorny trees with needle-thin leaves, one of which a goat was climbing to reach a few remaining bites of greenery. I directed my attention from that lone goat to the wide, gently flowing Senegal River now straight before us. At that juncture, our view of the river was blocked by piles of bramble protecting the banks' ripening crops from hungry animals. Demba steered left to follow the river upstream, while below us a dozen women and children labored on the riverbanks, hacking wooden jalos into the thick soil. Demba honked. The farmers stood, waved, and then silently stared as we passed by above.

"Sweet potatoes," Demba instructed. He tapped a final greeting on his horn.

Ten minutes of rough passage up and down parched ravines followed; then Demba ejected his new Baaba Maal tape, flipped it over for the sixth time, turned up the volume, and then suggested that I "hold on." Up we climbed over a rugged incline, then bounced up the side of a steep culvert. After cresting the top, Demba pointed out the first of Civé's homes in the distance.

Within a minute, Civé's western edge was upon us; on our left a rectangular mud-brick schoolhouse emerged next to a small one-room health clinic. Demba continued past, and soon the bramble on our right gave way to an unimpeded view of the muddy-green river flowing beyond a long, gently sloping bank. Upstream, the river veered sharply right to disappear behind the flat hazy banks of Senegal to the south.

On our left stood compact and small rectangular homes with thatched roof overhangs, wooden fences, and shade trees interspersed here and there. The rhythmic pounding of grain filled the air, accompanying the crying of babies and the playful afternoon shouts of children. Women and men dressed in flowing colorful boubous halted their activities and watched as our vehicle ambled by. Civé appeared to me like a carbon copy of the other simple, quaint villages we'd passed through that afternoon, only with one significant difference: my heart had now edged up to my throat.

On we crept another hundred yards further, whereupon a lone majestic palm tree loomed ahead, half of its roots jutting out over an eroded cliff. The palm's lanky trunk split into shapely Vs as it grew upward, each side topped by a spare tuft of palm leaves swaying in the breeze. On the riverbanks below were dozens of villagers, all noisily bathing, washing dishes, and collecting water into large tubs. Demba returned their waves and happy cries with a shout, a wide smile, and an occasional short toot of his horn.

How was it that our Peace Corps chauffeur seemed to know everyone? I wondered. It felt as if behind the wheel of our car sat a movie star or some celebrated sports figure.

Our arrival now thoroughly announced, young boys streamed out from the village center and sprinted up from the river. They encircled our truck as we passed the split palm tree that marked the end of the village's western flank. With boys swarming around us, we carefully turned left to bounce our way down a large wide gully that transected the village. Above us, I spotted a small community of round huts, each one containing large irregular but sturdy stock pens. In the distance beyond, ochre land rose to meet the red rocky outcroppings that ringed the village. *It's more picturesque than most,* I thought as I attempted a swig from my empty water bottle.

Demba then coaxed our truck up the small gorge's steep eastern embankment while continuing to honk and holler joyfully at people in the distance. Meanwhile, I fidgeted with my head scarf, shooed away the boys so we would not crush them beneath us, and hugged the car's frame to keep from being hurtled across the cab. Cresting, a collection of spacious compounds greeted us, split left and right to allow a wide passageway for the rare vehicle that passed this way.

Suddenly, Demba jammed our vehicle into park, halting before a spacious dirt yard containing a small, two-room mud hut: my new abode. It looked bare and forsaken, with a closed door, no apparent windows, and a wood fence woefully in need of repair. It would have been a forlorn greeting indeed had my new hut not been overshadowed by the presence of a large and welcoming neem tree swaying in the breeze.

I descended the cab and drifted over to inspect my new residence. With delight, I found the backyard bordered a steep, craggy cliff that looked down on the river fifty yards below. I had no neighbor to my right, the locale instead offering a prime view of the dense maze of mud houses, sandy paths, and spare trees that lay across the gully. The compound bordering mine on the left contained a couple of mud rectangular huts visible across our shared wood fence, a fishing net sprawled out between them. Beyond that, I glimpsed the river which upstream gracefully curved right before slipping from view. I took a deep breath, enjoying the pleasant smell of burning wood and fried onions, grateful for this surprisingly fine locale offering the luxury of private accommodations.

With a growing swarm of young boys buzzing around me, I turned back to find Demba unloading my belongings, including the motorbike Peace Corps had sent me with, a possession that proved so useless in this sandy, irregular, and thorn-ridden terrain that in due time I dispatched it back to Nouakchott.

Behind Demba I spotted a large cinder block building beyond a wobbly pen containing several humped-back Zebu cows. Some people there were looking our way, so I decided to go introduce myself. As I entered their compound, I caught the lingering smell of smoldering charcoal and cattle dung; ahead four women stood beside a frail old man encased in a hammock and now struggling to emerge. Tin cans, handfuls of hay, plastic containers, burlap bags, various shaped gourds, and broken rubber slippers were scattered about.

Up I walked to the women. A thin matla was produced and someone patted it to show I was welcome. I sat as Demba entered to explain who I was; word spread, and soon I was surrounded by a dozen villagers who now loudly proclaimed that I was the village's new *Americanaajo*.

"Here, for you." Demba was suddenly by my side and handing me a thick bronze key. "Time to head out."

I stood and tried to say something, but my mouth went dry, and my legs felt weak. I looked about, then with a bit of confusion, followed Demba as he headed back to his truck. With his engine soon revving, Demba hung out the window and clasped my hand.

"Civé is a great village," he promised me.

Then he added: "It will be your new family." He put the truck in gear. I imagine I looked to him like an abandoned puppy. "They'll feed you dinner," he said while pointing beyond me to the compound where the old man in the hammock was now bent over but standing. Demba called out some blessings to him, then turned to give me one final smile. I tried my best to return his good cheer.

Then the truck lurched forward. Once again, Demba's head emerged from the window as the vehicle continued on. With Baaba Maal's loud but melancholy voice now filling the air, Demba hit the gas pedal, and left in his wake a growing dust cloud, a rising mass of cheering kids, and one deserted Americanaajo.

With some trepidation, I crossed the lane to enter my compound. After a slight tug, my front door swung open, sending chunks of mud tumbling to the ground as it did. I realized then why Demba had handed me a key; it had been 'locked.' To my left a colorful agama lizard stood attentive, his eyes growing wide each time he emitted a loud clicking noise from his throat, a signal seemingly designed to alert his fellow lizards that a home invasion was in the works.

I entered the dark, cool, and very musty room, leaving everything but my duffle bag outside. Before me, embedded in the back wall, was a wooden shutter. The small opening gave way to my expansive backyard. To the left a few dozen feet beyond my hut stood the remains of a U-shaped stall, standing five feet tall with walls looking like a half-melted ice cream cone, deeply weathered as they were by rains. The stall's U opened toward me, and in its middle lay an overturned, misshapen rusty bowl. This, I now realized, was my toilet, the sole one in the village. While it lacked much in the way of privacy, at least I had one; going out in the bush was more 'adjustment' to village life than I cared to make. But clearly a door to my privy would make for a nice home improvement project.

Meanwhile, the crowd of boys lingered at my entry, whispering incomprehensibly, toes out but chests and heads in. I continued my inspection. Above me, a mud-and-thatch roof had weathered the last rainy season. I entered a dark second room identical to the first, also containing a small wooden shutter emitting thin rays of light around its leaky seal. I crossed to open it, and once again dried mud fell to the ground and shattered. The pressing mass of boys burst into giggles, unsuccessfully stifling them as I returned to the entry room. Beams of sunlight streaming through my open windows revealed my new home's barren brown mud walls and cracked concrete floor.

For some time, I busied myself with obvious tasks. Michael, the volunteer before me, had left four months earlier, and the floors were now carpeted in sand, dried mud, thatch, and the weightless remains of scorpions. Bent over, I began sweeping all this into a pile with a foot-long 'broom' made of stiff straw that I'd purchased in Kaedi.

Thirty minutes on, I had my belongings inside and unpacked atop my two foam pads. The dozen shoeless young boys with protruding bellybuttons continued to squirm at my open door, observing and commenting on my every move. Nothing of their whispered exchanges made any sense at all to me, except for periodic utterances including the word *tankal*, or candy. I regretted that several nights earlier, Julie, David and I had consumed two bags of it (along with a fine bottle of Lebanese wine) while playing the card game Hearts deep into our final night together.

With my new home swept clean, and with the realization that

I was 10,000 miles from home, I suddenly felt overcome with self-doubt, confusion, and exhaustion. I turned my back to the kids and closed my eyes. Suddenly I felt very dusty, sweaty, and thirsty.

A trip to the river will help, I decided.

I closed my front door, passed through the opening in my listing fence, then turned left to make my way to the river, blindly following a thin veneer of sand that gave way to smooth clay as hard as concrete. Seeking a bit of privacy from the women and children on the shores before me, I veered left, then looked up to where I figured my new home was. Yet unbeknownst to me I had stopped at an inconvenient place to enter the muddy river, as the bank at this spot was muddy and steep, just the place *not* to enter the water. I was also completely oblivious of the fact that from a distance, dozens of children and adults were shouting this information out to me, surely baffled by my inattentiveness—and plain lack of common sense.

As I had learned to do during training, I slipped off my boubou and T-shirt and laid them on the mud bank above the river's edge. Now wearing only my wrap-around pagne, I waded bare-chested into the mud. It squished up between my toes, then oozed up and over as my feet sank. I struggled to walk. When the river reached my knees, I awkwardly tumbled forward, my pagne ballooning up behind me. The brown water was surprisingly cool, and I hesitated a second before sinking below. After a few moments of quiet solitude, I reluctantly surfaced, the silky mud underfoot holding me captive.

Turning I found a large silent crowd observing me from the banks above. With no better notion of what to do, I simply lifted my hand and waved. Smiles broke out all around, and a few spectators called out to me. Within seconds a spirited and excited group of young boys had me surrounded in the water.

The air was now charged with excitement as the encircling boys bobbed up and down. Slowly I sank beneath the water. Then, after a dramatic pause, I shot up into the air. The youth's joyful shouts and jubilant squeals happily evoked memories of my younger sister when ages ago, I had entertained her with this exact same stunt.

The awkwardness now broken, I felt strangely lighthearted and calm.

Maybe, just maybe, I could learn to like this new life of mine in Civé.

Chapter 7

The Location

Civé was home to about a thousand people, most of whom lived squeezed into two acres of sloping land on the village's western flank. The upper part of this slope was called Civé Dow, or upper Civé. The bottom was Civé Less, lower Civé. Other villagers lived as I did on the sprawling eastern side of the village gulch in a neighborhood referred to as *Moderne*, signaling its more recent origin.

"My hut is in Civé's suburbs," I jokingly wrote to those back home. But the location indeed had a bit of that feel.

West-side, where nearly everyone else lived, the compact mud homes were laced together into a maze-like network of narrow sandy paths used by roaming goats, braying donkeys, and sprinting kids. To separate one compound from the next, men drove sticks into the ground and then wove them together using the rubbery bark of gonakie trees. Early in Civé's history, such a fence separated Civé Less, where lived the slave caste, from Civé Dow, where lived the fisherman and noble castes.

Entering a compound, one typically encountered a large court-yard with open pits off to the side where women cooked. Unless men gave them money to purchase the rough bread baked in the dark by the village baker Alasanne, each morning women cooked a thick porridge from whichever grain was on hand. For the main meal of lunch, the women cooked oily rice topped with vegetables and dried fish, or in good times, meat. Dinner was nearly always haako, a tasty bean leaf sauce plopped on top of a bed of finely ground warm sorghum. If made with meat and several scoops of ground peanuts, haako is hard to beat.

In large compounds, the courtyard was usually ringed by a series of rectangular mud buildings, each one housing one nuclear family, with those in separate dwellings somehow related to one another: siblings, parents, kids, aunts, step-cousins, or some complicated combination of categories. While there weren't many wealthier men in the village, those with a bit of extra cash frequently splurged on a second wife, and on the rare occasion, a third. Each wife had her own bedroom, which perhaps explains why the Pulaar word for wife, *jom suudu*, means something like 'master of the room.' To put things in their proper perspective, the term for husband, *jom galle*, means 'master of the household.' And *jom wuro*, master of the village, would be the village chief. Civé's fifth jom wuro happened to be the old man across the lane from my hut who laid in a hammock most of the day, and who was now considered to be my host. Samba Ba earned his title of village chief by being the grand-nephew of the revered Weli Alpha Seydi Ba, a man credited with settling Civé toward the end of the 19th century.

Men who did have more than one wife followed strict rules governing the treatment of each. For any sign a husband favored one wife over the other risked a corrective visit from the imam. Not to mention the disapproving tutting of villagers, as such things were hard to hide, especially since any jom suudu on the short end of a marriage never kept this to herself.

Each of the village's mud huts sported the obligatory shade structures, called *caali*, built over *dinndeeres*, or raised platforms constructed out of mud or thatched branches. It is on these dinndeeres that people hung out, typically on worn-thin matlas placed on top for comfort. Except during the cold season or when it rained, people lived almost exclusively outside, and these dinndeeres served as living rooms during the day, then bedrooms at night.

The main construction material in Civé was the thick

chocolate-colored mud dug up riverside. Tradesmen formed this mud into bricks down on the banks, then left them to bake in the sun. Two cents would buy you a single brick, which when layered on top of another—mud serving as mortar—could be shaped first into walls, and then a home. Once finished, you'd seal the structure from the rain with a thick layer of brown sludge made by kneading a bit of water into fresh cow dung. For when the rains come, don't expect sprinkles, as this is not a land of moderation. Torrential downpours carve deep gullies, create jagged cracks in the bluffs, and dig deep ravines that channel water to the river. Sealing homes was thus crucial if any dwelling was to survive even one downpour. Once dry, this cow-dung paste forms an enamel-like finish that is amazingly effective at repelling rain.

Most residents topped their homes with roofs made of thatch and mud, although a few families splurged on corrugated tin ones; a choice I never could quite fathom, since during the hot season the tin turned the rooms below into ovens, and when the rains came, the clatter within sounded like unrelenting machine gun fire.

When I arrived in Civé in 1984, the village was almost entirely self-contained as hardly anyone came or went, except for the occasional nurse and the few elementary school teachers assigned to the village's two-room mud hut on the town's edge. And, of course, there was SONADER, the organization I worked for and on which the village's rice farmers now depended.

But villagers also survived on an inflow of cash sent by relatives living in urban centers or abroad. Stacks of bills arrived, always in unsealed envelops so that the currency could be hand-counted in public at handoffs along the way. This cash kept many households afloat. In fact, very few villagers were self-sufficient, and those who were usually lingered near starvation; far from the romantic image I held of a self-supporting lifestyle.

An outsider might look at Civé in the mid-1980s and conclude that life there was simple: no electricity, no running water, no phones, cars, or toilets, and only a few radios with just enough juice left to make sense of the noise emanating from within. But, as I learned, that premise would be incorrect: simple it was not.

The only real place to shop in Civé was at a closet-sized boutique run by Samba Anne, a Pulaar man from Senegal. At Boutique Samba, as his stall was called, you could buy the village staples of rice, oil, powdered milk, tea, sugar, 1-cent candies, tomato paste, bouillon cubes, cigarettes, and a yard of cloth from a dusty fabric bolt. Samba Anne also served as the village banker, providing loans to desperate villagers at interest rates revealing just how desperate they were.

Next to Boutique Samba stood a two-room schoolhouse attended by some of the village children until the age of eleven; when their instructor decided to show up, that is. Next to that was the village health clinic, a single cement room that off and on had a male government 'nurse' assigned to it. Like the schoolteachers, he too had spotty attendance.

Depending on one's point of view, a person might be tempted to describe Civé as isolated. If someone got up very early and was exceptionally lucky, after paddling across the river and spending an endless, exhausting day in a jammed-packed taxi, she might reach Dakar by midnight. Along the way, not much would catch her attention except for the occasional majestic Baobab tree in the distance, its massive trunk juxtaposed against its tiny, sparse leaves, like something out of Dr. Seuss's *The Lorax*. Or roadside, she would see women peddling their mangos and cashews while men herded goats or stretched out a thin carpet to face east toward Mecca.

Alternatively, a traveler could reach Nouakchott in a day and a half by heading downstream from Civé and then angling north. But that trip would require traversing body-numbing roads guaranteed to leave the soul with cramps, aches and pains, and the hair, eyes, nose, throat, and even lungs caked with sand. The distances, hassles, and expenses of travelling meant very few ventured to either of these two capitals.

Yet despite its seeming isolation, many considered Civé's location to be rather ideal. Most of its residents did at least. In fact, back long ago, at a time even before a French river boat plowed the Senegal, Civé was the ideal place to cross the treacherous river during the rainy season. After rains filled marigots and created inland lakes, and before bridges and roads offered good alternatives, the surest route from the commercial center of Matam, Senegal to the northern markets of Kiffa, Nema, and M'Bout passed through Civé.

During those times, the village was a verifiable regional hub. Herders from the north came to Civé to gather under a spreading tamarind tree named *Kampona,* the stump of which remains visible today. There they traded butter, soured milk, and kinkeliba leaves with residents from the south who offered up fish, honey, peanuts, and millet. Once machines replaced pack animals, merchants brought old but rugged Citroen T46 trucks to transport merchandise and food to inland locales cut off from trade. And everyone happily refueled at Civé's popular bakery and restaurant operating riverside.

Alas, such good times in Civé ended when shortly after Mauritania's independence from France, the new Moor government established Matam, Mauritania as its regional headquarters, with Matam, Senegal situated just a stone's throw away. Thus ended Civé's time as a humming commercial hub.

Most important to residents now, though, was Civé's proximity to the Senegal River, which in the 1980s flowed ten months a year and provided needed relief from scorching temperatures that hovered near 120. If you climbed aboard a long pirogue carved from the soft trunk of a thick red dounoube tree that ages ago had turned grey, you could cross into Senegal. A mere ninety-minute walk upstream lay the town of Matam, Senegal, with its lively population of 15,000. In Matam, you could ring anywhere in the world, buy fresh meat and ocean fish, post a letter, hire a carpenter, find a wide range of pharmaceuticals, or enjoy a cold Coke. Or even a warm beer: although most Senegalese were Muslim, alcohol was legal, and you could occasionally find a few cans of *33 Export* on a merchant's shelf.

Confusingly, there was also the Matam on the Mauritanian side of the river, the two towns staring across the river at one another. But that small, bleak, and lifeless government outpost which decades earlier had siphoned away Civé's vibrant commercial life, was inexplicably built on mudflats that rain transforms into a giant shallow mosquito-infested lake. This Matam offered a stark contrast to its delightfully lively Senegalese counterpart.

In the opposite direction from Matam, located a mere hour's walk downriver, was Tokomadji, a small Fulbe village. Tokomadji always promised enough gossip to while away a day, as did the upriver village of Garly, another small village where residents all seemed to have the same last name. There was so much intermarriage between Civé and these two villages, however, that any visit to either inevitably took on the festive air of a family reunion that must not end before the sun touches land.

And finally, there was Kaedi with its booming population of 30,000. You got to Kaedi by climbing into the back of a pick-up truck that passed through Civé each afternoon—although occasionally the rains left the roads impassable for days and sometimes weeks at a time. This truck stopped at Samba Anne's stall and could reach the downstream Kaedi in three hours or the next day, depending on the number of times passengers had to push the vehicle out of a sand trap or up a steep gully, dig it out of mud, or find shade while a flat tire (or two) were repaired. Locals referred to this transportation service as the *Rapide*, revealing both their sense of humor as well as pragmatic observation that this unreliable vehicle was *almost* always faster than the alternative, which would be to walk the fifty hot miles to Kaedi. And since many in Civé could recall the days when feet were the main mode of transport, this Rapide served as their daily reminder that progress was possible.

***

My long-awaited arrival of in Civé was followed by the uneasy, awkward process of settling in. Each day felt endlessly long, lonely, and clumsy. Each ended with lengthy letters home, each jammed packed with youthful enthusiasm and colorful descriptions, recorded on tear-stained paper. Yet to say I was a misfit suggests I had more reason for being in this village than was at all apparent to me. By the time midmorning arrived and the villagers had swung noisily into gear, I was exhausted. By noon, spent, I futilely sought solitude in a culture that equated aloneness with loneliness.

"I'm here to be with you," some young girl would murmur with averted eyes whenever I was home alone. Then she'd sit at a distance, swing her legs, or play with a stick while curiously observing my every move.

To keep myself from fleeing on the afternoon Rapide, I embraced the discipline of a strict routine. Mornings I swept. Then I gathered my daily tub of water and carried it up the river's hard cracked banks. To make it drinkable, I sprinkled alum on top to get the suspended particles to sink. Then I ran it through a filter. Finally, after adding two capfuls of bleach, I poured the tubful into my calabash. Mid-day I wrote detailed notes on the people and happenings around me. Afternoons, I entered the village to greet people and eventually wind my way around to the riverfront home of a man by the name of Tall, who for $3 a day was now giving me Pulaar lessons. Once the lesson was over, I completed the day by heading to the river where I worked on mastering the difficult skill of bathing, one which required keeping secret all that lay between waist and calves. Along with my loneliness, this was another part of me I was to keep to myself.

Chapter 8

Casio

It was early November when I arrived in Civé, and the cool season, *Dabunde*, had already settled in. The midday sun was weaker, the sky clearer, the nights chillier. One cool morning about a week after my arrival, I stood draping wrung clothes on the crooked remains of my fence. A man's bobbing head bustled up the ragged gully, called *Caangól Laddéegi*, that split the village. Shooing away a goat that was nibbling on a strung pagne, I hung out my last boubou while scrutinizing this figure heading my way. Even though we'd spent only five minutes together in Kaedi, I recognized the man's long gait, urgent stride, and imposing stature. It was Mamadou Konaté.

Since greetings are an essential feature of Mauritanian life, I began rehearsing mine. I'm not sure why Mauritanians spend so much time greeting one another. Some historical artifact, no doubt, perhaps dating to an era when encounters among the region's once-roaming residents provided an occasion to learn about forage, ferocious animals, or foes. Or maybe greetings gave information on one's position in the social pecking order, one historically nearly as rigid as feudal Europe's. Or perhaps you could trace their endless greetings to longstanding conflict over the region's few resources, where prolonged ritual-like salutations evolved as a type of diplomacy. Think of the movie *Lawrence of Arabia,* when Omar Sharif's character Ali and Lawrence's guide, chanced upon one another at a watering hole. Maybe if that encounter had first involved long warm handshakes and extended greetings rather than pointed guns,

Lawrence's of Arabia's guide would have survived that scene. Well, maybe. I know I always felt warmer toward someone after holding their hand while inquiring into their health and wakefulness, learning their name, and hearing them praise each member of my family.

In any case, Mamadou had just returned from Kaedi. This meant I should query him over the health of those he left behind, ask about his journey, and learn whether he arrived in peace before moving to the more routine greetings.

Yet I had barely managed the 'welcome home,' when with a wide sweep of his arm to smooth out his boubou, Mamadou was sitting erect on my porch's mud dinndeere, ready for business. One moment later and he had outlined an appropriate rental arrangement with my landlord—for some reason Mamadou insisted I pay my rent to him and not my landlord—and agreed that I needed my wayward fence repaired to keep wandering goats out. He also concurred that the crumbling structure in my backyard serving as a latrine required a greater modicum of privacy than offered by the fabric now stretched across its gaping doorway.

Before arising to leave, however, that morning Mamadou had one further order of business. The Peace Corps volunteers before me had each undertaken a project, he informed me. Tom had introduced vegetables; Michael, whom I had replaced, brought chain-link fences to protect the village's fields from hungry roaming animals. Mamadou stretched to his full height, shook out his long thick robes, and then while looking about, adjusted his turban.

"Done," he announced. He hesitated for a moment as he looked toward the village. Then he turned with what seemed an afterthought: "We know about rice. We know about vegetables. We know about corn, millet, sweet potatoes, melons, beans, peanuts, and sorghum. We need something new. Something like fruit trees."

With that, off he strode with the same sense of urgency with which he had arrived, breaking stride only to shout greetings to my neighbors, assuring everyone that all was well in Kaedi, that such-and-such a person sends her greetings, and yes, that he'd delivered my neighbors' message, but no, the receiver hadn't sent money back, but promised to do so 'next time.' At the time, of course, I understood little in these exchanges. But eventually I learned that the topics of conversations and daily activities in Civé were very, very predictable. Or so at least they seemed.

***

Mid-morning the next day, a young boy with a shy smile and large expressive eyes stood in my open doorway.

"You…soap…dog," was all I was able to make out. The youngster repeated his message while all I could do was watch his bare foot as it pushed a large thorn on my porch to the side. Finally, I ushered him across the lane to my hosts, the Ba's, who in exchange for periodic gifts were now feeding me lunch and dinner.

Approaching the narrow entryway to the Ba's compound, the young boy and I stood aside as a local shepherd escorted the Ba's cows out; they were headed, no doubt, to the sandy uplands, called the *dieri*, which contrasted with the muddy lowlands called the *waalo*. There in the dieri they'd pass the day under this sleepy herder's watch. The sound, smells and dust of the exiting cows filled the Ba's compound as we entered.

That morning, the half dozen resident kids were off to school on the opposite side of town, and the Ba's courtyard felt empty. Some dry cow dung smoldered in the cooking pit on our right, and next to it a goat noisily scraped the remains of the morning rice porridge from a large cast-iron pot. Nearby, a scrawny chicken bobbed and clucked, seemingly on high alert for any wayward tidbit.

Two women were absorbed in an animated conversation involving a few coins in the hand of one. The woman on the left was my new 'mother,' a small, lean but quite muscular woman by the name of Taanooy, who with her toothless grin had taken great delight in giving herself that moniker. Over to the far left, a teenage girl named Habi was piling dirty dishes into a large tub to take to the river; Habi's aunt lay nearby under a shade structure nursing one of two newborn twins while the other impatiently shrieked.

"I hope you are having a peaceful morning," I called out as I entered.

The chicken noisily scurried away.

"May we all have a peaceful morning," the adults responded in unison as they looked up from their various tasks, the air suddenly still as the shrieking baby began to suckle.

"Did you sleep in peace?" came a weak voice from afar, and I noticed that Taanooy's husband Samba Ba lay twenty feet away in his hammock. Samba was well into his eighties, probably twenty or so years older than his bride.

"I slept in peace, thanks be to Allah," I called out so he could hear. Nodding his approval, Samba lay back down, mumbling something I couldn't make out.

"*Neene*," I said, addressing Taanooy as my mother. And then putting my hand on the young boy's head, I continued, "Here, boy, no understand. He say?"

Taanooy broke into a wide-eyed grin. "*Neene. Neene.* You hear? I'm her mother. I have a *tubaak* child."

The adults all laughed, although the old man Samba's barely audible mirth quickly turned into a coughing fit.

In a faint voice using words that conveyed nothing to me, the boy mumbled again about soap and a dog. *Did I hear the word tree?*

After a moment of listening, my neene turned to me. "Mamadou Konaté. The President. He…where you…" I looked at her vacantly, my mouth open but no words emerging. "Go, go," she said, pointing northwest across the gully to the main part of the village. "…calls you!"

My adopted mother then said something to the small boy, and I understood I was to follow him. My heart oddly pounded as we left the compound, and once again I heard my mother delight in her new status as 'the tubaak's neene.' Tubaak, the common term for *Westerner* in West Africa, comes from a local word for shorts, presumably because of Europeans' odd preference for this scanty and child-like apparel.

Ill at ease, I followed my small guide, clueless as to our destination, thinking that maybe it was some sort of a…dog wash? Meanwhile, this sweet boy wearing a T-shirt two sizes too small led me down the gully, casually swinging a stick as he did, each swipe clearing yet another of the fat, industrious dung beetles from our path, their balls of dung bouncing out of their clutches as they tumbled away. Down one, then up the other side of *Caangól Laddéegi* we went, a line of irregular shaped compounds now lined up in front of us. Following my barefoot guide along sandy paths winding through the village, I called out greetings to people I recognized, as well as the vast majority of those I didn't.

Shortly we came across two dark-skinned Moors hard at work. I knew they were outsiders, as Civé had no Moor residents. They were Haratin, the so-called "Black Moors," the result of centuries earlier when Moors swept down from the north to ride off with cattle, millet, and slaves. The Haratin usually lived north among the Bidhan, or White Moors, having long ago adopted the Moors' language, culture and religion. In this part of Mauritania, they often settled in small hamlets on dieri lands to the north, residing on land claimed by their former (or perhaps in some cases current) Moor masters. As had these two, many such members of the Moor slave caste regularly hiked south an hour or two to villages like Civé to trade hard manual labor for a few coins or a gourd-full of rice.

I approached these muscular men whose dark skin emitted a musty odor and gleamed in the cool morning air. The feeling of a strange bond with them arose within me. I halted to observe their work, thinking they too might view me as a kindred outsider. Yet instead, they both froze and stared open-mouthed, a dreaded look in the eye of one suggesting the presence of a ghost. My heart sank and my legs grew heavy. Immediately wanting to turn around, I instead simply asked if they had passed the night in peace. To which they stammered out that they had. Gazing over their work, I saw they were constructing a small odd-shaped building with no windows, one arising in the lane and strangely unattached to anyone's compound. Was Boutique Samba expanding, I wondered? Or was this to be a place to wash dogs?

The guide by my side decided this delay had gone on long enough, and he tugged my boubou while silently gazing up at me. He then led me into a nearby compound. I entered and was greeted by a large handsome neem tree surrounded by a dense U-shaped configuration of mud buildings, each sporting large, thatched hangers shading numerous raised wooden dinndeeres. Off to the right grew a tall, impressive date tree.

Unlike the Ba's compound, this one was orderly, the dirt grounds tidy and freshly swept. Some women just up from the river were expertly tipping large tubs of water from their heads, directing the streams into a half-dozen elevated clay vessels around the compound. Older girls were in the early stages of preparing lunch, their hands rhythmically pounding paddy rice in deep wooden mortars with heavy pestles. The loud, steady thump, thump, thump, of their pounding filled the air.

In the compound's left corner, a dozen men mingled under an expansive shade structure, the smell of their cigarettes wafting my way. Smack in the middle of these men, upright on a wood dinndeere, sat Mamadou Konaté. There was no doubting now that it was he who had summoned me.

Unsure what to do, I stood uneasily, and then reached beneath my boubou to retie my pagne. A young man noticed my presence and called out greetings. Mamadou looked up and brusquely called out, "*Ar gaay.*" Come here. I approached and was aware he was asking for something. I struggled to let his words pierce my isolation, but they would not.

"What? I not hearing?" was all I managed. Mamadou babbled on, and I probably stood looking at him like my dog Cher used to look at me. But eventually I thought I caught the word 'calculator' in his jabber. "Calculator?" I poked the air with my index finger.

"Of course," he replied switching from Pulaar to broken French, his tone conveying clear exasperation. All eyes were now fixated on me and the fact that I'd arrived empty handed.

Some music across the courtyard served to remind me that I needed batteries for my cassette player. "Home," I replied. *But why does he want a calculator? How did he know I had one?* After all, I wasn't even sure why I had brought one. And does it have batteries?

"Home, it home," I repeated, indicating I would go get it. Mamadou waved me off while turning to give loud orders to all those about.

Unsure just what had transpired, except that it had nothing to do with either dogs or soap, I hurried back across the gully then dashed into my latrine. With great relief, I opened the door to my darkened hut to dig out my calculator, which indeed did have batteries. I then called out to the Bas with a wave of my arm, "I go back." At least this day my Casio Calculator was on a mission.

"Go my tubaak child," chuckled my mom as she looked up from behind the cow she was milking.

Once more I crossed the gully. By now, morning activities in the village were in full swing. Compounds rang with banter, laughter, howling babies, the rhythmic she, she, she of sweeping, the banging of pots, the braying of donkeys and cackling of chickens, and the snapping of freshly washed clothes that chattering young girls had lugged up from the river.

A million thoughts ran through my head as I re-entered Mamadou Konaté's compound. Casio in hand, I felt the strong pull of my unfinished morning chores back home. The thick dusty air that morning gave me a headache. Let this be short, I prayed.

By now, the dozen men surrounding Mamadou had swelled to

a crowd. One of them eyed my calculator and quickly announced its arrival.

"Come, come, are you awake?" the man greeted me while ushering me to a dinndeere where I soon sat an arm's length from Mamadou. Surrounded by two dozen men, I looked awkwardly toward the women across the compound, and tried in vain to make eye contact with them.

To my left, a young girl cautiously approached, then handed me a leather pillow with geometric designs that reminded me of the wallpaper that one summer my mom had carefully steamed onto my bedroom walls. Slowly this girl climbed up next to me, her finger soon running up and down my pale arm until Mamadou leaned over and swat! Off she fled. More women entered with more tubs of water while the thumping of the rice pounders continued, my headache and cramps grew, and in a disoriented state up popped images of my mom climbing atop a stool to steam on one more wallpaper strip, starting at the ceiling and carefully working her way down to the floor.

Just then, the men around me lifted their voices in argument, a few pointing to some papers Mamadou Konaté held in his hand.

I listened without understanding as angry words erupted around me. My body tightened, then relaxed a bit as laughter followed. Mamadou turned my way to hand me a large, thin, bound book with a black cover.

"Here, Fatou," he said, using my Pulaar name as he placed the open book in my lap. I could see that it was a ledger of sorts, filled with names and columns of numbers. Mamadou ran his long finger down some of the columns and tried to explain. Everyone chimed in, and more brusque words were exchanged. I sat up a bit, blinked, and then examined the page before me to see if I could decipher its meaning.

"Kebe!" Mamadou called out sharply above the din. On cue, a young man with a frayed blue knit hat, a long thick scar on his forearm, and a threadbare boubou worn over a T-shirt appeared at my side. *"Firde haala,"* Mamadou commanded. "Translate."

And so, I met the cooperative treasurer, Kebe, who mercifully switched into French, and patiently explained that the final rice campaign expenses were in, and we were to calculate the amount each cooperative member owed. He showed me the column of names, and then pointed out the kilograms of fertilizer and insecticide each member had used. He was methodical in his explanations, articulating his words carefully by exaggerating the cadence of each. A burst of clarity overcame me, a sensation thus far I'd only had with my Pulaar instructor, Tall. Relieved and alert, my headache now abating, I felt as if I had emerged from some prolonged period beneath the waves. Taking a deep breath, I wanted to remember this friendly man with the broad pearly smile and tattered blue knit hat. I made a mental note to locate his home.

Kebe then drew my attention to a line halfway down the ledger.

"You see, Fatou? Here. Here I am." He pointed to his name written in letters so small I had to squint to read them. "I had 0.7 hectares of rice, see?" He indicated the column containing this information. "But I also had 0.2 hectares of sorghum, here." He pointed to this detail. "Now we must divide up the diesel, oil, and motor pump expenses among each cooperative member based on their land. Do you understand?"

"Yes," I answered, my focus sharpening. Then I paused before asking, "You know how do this?"

I had begun to hope that I might actually prove useful that morning, capable of accomplishing more than re-sweeping my floor or getting Taanooy to laugh by calling her *neene*. I sat up straighter, put my wallpaper-pillow to one side, and tucked some wayward locks of hair back into my headscarf.

"Yes, but we should do it together," Kebe replied. "I have paper here to write down every member's final bill. When we're done, we'll give each man his bill. Do you understand?"

"*Mi nani*," I answered him confidently in Pulaar. All the gathered men, listening intently though they spoke no French, registered their approval.

"She understands," they chuckled.

I took quick stock of those around me. A middle-aged man with a toothless grin, a worn blue tunic, and a graceful piece of white cloth intricately wrapped around his head, its end resting on his chest, urged me on by jabbing the air with a leathery index finger. My discomfort with being amidst lounging men while the compound's women steadily worked, began to abate. I too had work to do.

I turned to study the accounting book. Some things were not clear, and I didn't understand a few words, like the line item for something labeled '*Pawgol.*'

"What's this?" I asked, pointing to the word at the top of a column.

Kebe leaned over. "*Pawgol?*" Some men chortled, and a man with a cigarette drooping from his lips slapped the shoulder of another sporting a goatee, sunglasses, and white skull cap.

"*Pawgol,* that's when members owe the cooperative a fine," Kebe explained.

I looked up at the man with the white skull cap, who answered my look with a crooked, apologetic tobacco-stained grin. I turned back to Kebe and the black ledger now laying before me, then nodded as the delicious smell of frying rice and the shouts of young boys drifted our way.

Kebe and I spent the next three hours on Mamadou's dinndeere. With Casio's invaluable help, we calculated and recalculated each man's final bill under the watchful eyes of the milling observers. By the time we were done, I could see why both Casio and I had been called to the task. Divvying up the cooperative's expenses was far from easy. Kebe described the group's rules to me, such as the fact that land planted with sorghum got half off the diesel and motor pump expenses.

"Sorghum's not thirsty like rice," Kebe explained.

But other issues were knottier, such as what to charge a member who had fled to Nouakchott for medical relief when a lump in his neck had grown from the size of a thumb to the size of a fist.

"*Two* fists," insisted one, while turning to demonstrate to all present the tumor's size and precise location.

To resolve such conundrums, Kebe gathered the men, sometimes producing Casio and calling upon the few who were literate among them. Some discussion would ensue, and accompanied by a loud explanation, Kebe would punch numbers into the calculator, then pass around the resulting figures for inspection. Nodding followed, and sometimes more discussion. Occasionally a woman sweeping or pouring river water into a baked clay pot would pipe up with some confirming or dissenting comment. But eventually, Kebe would turn to me to report, "OK, everyone agrees." Then on we'd plod.

As morning turned to afternoon, odd memories of my high school comrades cropped up; for instance, the long Saturday spent figuring out how many floats would fit in the upcoming homecoming parade. But I shook such images away and applied myself to the project at hand.

Eventually we finished. The youth who had led me here was dispatched to the mosque uphill in Civé Dow, and in short order, in strode Mamadou, his headdress piled high, his long dark blue shiny boubou fluttering behind, this arresting ensemble topped off with smart hand-crafted pointy mustard colored leather shoes. Straightaway, Mamadou strode over to Kebe to retrieve the cooperative's thin black ledger.

Surrounded now by dozens of men, with an air of authority Mamadou launched into the final task of delivering each man his bill. One-by-one, Kebe gave the cooperative president a bill, quietly stating whose it was and what was owed. In a loud voice, Mamadou then took this information public:

"Sidy Barry, 15,124 ouguiyas. Ousmane Kadiatou, 15,252 ouguiyas. Mamoudou Aissata, 14,224 ouguiyas…"

Soon most of the cooperative members had their bill, their amount owed recorded on tiny scraps of paper that Kebe had meticulously measured, folded, and then torn from a single sheet of lined school paper. As I watched him so engaged, I silently reproached myself as someplace in my back room lay crumpled up a dozen sheets I deemed unusable.

The announcements continued and while the men busily inspected and compared their bills, I slipped over to playfully tousle the young errand-boy's head.

"What you name?" I asked, leaning down toward him.

"Abou," he replied while bending over to pick up a small rock.

"Abou," I said more to myself, committing yet another name to memory. "Abou…Konaté?" I guessed. Abou straightened up while closely inspecting his smooth stone. He nodded. Then, responding to the loud shouts of boys in the alley, off he bounded.

I crossed the compound to greet the women now cleaning fish and picking dirt and tiny pebbles out of a bowl of unpounded sorghum. I felt awkward, wondering if they'd see me as a traitor or worse, a complete misfit, neither male nor female. They stopped their *thump, thump, thump* and incomprehensible chatter long enough to greet me warmly. I fumbled with Casio, for some reason wanting to show it to them. They smiled, and we wished each other a day of peace. My work now done and suddenly feeling starved, I exited the compound to the final pronouncement of our achievement, "…and Moussa Maladel, 9,460 ouguiyas."

On the way home, I felt competent, proud to have played such a central role in village affairs. And I had a new friend, the cheery blue-capped Kebe. Then a memory of myself as a young girl came from nowhere. I was sitting on a bench as my dad's Little League team played. I longed to play, but being a girl, I couldn't. Instead,

I kept score, sitting quietly and invisibly alongside all the boisterous uniformed players. Crossing the gully, I unconsciously flipped Casio around in one hand, buried in thought. By now I had become used to feeling my white skin constantly on display. Now this was joined by the long familiar one of gender.

Chapter 9

Mud Stoves

A few days later, I had a date with Djeinaba Deh. Djeinaba was a strikingly beautiful Fulbe woman with an easy laugh and playful smile, the wife of my Pulaar instructor Tall, a man who also taught at the mud-brick elementary school on Civé's western edge. Djeinaba was my age, short and strong in build, with an open and intelligent demeanor. With a salaried husband, she displayed uncommon signs of wealth; each day she wore a different, well-coordinated outfit, the fabric stiff and shiny from a long soak in patouki tree sap, a signal to all that her day was not one spent in toil. And indeed, despite having a toddler and infant, Djeinaba enjoyed more free time than most as hired hands and girls in servitude pounded her rice, collected her firewood, and delivered her household's daily tubs of water.

With Tall's help, a few days earlier I had explained to Djeinaba (who spoke no French), that I wanted to build her a clay stove. Operating like wood-burning ones, these appliances took less wood than did the open fires over which women cooked. This could help spare a few of the region's diminishing stock of trees. During our Nouakchott training, we had learned to fashion these stoves out of clay bricks and mud mortar. Getting women to convert to them was part of the Peace Corps' effort to halt the Sahara Desert's steady southward creep. Could I showcase this new technology in her compound?

"Of course." Djeinaba had replied while pouring out *lowwol*, the first round of tea.

Djeinaba and Tall's small compound was located in Civé Less, the flat part of the western flanks. Consisting of a mud hut a bit larger than mine, their home was located at a bend in one of the sandy paths that laced the village's irregularly shaped compounds together. Djeinaba's small courtyard was always freshly swept, and the wood fence around it upright and sturdy.

Upon entering Tall and Djeinaba's homestead, a small cooking area situated in the mottled morning shade of their spiny murotoki tree greeted you. Just beyond that stood a diminutive pen enclosing a single goat, 'my herd' as Tall liked to call her. On the right arose a sturdy well-maintained shade structure, behind which lay the compound's sole dwelling. Large panels woven from doum palm leaves lined this portion of their compound, providing the young family with a tiny but rare modicum of privacy. Beneath the freshly thatched shade structure beckoned several thick matlas generously sprinkled with soft embroidered pillows.

Except for her infant son asleep under their hangar, Djeinaba was alone that afternoon when I entered. As promised, she had already assembled a stack of hardened clay bricks alongside a large pile of wet mud. She located just the right spot for our desert-stopping stove, and we set to work.

As our stove took shape, the school day ended and Tall arrived.

"Afternoon peace, how is your work?" Tall greeted us. Then he sat cross legged on a matla across the courtyard to tune his short-wave radio to news from Paris.

About halfway through our stove-building exercise, Mamadou Konaté stepped through a gap in the fence and called out greetings to a now-napping Tall:

"Afternoon peace, may we live." Turning to us, he then asked: "What's that?" A surprised look crossed his face as he brushed dirt from his hands before smoothing out his boubou.

"A mud stove," Djeinaba responded, while holding a large cooking pot over two bricks in my hands.

"Keyti is teaching Djeinaba to build it," said Tall as he stirred to life, turning the radio's volume down as he did. Ever since we met, both Tall and Djeinaba insisted on calling me by my American name.

"Keetheey?" Mamadou said with wrinkled brow.

"Keeeyyyti," Tall corrected him with a chuckle. "Fatou Waaaannnneee," he continued as he and Djeinaba swapped knowing looks. Tall found my Pulaar name funny—something to do with a family connection my name implied—and both he and Djeinaba snickered. Not in on the joke, I returned to our project, hoping to finish it before the mud dried.

"A mud stove cooks faster and saves on wood. It will help spare trees. Keyti wants to help women in the village build them," continued Tall. That was *my* spiel, at least, one I was trusting that Tall had just accurately conveyed, although I noted his sleepy tone lacked the requisite sense of urgency.

Intrigued, Mamadou lifted the sleeves of his boubou up around his shoulders, and circled the half-built stove, curiously bending over for closer inspection. Then he straightened up, pursed his lips, and pronounced, "Fatou. Come to my compound in the morning and you will make one there." Unwinding the long strand of fabric wrapped around his neck and converting it into a tall turban, he held his head high and stepped back over the same open spot in the fence. Then off he strode.

***

The next day I awoke to morning air so cold I could see my breath. I made coffee and waited inside my sleeping bag for my daily loaf of bread which the yawning neighbor boy Kalidou delivered each morning. Soon I was mulling over Mamadou Konaté's 'order' the previous afternoon. I wanted to ignore it. I had planned to spend the morning in the irrigated perimeters. Agriculture, not stoves, is why I was sent to this village, I grumbled to myself.

For sure I was intimidated by Mamadou's imposing presence. Yet his bossiness simply annoyed me. For four months I had lived crammed together with two dozen others, enduring the stress and rigidity of our training schedule. I longed for my independence—although, granted, if that was what I sought, living in a small African village where I *maybe* mastered 200 words was probably not the best of choices.

Perhaps it was the indelible image etched in my mind of the Sahara blowing southward, covering all in its path that eventually compelled my decision. During our recent trip from Nouakchott to Kaedi, we'd traversed a portion of Mauritania's sole east-west highway, a trip requiring numerous off-road detours to circumvent the large sand dunes swallowing the road. Images of those migrating sand dunes stuck with me, and on occasion I gazed northward wondering when the first wave of them would begin rolling in.

So, at ten that morning, with a fresh light blue sky above me and a pleasant cool breeze at my back, I entered the village, once again encountering the two Haratin workers now putting the final touches on that small windowless room with tiny ventilation holes at the top. What was this building for? I wondered, as I turned into Mamadou's busy compound.

Several women with empty bowls on their heads and jalos hanging from their shoulders greeted me as they exited. Two others were exchanging Mauritanian ouguiyas for Senegalese currency; behind them a teenage boy was corralling a chicken that squawked while hopping in terror, seemingly understanding that its capture should be avoided at all costs.

I was ushered over to Mamadou's empty dinndeere, and the same small girl appeared at my side, once again handing me that familiar leather pillow that in a flash transported me back to my childhood. I uneasily waited for Mamadou while looking for someone to talk to. Off in a corner, I caught sight of a candidate: an elderly woman propped up on a rickety wooden dinndeere. Once beside her, I explained that I wanted to build a mud stove.

"Good, good. That's good," she responded in a hoarse voice. Did she have any idea what a mud stove was? Probably not, I figured.

"Do you cook?" I asked, noticing that her eyes were obscured by cataracts, sagging eyelids and puffy cheeks.

"No, no, I'm old," she chortled, exposing teeth-stained orange from kola nuts, small pieces of which lingered on her gums.

"But you eat," I countered, and we both laughed. "I like to eat," I said, and we both laughed again.

"Yes, yes, I like to eat," she responded while leaning over to blow her nose on the ground. "You can't laugh when your belly is hollow," she reported while patting hers.

Just then, Mamadou strode into the compound, followed closely by a slew of young boys dutifully carrying mud bricks on their heads, and an older girl carrying a heavy tub full of wet mud.

"Come here, Fatou," he called out, once he located me sitting aside this elder. I bid the woman farewell, grasping a rough and calloused hand as I did.

"Go, go," she said, "that's my son." She demonstrated her relationship with Mamadou by slipping her hand from mine then shaking a flaccid breast beneath her frayed boubou.

"Oh," I said, taking a closer look at her kindly face, guessing she was over eighty.

She broke into a wide orange smile, then put the last bit of a yellow kola nut into her mouth and gave it a loud crunch.

I wasn't sure what I made of Mamadou, but I sure liked his mother.

"To you I bring kola nut," I promised as I rose. She grabbed my hand, praised my name, and shooed me off.

Meanwhile, Mamadou was already setting up the bricks and orchestrating the deposits of mud on a growing pile. I was taken aback by this one-man show, as I had expected to undertake the project with women, not him. Women, after all, were the ones who cooked.

I walked to the spot already identified for the stove's location, and asked, "Who cooks? Who cooker?" It wasn't Mamadou, I knew, and I was sticking to our lesson plan; the women must choose the stove's location, since they were the ones who cooked. Mamadou's imperiousness was dooming my project.

With a sweep of his arm, Mamadou ordered the young girl back to the river for more mud.

"The women," he eventually responded from his bent-over position.

I looked around. A dozen people of different ages were scattered about the compound observing the scene before them. With no obvious lifeline, I tried again.

"Women build, women make," I insisted, a statement I knew would be about as effective as had my suggestion days earlier that men should help women hoist water up from the river. No surprise that this day's entreaty was similarly ignored.

And so, an hour later Mamadou and I had a stove built in the middle of his compound. With lingering annoyance, I stood back and inspected our work, my arms now covered in mud. As Mamadou ordered someone to bring him water, I told the women to wait two days before coating the oven with the cow dung treatment that would give it a hard, protective shell. They nodded and we smiled at one another. Despite the breach in building protocol, I felt optimistic.

And with good reason. In the months that followed, Mamadou and Djeinaba's stoves became the village's conversation piece. Each day I filled orders for more, and soon a good share of Civé's compounds proudly displayed this new energy-saving technology.

Too soon, though, those stoves fell into disuse, seemingly never able to replace the comfort and familiarity of their old-fashioned counterpart. Like new shoes that don't quite fit, I figured. Once the rains arrived, slowly but surely each stove washed away, eventually leaving not a single trace behind of their temporary presence in Civé's compounds.

One more lesson learned: Making a difference in this village would take something more than shaping the riverbank's mud into brick stoves.

I knew I had my work cut out for me. Yet lacking a blueprint, I somewhat blindly stumbled onward. Hopefully I would not wind up like my neighbor's goat, which that week had been swallowed up by one of the countless crevices that the parched land around us offered up.

Chapter 10

My President

My first friend in the village was a middle-aged man named M'bu. Short and scrawny, M'bu wore ragged shorts, had a patchy beard, and always carried a broad toothless smile. M'bu's happy-go-lucky demeanor attracted me. Plus, I had everyone's endorsement for my fine choice: '*M'bu ko kangaado,*' they would tell me. M'bu's a great guy. "Yes, *kangaado,*" I responded happily.

Every day M'bu dropped by. Generally, such constant attention would drive me crazy, particularly since visitors never left without demanding some gift. But once I shrugged 'no' to M'bu's request for a cigarette, he waved away my empty hands with a wide grin and twinkling eyes. Most importantly, he seemed not to care the least that I couldn't get beyond the 'hello, how are you, how is everyone at your house' greeting, nor that my language skills matched the babble of a toddler. M'bu just chattered away at my porch, his soothing steady patter allowing me to pretend some meaningful exchange was occurring. For sure it wasn't perfect, but his mere presence gave me a welcome respite from my long mute days. I kept watch for his approach.

But once my senses were no longer on overload, some things began to stand out about M'bu. Like he was always barefoot. That he never headed to the fields. That he wore shorts, not a boubou. Then it struck me that his soothing voice had an unusual sing-song quality to it.

"*Neene,*" I asked my adoptive mom one crisp morning, "M'bu.

M'bu ko… o andaa…." I struggled.

With characteristic impatience, she ended my sentence for me. *"M'bu andaa hay batte."* *He knows zilch*, she had declared with a chortle, her 'zilch,' *hay batte*, articulated with great emphasis. Thus, finally, it sank in. *Kangaado* didn't mean 'great guy' after all. It meant 'crazy'.

Those initial weeks were indeed awkward and confusing; I was uneasy in my surroundings and uncertain in my mission. Any bearings I might gain, for instance through a new friendship, a successfully built stove, or a conversation understood, was short-lived. I continued my sweeping, letter writing, and walks to the fields; anything to create the illusion of days fuller of purpose than I felt them to be.

But there was another reason for maintaining a strict routine. I wanted to ward off Civé's unoccupied teenagers. The least sign of inactivity on my part—like reading a book—and a slew would appear at my fence unannounced, stroll in and greet me, and then plop themselves down and make themselves at home.

At first, a long list of questions would ensue, typically about my parents, my family, the river in my hometown ('None? Where do you get water?'), whether I liked Pulaars, how much money I made, and when I was going to take them for a ride on the useless grey motorbike still stored in my back room.

Eventually someone would insert a cassette into my radio, and all would settle in for an excruciatingly long stay. Before the time arrived to flip the cassette over, all of my personal items were under inspection. One would rummage through my clothes, holding a few odd items up for the amusement of others. Another would apply hand cream, passing it around before sending a child with a handful of it off to some distant locale. Then out came my books, searched for illustrations; *Where There is No Doctor* was an unsurpassed hit, especially the chapter on childbirth. My toothpaste was tasted, my flashlight batteries borrowed, the rubbish in my back room sorted.

Our Peace Corps trainers had warned us that villagers would push our personal boundaries. They recommended that initially we avoid being overly friendly or generous. "Figure out who you want as a friend rather than the other way around," were Tyler's parting words to us.

I took this advice to heart and arrived in the village wary of everyone. Each request I received, whether it was for aspirin, a hundred dollars, a bottle of shampoo, some hand cream, a hairbrush, batteries, my motorbike, a cigarette, my diesel can, a picture of my mother, or most commonly, my hand in marriage, I said no. And yes, marriage. After a minute of conversation, most males over the age of twelve would propose it after confirming my unmarried status.

"Single? Then I'm your man."

"I want a tubaak wife. I will marry you."

"Pulaar men make good husbands. How about me?"

I did make one exception to my otherwise cross-armed responses to villagers' requests. That was with Mamadou Konaté's eighty-plus-year-old mother Koumba, who had all the appearances of someone in the twilight of life. Her eyes were milky and unfocused, her legs often swelled, and flabby butter-soft skin looking like cloth, hung from her upper arms. When someone talked to Koumba, they often shouted, then grinned when with raspy voice she responded. But what really endeared me to Koumba was that each day her legs allowed, she arose from her dinndeere, plucked a rusty enamel bowl from a pile, ordered a boy to bring over her short jalo, then wriggled on thrice-repaired rubber slippers. Out she then ambled to the fields, often several miles distant, where she toiled until that rusty bowl of hers was filled. Touched by such tenacity, I took to periodically delivering her a small handful of kola nuts.

Despite being otherwise stingy, and despite not welcoming marriage proposals, my popularity rating seemed to soar, particularly among the town's teenagers. Without notice, they strode jovially into my house, then roamed freely while ignoring my inhospitality. How was I ever to establish boundaries when they seemed to recognize none?

A month or so after my arrival, a ringleader of this teenage group, the teenaged niece of my neene Taanooy, came over. Habi had long ago dropped out of school, and while living with the Ba's came with a full slate of household chores, she also had plenty of free time.

On this particular morning, I was grumpy as I'd spent a sleepless night serenaded by the raucous grunts of my neighbors' mating goats. It was early, and I was standing in the backyard brushing my teeth while ruminating over a restless dream featuring an old boyfriend riding my motorbike over sand dunes. Below me the wide river murmured as it rippled west.

I spit the remains of my toothpaste into my sandy backyard, stretched, then watched my next-door neighbor Harouna stand up in his long grey pirogue as he cast a thin net out over the calm river. The net spread, briefly floated, then sank. Harouna next slowly reined the net in to inspect its contents as the languid river leisurely carried him my way. The quiet peaceful beauty of that early morning was reviving me.

For a moment, anyways. Alas it broke when I turned to see Habi entering my property trailed by twin girls, each carrying a wide assortment of cooking supplies.

Within minutes, Habi had set up shop in my entry room and was firing up my miniature gas stove. A large gourd spoon in hand, she straightaway began scooping out the contents of an oversized tin can, one stamped with the words 'DRIED WHOLE EGGS' and 'USA.' Unbeknownst to me, the day before a truckload of food aid had arrived in Civé, and each household had received a large tin of powdered eggs, five gallons of cooking oil, and a fifty pound sack of flour. Habi had decided to use my premises and gas to cook up a meal. Word of this activity quickly spread, and soon a large handful of youth came sauntering in. In short order, my home was overrun with adolescents I barely knew. I had nowhere to go and no idea how to rid myself of them.

So, I turned to my morning tasks, trying to appear too busy for either eggs or socializing.

"*Kinidi*." Habi smiled at me as she stirred her simmering eggs amidst the developing crowd, as I, bent over, swept sand and a live dung beetle from my porch.

"*Kinidi*?" I asked. I wondered if she would once again instruct me on how to tie my pagne and braced myself for another condescending lesson.

"*Kinidi*," she repeated, and then the unusual utterance: "Thank you."

A young man laying by her side dressed in brightly printed baggy cotton pants, a T-shirt, sunglasses, and a knit hat, pointed to the small gourd of oil that Habi now held, and repeated, "*Kinidi*." I could tell this was important because just as the African pop star Youssou N'Dour was reaching the climax in his piece—right when someone usually ratchets up the volume to drown out all interference—a youngster relegated Youssou to the background. Habi stirred the eggs now frying in oil. A deliciously evocative smell entered my brain through both nostrils.

"*Nebam*?" I asked, using the Pulaar word for oil, my eyes now drawn to this irresistible bubbling dish cooking on my floor, while out of nowhere came memories of late Sunday breakfasts. I wondered if she could learn to make hash browns. *And how exactly does one dry eggs?*

"No, no, not nebam. *Kinidi*." The others in the room looked at me and concurred that I must understand this word. Frustrated but curious, I stopped sweeping completely. Did kinidi perhaps mean gourd? It didn't. Eggs? Cooking? No and no.

"No, no. Kinidi means Kinidi. Ki-ni-di," said a young man who, now wrapped up in my sleeping bag, was taking photos of my family out of my small album and passing them around. With his helpful explanation, I gave up. I disappeared down to the river to wash clothes, then returned to drape them along my fence.

An hour later, my laundry dried and folded, my entire compound swept, and a rip in my boubou mended, I announced that I had some writing to do.

"Me write," I said, waving a spiral notebook, expecting to go sit under my neem tree and abandon my house to these intruders.

Inexplicably, though, all activity immediately halted. Off went the radio. The dishes were collected, and the pans, utensils, pots, gourds, and platters gathered. In a few short minutes, I sat alone, pen and blank paper at my side, the air suddenly too quiet.

What now? I wondered, as I watched the youth stride merrily down the lane in the best of spirits. Worse still, they had left no eggs. What now?

With these mysterious events in mind, I eventually set about to writing letters and jotting down questions I would ask my instructor Tall that afternoon. Top on my mind was why teenagers descended on my house, and how I might keep them at bay? And what the heck did this word *kinidi* mean?

***

My afternoon walk through the village that day led me to a wide, shady compound on a rise just down the lane from the village mosque. I wasn't sure who lived there, but was soon strolling from one dinndeere to another, exchanging handshakes and good cheer with everyone present.

Across the courtyard, a large woman with indigo-colored lips and decorative scars adjacent to each eye set down a bowl brimming with deep-green bean leaves. She approached me smiling broadly with both hands extended.

"Wane, Wane, Wane," she said, praising me and all my ancestors. She inquired into the health of all as we warmly shook hands, her large muscular arms and half-exposed breasts jiggling with enthusiasm as we did.

"Wane. Wane," she continued, finally clapping her hands. "Come. Stay for dinner."

Before I could answer, this matronly woman smelling of charcoal and incense and bursting with goodwill led me by hand to a prone elder on a nearby dinndeere who was now struggling to rise.

"This is my father," she announced, our hands joined as we stood above him.

The man appeared to be at death's door; his eyes stared blankly, and his voice seemed trapped in his throat. I sat by his side as he slowly rose to his elbows and asked for his skull cap. Then I swore I heard him utter the word '*kinidi,*' followed by a blessing.

"Here, here!" Nearby a middle-aged woman was drawing my attention to a large burlap flour sack propped upright in a dark entryway leading to some back room. I figured this bag contained the flour Civé's households had received the day before. The woman continued slapping the bag, and I found myself scrutinizing it. Then I realized it was decorated with an American flag, above which was written in English, 'A gift of the American people.' Placed below the flag was the image of two shaking hands, one a white countryman's, the other some generic, brown-skinned beneficiary. I stared at this startling gift from my country, one that in some very circuitous manner had just found its way to this remote Mauritanian village.

"*Kinidi,*" the woman said clearly while pointing to the sack. My ruminations broken, I looked up at her wide welcoming smile.

My attention returned to the familiar red, white and blue flag emblazoned on the front of that upright sack. Then a flicker of light.

"Kennedy?" I looked up at her.

"Yes, yes, *kinidi*" she responded while nodding and giving the sack a friendly smack.

"President Kennedy?" I asked. Her wide smile told me I'd finally got it. She and the other women laughed merrily while I blinked away a sudden sting in my eyes.

"Kenedi," repeated a young girl with a giggle, making fun of the odd way I pronounced our long-deceased president's name. Countless thank yous and blessings followed. Regaining my composure, I beamed as we exchanged more handshakes, delighted with the realization that villagers considered me JFK's next-of-kin.

***

An hour later and my daily Pulaar language lesson with Tall was under way. I was eager to ask about food aid, and Tall was happy to explain. The first truckloads of it came in the early 1960s, shortly after Mauritania gained independence from France. Now with the prolonged drought, deliveries came twice yearly.

"When the first load appeared, we were told it was a gift from President Kennedy," Tall explained with a chuckle as we lay on mats in his courtyard, sipping lowwol. "We named a boulevard in Nouakchott after him, and everyone just started calling food aid *kinidi.*"

The oil, which was the most common delivery, was soon termed '*kinidi oil*,' and an active trade in it occurred whenever it arrived.

"Before, Moors in big trucks followed each delivery. They bought up the food aid, paying hardly anything. People were more desperate for money than dried milk," he explained. The aid then wound up in urban centers for sale. Even today, kinidi oil can occasionally be found in local markets—if you ask for it.

"But the kinidi oil is cheap…you don't pay much," Djeinaba snickered as she switched her infant son from one breast to the other.

Tall tried to fill in. "President Kinidi doesn't know oil," he explained, adding some detail I didn't quite understand. Djeinaba nodded. Puzzled, I decided not to pursue the topic, and soon our conversation turned to their lone goat and the two kids she had delivered the night before.

But eventually I did come to understand. For some reason, the flavor of kinidi oil was always off. I don't know why. Maybe the heat and transportation degraded it. But after eating a single meal of rice fried in it, you would know. Only people too poor to buy Mauritanian oil would use President Kinidi's. The first bite of my inaugural meal cooked in it was, to put it politely, unsavory. From then on, I cut any visit short once I detected the sharp aroma of kinidi oil emerging from a sizzling cast iron pot.

***

Whether or not food aid—actually any sort of aid—is the right response to poverty and hunger in poor countries is today hotly debated. Some believe aid undermines local institutions and stifles more organic, effective solutions; that outside help from rich countries should be directed toward enabling rather than supplanting the local economy and assisting rather than replacing the government. Others argue that the aid rich countries give is totally insufficient in amount and type to make a difference, and that we must be vastly more generous.

The lives led by those I came to know in Civé were complicated, and far more trying than the typical ones in rich countries. So much so that I have become wary of simple explanations for why poor countries stay poor and what we in rich countries can do to help. While in Civé, I came to feel ambivalent about those burlap sacks of flour or gallon cans of oil scattered throughout the village, each one emblazoned with an American flag and hands grasped in friendship. On the one hand, the logo offered momentary relief. For a passing instant I felt the presence of my countrymen in our joint mission to help the people of Civé. On the other, my nation's gestures seemed cheap, even disingenuous. There was no real handshake. No genuine understanding of what the oil they sent tasted like, nor whether people even needed dried milk.

Those periodic deliveries of food aid to Civé served to remind me of my country's awkward, ill-chosen way to help the people of Mauritania. Whenever I saw those woven bags and large tin cans being offloaded from trucks, I always stood wondering if my own presence in this village wasn't just as misplaced as was the foul-tasting oil now being carted off to each of the village's compounds.

Chapter 11

Cóndi Hiraande

To those in Civé, I was an Americanaajo. No other identity seemed necessary to explain why I had settled among them, wandered their lanes, scrubbed clothes on their riverbanks, and wobbled uneasily along the diggettes in their fields. I on the other hand, desperately needed a fuller identity.

So, I worked on building one. Whenever possible, I reminded villagers that I was an *encadreur*, or extension agent, working for their own Mauritanian Ministry of Rural Development.

"Once rice come, I help you," I told them cheerfully, all the while sensing the presence of a smirking Mr. Okamoto thousands of miles away. Still, I did know there were things I could help with, like making sure the fertilizer was correctly applied; the rice shoots were uprooted at day twenty and transplanted into fields one palm apart; and that all bugs were doused with the requisite powder as soon as they dared appear.

This 'once rice come' comment of mine, not surprisingly, often led to an astute observation:

"But rice comes after *Ceedu*, when *N'dungu* arrives." It was as if I had told them in February that I was here to help with Christmas decorations.

Honestly, I had no idea why I was sent to help with a crop that had just been harvested. But I had a response: "Because I must learn your tongue." Which was true. And as a side benefit, the long interlude gave me time to study each of the International Rice Research

Institute's manuals stacked in my back room.

SONADER, as everyone called the Ministry for which I worked, was short for Société Nationale Pour Le Développement Rural. Only a decade old, its sole purpose was to bring irrigated rice to the right bank of the Senegal River Valley. This brown, dusty, and windswept locale was not one where you'd imagine rice growing; you could, after all, count on two hands (*if Allah willed it*) the number of days each year the rains fell. Photos in SONADER offices of lush Asian rice fields with palm trees swaying off in the distance only emphasized how poorly adapted our surroundings were to rice. Whoever heard of growing rice in the desert?

But it turns out the Senegal River basin's heavy clay waalo fields and long hot sunny days make it a rice-growing haven. The missing ingredient, water, is more or less abundantly present in the river that courses below its mud flats. All you needed were motor pumps to carry that water up and over the banks. *And* a reliable infrastructure for a few other necessary ingredients: oil, fertilizers, tractors, pesticides, spare parts, mechanics, and technical advice. Providing all this was SONADER's role. And now mine. Together we were helping to bring SONADER's resources and guidance to the region's farming talent so this fertile valley could blossom with rice.

Simple math during our Nouakchott training sessions had convinced us SONADER volunteers of our mission's urgency. If farmers would convert their clay waalo lands to irrigated rice, they'd triple or even quadruple the calories produced. For this reason, and this reason alone, villages up and down the river valley were lobbying for SONADER's bulldozers and backhoes to come convert their waalo plains into neatly arranged perimeters. When that happened, SONADER's loans, fertilizers, and expert technicians—like me—followed.

When I arrived in 1984, the region's first rice perimeters were barely ten years old. The impetus for this historic switch from rain-fed to irrigated crops was the severe, prolonged, and still ongoing drought that in the 1960s hit the entire Sahel, from Mauritania in the west to the Sudan in the east. Some label it one of the twentieth century's most devastating droughts.

However it measures up to other awful droughts, this one left Mauritania absolutely destitute, its pastoral society transformed into a nation of squatters pressed into the margins of the young nation's sparse and impoverished towns. Countless acts of desperation were destroying the region's common grazing fields, shared woods, and public watering holes on which so many depended. Food production fell in half, and three-quarters of Mauritania's livestock died. Food imports and kinidi brought some relief, but malnutrition and starvation were everywhere. Moor camel herders descended farther and farther south from the desert, placing themselves in direct competition with Mauritania's black farmers for the country's dwindling forage and water supplies. The nation's newly established political order faced intense pressure to resolve these growing conflicts.

Meanwhile, international agencies urgently developed many 'action plans.' One proposal held special promise: sucking the Senegal River's bountiful water supply up and over the banks and into brand new perimeters constructed for rice. This plan eventually gained Peace Corps' support, and soon young unknowing Americans like me were dispatched up and down the country's river valley to help small villages, like Civé, manage this momentous transition.

***

The month I arrived, Civé's two irrigated perimeters were sprouting not rice, but corn and vegetables, the region's preferred crop during *Dabunde*, the cool season. Shortly after settling in, I began taking regular trips to the fields to observe the activities and bolster my identity as the village's bonified SONADER expert. The first field went by the name of *Cóndi Hiraande*. Located on a bluff above the riverbank a short half-mile from my hut, Cóndi Hiraande spread out over thirty hectares divided into 40 family plots. The second field, called *Becce,* lay another three miles upstream, and Mamadou Konaté was the cooperative's president.

It didn't take long for me to figure out that all was not well at Cóndi Hiraande. One obvious problem was its motor pumps. The cooperative owned—or more accurately, was in the process of buying from SONADER—three separate motor pumps. Yet for some reason, only one worked. A brand new, army-green pump, its steel still shiny, its yellow Lister label not yet splattered with oil, had inexplicably shut down at the tail end of the rice campaign. A few farmers had hoisted the heavy pump up from the river for closer inspection, and the machine still lay by the edge of the perimeter gathering mud and dust, as if awaiting transport to a machine morgue.

"The broken piece comes," one farmer told me. "We are waiting. It comes from your land."

"My land?" I asked.

"Yes, the land of tubaaks."

I learned that after a visiting SONADER mechanic was unable to awaken the broken beast, he had ordered a new shaft from Europe. But that was long ago. Meanwhile, a second pump had also given up the ghost and now lay abandoned, half-hidden by weeds.

Yet the farmers continued to receive bills for all three pumps. Why they must pay for two defective pumps baffled me. I asked, but the answers I heard perplexed me.

"Hendu ndu. Lewru ndu. Apollo," explained a short, sinewy, barefoot farmer one windy day when the air was so thick with dust that villagers insisted that I cover my face with a scarf, even though they did not. He made a click clicking noise of approval while I, standing on the canal banks above him, recorded his pronouncement in my notebook.

This man's references to the wind (hendu) and the moon (lewru) I caught. But Apollo? This, my instructor Tall explained that afternoon from behind his scarf, meant conjunctivitis. Apparently a particularly virulent and long-lasting attack of the inflammation coincided with news that Americans had launched a ship out to where the moon lived. From then on, the word Apollo became synonymous with *ñaw gite*, or rotten eye, as Pulaars traditionally call conjunctivitis.

But I still didn't know what Apollo, let along the wind or the moon, had to do with Cóndi Hiraande's broken motor pump. Tall and his wife Djeinaba only chuckled when I asked, then shrugged their shoulders.

To explain their predicament with these broken pumps, others in the cooperative directed their ire toward the cooperative's president, an older man by the name of Doro Thioub.

"Doro! He knows nothing," exclaimed more than one.

Suspicion was also cast on Thiamel, a wiry man who wore a faded camouflage jacket in the fields, and who oversaw the cooperative's motor pump. "Thiamel. You can't eat rice with no oil. Why should a machine live without it?"

A few blamed the rains, evoking the days of old when farming required neither SONADER, motor pumps, nor the trouble of working with this complex organization called a 'cooperative.' These farmers simply threw up their hands, then plucked out a penny they'd stashed in their thatched roof, and bought a single sheet of paper. Some youth would be recruited to write a relative in a distant locale, imploring this family member for a few ouguiyas to get them through 'times only Allah understood.'

Most commonly, though, the farmers' fury over the two non-functioning pumps was directed at SONADER.

"SONADER is a *mbuutu*," exclaimed a farmer one day while vigorously weeding her plot. "… bad pump. They make us pay… all *booti*." I wondered if she understood that I, too, worked for SONADER, which would make *me* an eel as well. Probably best not to remind her.

Still, I took my association with SONADER seriously.

SONADER's problems were mine to fix. Every few days, I handed the driver of the afternoon Rapide an envelope as he headed downstream. On it I had written 'Guisse, SONADER' in clear, tall letters. Each day I asked the shopkeeper Samba Anne, whose small booth stood adjacent to the village's "taxi garage," if the Rapide had brought me a response from my boss. Each day he crossed his arms across a wide middle, and with a bemused look shook his head no.

Frustrated by SONADER's silence, early one morning I hiked ninety minutes to Matam, Senegal. There I posted a letter to my boss Stan in Nouakchott, asking if he could let those at SONADER's headquarters know that Civé's two motor pumps were busted and needed fixing. But writing Stan proved as successful as did writing my boss Guisse. That both my SONADER and Peace Corps partners went mute when presented with such urgent needs, filled me with despair and a sense of abandonment. It was as if I too lay wounded and helpless with dust and sand settling over me.

Meanwhile, the cool season continued to chug along, and so too did Cóndi Hiraande's vegetable crops. Soon the fields required more water than the cooperative's single working pump could deliver, and each day fresh disputes broke out. Arguments now turned from whose fault it was that the pumps were broken to the more pressing concern—which farmers would get the limited water the single pump could deliver? And should farmers be able to put more land under cultivation, as many were already doing?

"There is water, and my family needs food," a farmer grunted to me one day, while emphatically thrusting a long heavy wooden rod shaped like a gigantic pencil into the hard clay soil, a pre-adolescent boy trailing behind to leave dried corn kernels in the hole.

Yet many were unhappy with such neighbors, pleading for patience because, "The road will bring us a motor pump." But the farmers went on planting, swatting at the air when others complained as if a bee were buzzing around them.

"No water for corn," I instructed a farmer one dusty morning as

I stood beside her. She was an older woman who had earlier caught my attention when I spotted her wearing a torn Boston Celtics T-shirt, complete with a shamrock and leprechaun. A bit mesmerized by her apparel, I now stood aside her as she jabbed her wood pole into the ground, her large muscular arms straining with each forceful thrust.

"I... don't... care," she grunted rhythmically. Standing up straight, she eyed me and then added, "Write that." I did, drawing a shamrock next to my entry.

Just then, a shirtless younger man in a neighboring plot halted his weeding to spit out loudly, "She doesn't care." As I turned his way, he spread his arms wide and twisted his face in anger. "But I do care. I pay her water," he continued before ordering me to, "Write that." Obediently I did, drawing a bald man with bare feet next to the entry.

Several times, I attempted to discuss the dilemma of too-little-water for too-much-land-under-cultivation with Doro Thioub, Cóndi Hiraande's president. Doro was an older man who always wore the same muddy ice blue tunic to the field. This along with his yellow bloodshot eyes, protruding front teeth, and grey goatee peering out from the deep shadows of his cone-shaped straw hat made him easy to spot. But my attempts at persuasion went nowhere. Doro had little patience for my broken Pulaar, and (fair enough) even less for any suggestion that I might have good advice. Each conversation was cut short with a final 'Allah is great' or 'too many problems,' and off he'd trot to shout something at some farmer in the distance. Meanwhile, I watched helplessly as one-by-one, Cóndi Hiraande's members arrived in the fields lugging oversized pencils with seed-bearing children trailing behind.

As the corn-growing ranks grew, so too did passion. Every morning Thiamel fired up the one working pump, and on it labored until the fourth prayer of the day approached. Some days it sputtered for hours only to deliver water to a distant plot with two-foot-tall bright green corn stalks located adjacent to a plot with eight-foot-high, sun-dried ones. Such jumbled practices were never discussed during our classroom sessions, nor did any passage in my agricultural manuals address them.

Clearly some intervention with the farmers was in order, but what could I do? My instructions were, more or less, 'to work with the rice farmers.' What exactly that meant in this precise instance stumped me. More seasoned volunteers had counseled us to just do what made sense.

One night, after another frustrating day at Cóndi Hiraande, I dreamt that I and other volunteers were frantically paddling a leaky rowboat, while beside us steamed a luxurious liner. On deck stood our Peace Corps director, helpfully bellowing through his bullhorn, "Do what makes sense!"

Feeling bereft of options, I blindly continued on with my campaign of reason, repeating helpful pieces of advice such as "This wastes water," or "Water is money," or sometimes an inspirational, "Work together as one!" And while everyone listened to me, so too did they heed the rustle of wind that passed through bushes and stirred up dust, or the occasional mangy dog that barked in the distance.

The more I visited Cóndi Hiraande, the more bewildered I became with its state of affairs. Broken pumps were its biggest problem. Yet there were more. The perimeter had never been properly leveled to allow water to flow smoothly through its canals. In some places, water faced the interesting challenge of flowing uphill. Where it ran downhill, sometimes it flowed so rapidly that the canals eroded, the water spilt over, and the fields flooded. In several places, fast-flowing canal water had so worn away the banks that the canal was transformed into a ten-foot-wide river.

Meanwhile, Cóndi Hiraande's members coped by manually lugging water around the perimeter, digging out waterways, patching holes, and occasionally shutting down canals that no longer functioned. Finally, the cooperative hit on the idea of rotating the location of its only working motor pump, one day placing it on the down river end of the perimeter, the next day on the upriver end. This task required a full day to drag the pump's floating platform several hundred yards upstream or downstream, then relocate and reattach the heavy irrigation pipes to the pump. Back and forth that pump shuttled so that water could reach all the plots scattered hither and thither.

And then there was the fact that the thorny dense bramble of murotoki branches that encircled the perimeter to serve as its fence had gaping holes in it. These openings made it hard to ward off the hungry camels, cows, donkeys, and goats out searching for a meal. As temperatures rose and wild forage withered, the challenge of keeping out those gatecrashers grew. Next to their plots, farmers began driving young patouki branches into the ground, then weaving doum palm leaves and millet stalks around and above those sticks until a tiny temporary dwelling arose. Come nightfall, men with dinner bowls tottering on their heads began passing my house, a small blanket draped across one shoulder.

"May we pass the evening in peace," I called out to each as he passed.

"May we live," each would respond with a smile and friendly wave as he headed out to pass a watchful night aside his Cóndi Hiraande plot.

Chapter 12

Becce

Members of the Cóndi Hiraande cooperative did not seem particularly cooperative. But the second one, Becce, operated like *Liwoogu*, the river manatee I occasionally spotted gliding up and down the river. No splashing, no struggling, in fact hardly a ripple: just smooth, effortless, indeed elegant progress forward.

After clambering over the thick branch that marked Cóndi Hiraande's far boundary, you would reach Becce after forty minutes of navigating gullies and steering through the long thorns scattered everywhere across the flat baked soils. Then, with the river some distance below, Becce's fields spread before you.

While it was a hike to get to Becce, it was a worthwhile one. There I visited with farmers and occasionally lent a spare hand: weeding one farmer's hot pepper plants, plucking the ripe cherry tomatoes of another, or distributing fertilizer doses to those toiling in the field.

And Becce was organized.

Members were grouped into small contiguous clusters sharing identical irrigation schedules. If a farmer wasn't present when water arrived, the treasurer Kebe would duly record a 100-ouguiya pawgol in the cooperative's black accounting book. And when Mamadou Konaté sent Civé's town crier Ballal striding through the village lanes, singing out in loud, harmonious tones that the next day was a *dawol*, or obligatory workday—the canals needed work, or vegetable seeds needed dividing—each member appeared or else Kebe's black pen would mark him for that dreaded pawgol.

Becce also allowed me to work on my language. By day's end, I could discuss how to transplant onions, explain the irrigation sequence, or describe the precise look of that day's dusty sky. Once home, I'd visit my family's compound to try out my new-found literacy.

"Today we transplant onions. You put each seedling one palm apart…" Most encouraged me on. My adopted mom, not so much. With a dismissive laugh, she'd find good reason to announce to all, '*O andaa haay batte!*' She knows zilch. Taanooy was like the person watching a magician's show who takes it upon themself to figure out the magician's trick, and then announce it to all.

***

One day late in winter, the hot winds foretelling what season was headed our way, I was out at Becce. Kebe called me over to examine his discolored eggplants. He pointed out spotted leaves and held up a few sad looking shriveled eggplants for inspection.

"Eggplants don't turn to money," he said with disappointment. "We need something that does." Suddenly he turned to me grinning. "Why not an orchard?" he asked, immediately reminding me on the spot of Mamadou's suggestion a few months prior. "See, there?" He pointed above the place where the motor pump's dull aluminum pipes jetted up from the banks. "They have them."

"Senegal?" I asked. "What fruit?"

"Mangos," he exclaimed, his eyes widening and his white teeth flashing an irresistible smile.

"Mango grow here?" I asked in disbelief while casting a glance around. My dusty, austere surroundings were not conjuring up images of thriving tropical fruit.

"They do in Senegal. And bananas."

Walking home that day, I gazed across the flat expanse of Senegal, wondering where exactly the nearest mango tree was. Not close, I imagined.

Those early days in the field allowed me to become acquainted with most of Becce's farmers; in addition to Kebe, my favorite became the fellow in charge of the motor pump, a slight man with an oversized grin and undersized boubou by the name of Amadou Demba. Amadou Demba sported a turban wound *out* rather than *up*, sunglasses, a button-up shirt that lacked all buttons but one, and rolled-up baggy pants. He instructed me on motor pumps, irrigation schedules, and the cooperative's rules for maintaining the canals.

One clear day, I was trailing Amadou Demba along the banks when he stopped and turned my way. "You know, we'd like mangos," he pronounced. Beaming, he added, "We make looooottttssss of money."

"Mango grow here?" I posed the same question to Amadou Demba that I had a few weeks earlier to Kebe.

"Ooooooooooffffff courrrrrrssssee," he said with great enthusiasm. "We would sell them in Kaedi, in Matam. Even…Nouakchott." He searched around in the front pocket of his tattered shirt for the butt of a cigarette, then lit it up. After exhaling, he added with a deep laugh, "Maybe even America!"

That afternoon, the lands beyond the ripening melon, beans, and corn on Senegal's distant banks once more drew my gaze. Just how far away *were* those mangos?

Becce's president Mamadou Konaté was ever present in the fields. We frequently crossed paths, briefly and politely exchanging greetings when we did. Occasionally Mamadou sent his son Abou around to alert everyone to an impromptu meeting; when he did, the men laid down their tools, stretched out sore backs, and headed to squat under a sprawling handsome dounoube tree in the perimeter's eastern reaches. I too headed that way to observe the discussion and catch what meaning I could.

After one such meeting involving some heated exchanges I

could not follow, I joined Amadou Demba as he returned to his plot. While traversing the canal banks, he patiently explained that the cooperative had just voted to pay the princely sum of 20,000 ouguiyas (nearly $350) to a Moor herder on behalf of a Becce farmer. Some weeks earlier, this farmer had encountered an unattended camel chomping on ripening sorghum in the sandy dieri fields behind the village. Deaf to shouts, the camel soon received a hard whack on the head from the exasperated farmer's jalo. With that, the beast crumpled to the ground.

"Thud. It fell. It didn't get up," was how this farmer later described the deadly encounter to me.

"You push one and it just falls dead," sighed another, commenting sympathetically on the frailty of camels.

Efforts to hide this deadly deed proved unsuccessful, and a few afternoons later the angry Moor herder arrived in the company of two Moor officials from the government outpost of Matam, Mauritania. The Becce farmer was given a choice: pay the fine or be carted off to some unnamed prison.

A few Becce members were unhappy with the cooperative's decision to pay this man's fine. But once the vote was in, everyone simply returned to their fields until hunger, exhaustion, and a sun touching the horizon signaled the workday's end.

***

I eventually came to see three factors that distinguished Becce from Cóndi Hiraande. One was obvious: leadership. To President Doro Thioub's credit, he did occasionally attempt to right the listing ship of Cóndi Hiraande. But whenever he announced *dawols* hardly a soul showed up. And those who did, came late and left early. Before realizing this, I always appeared whenever a dawol was called. Eventually, a few others would too, and we would gather at the most problematic canal or largest gap in the fence. But inevitably someone let loose a few choice words, and dramatic shouts, laughter, or displays of spitting followed. Finally, someone would shovel dirt into a canal or throw murotoki branches at the fence. And that was that.

At first, I couldn't understand why Cóndi Hiraande's members didn't respond to Doro as Becce's members did to Mamadou. But after one particular morning I did. I had agreed to help Doro divvy up the rice season's campaign expenses, the same task I had undertaken with Kebe months earlier, promptly becoming smitten with him in the process.

Doro lived up on Civé Dow, High Civé, in a home overlooking a deep ravine forming the village's northwestern border. That morning, my arrival was announced by a couple of chickens as two girls with tubs of dirty clothes balanced on their heads sauntered past me to the river. Off to the left sat Doro alone on his dinndeere while his two wives remained swaddled in blankets across the dirt courtyard.

As I entered, Doro looked up from the paperwork on his lap. With an impish smile, he rose to greet me. His groomed appearance caught me by surprise. He sported a freshly pressed midnight blue boubou with intricate gold embroidery on its large front pocket, and his square white skull cap revealed short hair turning grey, a round face with puffy cheeks, and protruding ears. He appeared very different from the rumpled and bossy farmer I knew from the fields.

After our greetings, Doro asked me if I had yet found a Pulaar husband. "Pulaar men are better than American men," he said with a mischievous grin.

"I carry calculator," I returned, holding up Casio for his inspection.

"Good, good," he replied. To my relief, it seemed he wouldn't return to his cure for my spinsterhood. Instead, he handed me a large, dirty torn yellow envelope. Out of it tumbled a few incomprehensible slips of paper.

"This all?" I asked, looking down at the fragments in my lap.

"And here," he grinned, tapping the side of his head.

Then he launched into a long story I couldn't quite follow, something about a son living in Nouadhibou.

"He has salary, you can marry him," he concluded. 'Having a salary,' meant his son probably worked for the government. Little in the Fuuta was more coveted than the secure and steady income that came with that.

"Ha," I replied, and waving the yellow envelope returned to the topic at hand. "No paper?"

"Oumar makes good husband," he continued. "Salary."

Seeing his wide smile and suddenly hearing how silent his compound had become, I took a chance. "And you: good father-in-law?"

At this, Doro roared with laughter, encouraging others to join in his merriment.

Encouraged, Doro attempted to settle a wedding date. "After two moons die, he visits. Then comes marriage."

Thankfully this banter came to an end when finally Doro gave up and called for Cóndi Hiraande's vice president. A short bald man with a warm smile and twinkling eyes, Saidou Thiam soon arrived and took over while Doro meandered down the lane to the mosque. But neither the VP nor I could make sense of Doro's 'records.' The amount owed SONADER that had to be divided up among the farmers—250,000 ouguiya ($4,000)—was gigantic. After several hours, we guessed as best we could, and wrote out forty different bills for Doro to distribute.

In my judgment, Doro seemed honest. He was remarkably consistent, and could provide detail on any figure, name, or circumstance that came up. Yet I could understand why others distrusted him. Civé had few of the formal institutions that support honest stewardship, such as auditable record keeping, a legal system, and democratic practices. For leaders to gain real followers, they had to compensate for these missing ingredients. Mamadou Konaté understood this, but Doro Thioub seemed not to. As one member once asked me rhetorically, "Why does Doro have two wives, eat meat each day, drink tea twice daily, and never skip dinner?"

So yes, one big difference between Cóndi Hiraande and Becce was a transparent leader others could trust. But another was more problematic: many Cóndi Hiraande members were not able to farm. For instance, one was a youthful widow with four young kids and a head-splitting toothache which she painfully endured until her brother tied a string around her tooth and yanked it out. Another was a squat man who lived across the lane from Djeinaba and Tall; after surviving a debilitating stroke, he now lay on a thin mat, unable to rise or talk. A tall young newlywed across the gully from me suffered from an incapacitating case of hendu (wind) that had entered his bones and left him unable to walk; yet no one in his family could afford the Senegalese Marabout who was the sole person capable of remedying this malady. A relative of my mom had recently lost her husband when a truck sideswiped the lorry he was atop, toppling it over and crushing him beneath. Now the widow, who farmed a riverside plot, was secluded for the obligatory four-month period of mourning. On and on it went, each Cóndi Hiraande member seemingly coping with his or her own personal tragedy.

Becce had solved this problem by keeping out those with limitations. Its distant location also kept membership to those capable of making the long trek there. If Cóndi Hiraande ran like a charity, Becce ran like a business.

Cóndi Hiraande's problems became even more complicated once I realized the role played by a third factor: my employer SONADER.

Chapter 13

SONADER

Late one morning, a SONADER truck rolled through town. Out at Cóndi Hiraande, Thiamel had just brought the single working pump back to life. I arrived late as the night before a villager returning from Matam, Senegal had delivered a stack of letters from my postbox there. The one from my dad stuck out. I left it to last. When that letter was all that remained, I slowly opened it to read what I already knew: my stepmother had died from cancer two weeks earlier.

I didn't know my stepmother well. My parents had divorced while I was in high school, and dad married Patti when I was away at college. Yet the pain from my dad's words sent half-way around the world struck hard. It left me melancholy and mournful, and I was slow to the fields.

Eventually arriving, and hearing the motor pump juddering in the distance, I climbed atop a diggette and watched while water crept through the canal network. In the distance, farmers were boisterously discussing the day's irrigation schedule. The few dramas taking shape were drawing me into the present.

I approached the loudest one, finding that a thin plucky woman named Ramata Thiapato had a vegetable plot that was somehow located uphill of the murmuring canal water. To get water, Saloum N'Diaye's plot had to be flooded. But Saloum's parcel still had standing water from the previous day; more water yet would mean his carrots and cabbages would rot. The local jury began gathering.

"You can put fish in Saloum's plot, and they will live!" one farmer observed while scanning the situation. The crowd began murmuring their agreement.

Desperate to shore up her faltering cause, Ramata threw her arms in the air, circling them like a windmill.

"But if fish might live, my onions will die!" she called out plaintively.

Suddenly, a revving truck's engine could be heard in the distance as it labored through a deep sandy patch in the road. The farmers fell silent as a large SUV approached and then parked just beyond the cooperative's perimeter. Emblazoned on the car's door was the familiar round SONADER logo featuring bursting stalks of plump rice. I turned to Ramata to discuss the problem at hand, but her withering onions no longer interested her.

Four men emerged from behind the vehicle's darkened windows, two wearing impossibly stark white boubous; garb that in this environment was to me as practical as long fingernails, high heels, or a fur coat. One of these two men was my boss Guisse from Kaedi, while the other Mauritanian I recognized from SONADER's Nouakchott office. The two remaining men were, like me, tubaaks, and were dressed in dark long pants and tightly fitted short sleeved shirts that accentuated a middle age spread. One was French, the other German.

Ramata dropped her pick, and along with a dozen others hurried toward the approaching men. Meanwhile, I finished up my notes on the dispute at hand. Taking a long look around, I slowly and reluctantly headed over to the gathering crowd, preoccupied as I was with imagining Patti's service and wondering whether any of my siblings had been able to attend.

By now, word of SONADER's arrival had spread. Except for the daily Rapide, very few vehicles passed through town, and when one did, everyone took note. Soon, a small crowd began to press around the four visitors now standing within the perimeter. I approached the group with no idea of what was happening and took up an elevated spot on a nearby irrigation canal to observe the proceedings from afar. I looked out toward the bank and for the first time spotted a rusty bent bicycle wheel dangling in some bushes. My eyes wandered upward, and I saw a bird's nest perched in a thorny tree. Beyond that spread the quiet grey sky, and I found myself wondering if ever anyone had heard an airplane screech across it. *Would they even know what that was?*

"Why are they here?...They owe us...Lies...Where's my fertilizer...The oil drum wasn't filled...Broken pump...Missing shaft... Tubaakland." Rising mutterings from the crowd began drawing my attention. Then the Frenchman from Nouakchott addressed the cooperative president Doro, who stood a few yards distant.

"You and your farmers must hold up your end. You have not paid your SONADER bill," he began in a loud scowling voice sounding thick with condescension. He waved and occasionally slapped a large accounting book.

Not waiting for a translation, Doro responded: "Look at us. We have no money because we grow food but you harvest it!" Doro jabbed a finger into the air for emphasis. More words were exchanged, making for a funny spectacle since neither understood the words of the other. Meanwhile, my boss Guisse acted like a boxing referee by inserting himself between the two, putting a clean, well-manicured hand gently on Doro's mud-splashed tunic. He alternated between speaking frankly to the Frenchman in French and calmly to Doro in Pulaar while the two continued to shout over one another. I watched Guisse closely, still finding him handsome but for some reason no longer attractive.

Just then a farmer came to my side to escort me forward. I obeyed, and soon found myself with a front row seat. Was I supposed to join these four men? I wondered. I was, after all, like each of them, a representative of SONADER. Yet I also felt adrift and unattached to everything around me. I felt like the small lone cloud that occasionally appeared out of nowhere in the vast grey-blue sky.

Why was it there and how did it get there? It also didn't take incredible insight that morning to know that I should avoid being associated with any of these well-dressed visitors.

A look of shock came over the Frenchman and German when they caught sight of me. I'm sure I appeared like some strange apparition, white-faced in a sea of dark, dressed in a long sack-like dress splattered with mud, a pad of paper in one hand, a jalo slung over my shoulder, an unintelligible juxtaposition of identities. The German opened his mouth as if to speak, but the Frenchman's persistent efforts to condemn Doro diverted his attention.

It soon became clear that the officials were on a mission of castigating the cooperative for all its past-due bills. Cóndi Hiraande still owed SONADER $4,000 from the last rice campaign, plus large outstanding balances from previous ones. According to SONADER's international funders, the region's cooperatives were eventually supposed to break even, putting an end to foreigners' ample subsidies. After a short transition period, farmers were expected to both make money *and* pay for SONADER's valuable services. Now in its tenth year of operation, this 'short transition period' was dragging on a bit too long. The time had come for cooperatives like Cóndi Hiraande—in other words, nearly every single one of them up and down this river valley—to pay up.

And so, on this breezy, cool morning, SONADER's funders were delivering tough love.

There's no doubt Cóndi Hiraande was an excellent candidate for such therapy. And the visitors saw this.

"Your fences are falling down, and your fields look like no one cares! Look! One canal three feet from another! Of course you have no harvest," the Frenchman exclaimed after casting his eye around.

Indeed, we were surrounded by unmistakable evidence that Cóndi Hiraande was not the tightly run organization portrayed in all of the "action plans" lining SONADER's shelves. It certainly was not the model cooperative described during our Nouakchott lessons.

The Frenchman's assault continued. The villagers were liars: They lied about how many members the cooperative had, and they misrepresented the amount of land they cultivated. They were also sneaky: What had they done with all the supplies SONADER had sent them?

"What happened to the hundreds of bags of fertilizer you received during the rice campaign?" he growled in words only a few before him understood, his syllables bursting forth sounding as if they first had been swallowed. "How could you have put *ten tons* of fertilizer on *twenty* hectares of rice?"

His distinct accusation was that the villagers had sold their fertilizer in Senegal, as across the river it commanded a higher price than what SONADER charged. I later came to discover that this seemingly *outrageous* allegation was in fact well-founded. It was one strategy cooperative members had hit on to pay their unaffordable SONADER bill.

The gathered villagers needed no translation for their mutterings to escalate into angry words, threatening disorder. SONADER, they protested, kept them poor by selling them motor pumps that didn't work, then never sending them a mechanic. As for the state of the canals, SONADER had promised them a backhoe for repairs. Where was it?

"How can we move dirt with this?" spat out one farmer while his skinny arm waved a three-foot long jalo in the air.

Another cried out, "You send the wrong fertilizer."

I had already heard this complaint from several villagers. Apparently during the last rice campaign, SONADER had mistakenly sent out all-purpose vegetable fertilizer rather than the nitrogen-rich urea that rice needs.

"The diesel was late."

"Yes, forty days before we transplanted."

This too I had heard; the fuel supply for the motor pumps

arrived so late that the villagers had to transplant rice long after its ideal age of twenty days. The mature roots were damaged in the switch, and the plants never completely recovered.

"I lost two sacks of rice because of very late diesel," charged another.

But it was the motor pump that really riled the crowd. SONADER had promised them a new part from Tubaakland. Where was this shaft they needed?

Squeezed amid sweltering bodies pressing in from all directions, I was getting hotter and thirstier by the moment. I flapped my arms to stir the still air around me, then strained to eye my canteen stashed beneath a nearby gawdi bush. But just then, a tall, lanky, barefoot young man pushed his way forward, jostling me on the left.

"You say we're thieves. But look…" He spread out his torn and stained boubou, held out calloused hands that long ago became too thick to close, and pulled up a ragged pant leg to reveal a festering sore. "Look you without callouses. Who is the thief? Who is the liar? I gave you rice, and you ate it; look at your fat stomachs."

He made a jabbing movement toward the Frenchman's middle, the visitor by now utterly drenched in sweat and looking very much like 'a duck in the desert,' which was the way my instructor Tall described visiting tubaaks.

I cringed at the leg wound. Looking down, I took in the leathery, thick feet surrounding me, and wondered who else was battling such festering infections. The sweep of Guisse's thick and splendid sleeves caught my eye as he bunched them up high on his shoulders. Beneath his boubou I caught sight of saw a beautifully embroidered tunic made from finely woven and intricately patterned cloth.

"Calm yourselves," Guisse said in a soothing voice to the gathered group, while at the same time taking a step back. I too stepped back, only in my case away from our visitors.

Guisse tried to continue, but all conversation was futile. The cooperative members sensed the tables had turned and grabbed their chance to direct this spectacle. Several followed the lanky fellow's cue and tore off T-shirts to contrast bony, muscular bodies with those of our soft and ample visitors. Others placed their deeply cracked and calloused feet on display, a stark contrast with the strikingly smooth skin and finely polished shoes of our guests.

The now exasperated and drenched Frenchman frantically waved a small pen, then thumped his accounting book as he tried to out-shout the chorus around him, sweat streaming from every pore. His condescension rose as the color in his face deepened. The four visitors turned to leave as one. But before they did, the German insisted that Doro affix an 'X' for his signature on some line.

This X procured, the visitors turned toward their vehicle, the Mauritanians serenely strolling off in their spotless white boubous while the two disheveled tubaaks picked their way through the thorn-filled terrain. Doro followed behind, the high-pitched staccato of his sharp angry words filling the air even after the visitors had rolled up their darkened windows, turned on the air conditioner, and engaged the gears.

**

Minutes later, Thiamel was back riverside yanking the short chord that brought the cooperative's lone motor pump to life. With restored solidarity, the villagers returned to where they had left off, arguing over whose turn it was to get water, whether fish could live in Saloum N'Diaye's plot, and how Ramata Thiapato's onions could possibly get water.

With renewed purpose and bucked-up spirits, I approached Ramata. There she stood amidst her onions, arms once again flailing while she barked at Saloum. As I arrived, Ramata halted her arm waving and gave me a long look. Hands on hips, eyes narrowed, and head cocked, she called out, "Fatou Wane. Were those men your relatives?"

"No… no…" I stammered while shaking my head emphatically. "Their land far from me. Across many rivers. They tongue, my tongue not equal."

Relaxing, a crooked smile appeared on her lips. "I didn't think so. Thanks be to Allah."

"Thanks be to Allah," I responded, feeling suddenly lightheaded. I shaded my eyes and cast my gaze upward, searching, I think, for either Allah, a sign from Patti, or a passing airplane.

"And may Allah… water onions," I managed to add, returning to the scene. Both she and Saloum laughed heartily. Then they resumed their dispute.

Chapter 14

Village Life

"Do you know what Cóndi Hiraande's problem is?" Tall quizzed me one afternoon.

The singular form of the word 'problem' stumped me. "No," was all I managed.

Tall fiddled with the dial on his short-wave radio as the 5 o'clock news from Paris began. With a chuckle, he then gave his pronouncement, "*So goo bonii limmore aayiima.*"

Eventually I got this proverb's literal translation. It is something like: *If you can't count to one, don't expect to count far*. Pulaars prize spare, clever humor that imparts wisdom. Nothing shows this more than their proverbs, such as my favorite: "No matter how long a log lays in the water, it won't turn into a crocodile." In this village, that log would be me.

Tall's proverb that afternoon evoked a key lesson I'd learned about building sandcastles: first build a thick high wall in front for defense. If you don't, the tides will swamp it. First things first. Sandcastles need walls, and cooperatives need leaders; although I wasn't sure I bought Tall's claim that Cóndi Hiraande's problems boiled down to the failed guidance of Doro Thioub. Still, I appreciated Tall's unmatched ability to explain things.

I valued my growing friendship with Tall, and others too. Like the smiling Becce motor pumpist and chain-smoking Amadou Demba. Some years earlier, Amadou Demba did what those in the Fuuta have always done when war arrives, trouble brews, or hardship descends: disperse to the south and east. In Amadou Demba's case, he packed a small bag, crossed the river, and struck out south, eventually winding up in the Ivory Coast. At the time, the Ivory Coast was West Africa's jewel, a place 'almost like France,' as Amadou Demba put it. There he spent several years selling merchandise out of one of those booths found on nearly every West African lane.

"I ate meat all the time and wore good cloth. They know how to live," he reported to me about his adventures abroad. "And," he added with amazement, "My friend owned a car. He even chauffeured himself." It seemed the ability to drive one of those contraptions was nearly as noteworthy as the ability to purchase it.

Most importantly, Amadou Demba sent envelopes stuffed with cash to his beleaguered family.

"Why you no return Ivory Coast?" I asked him one afternoon.

"Ha, ha," he said, his wide grin revealing tobacco-stained teeth. Taking a drag on his cigarette, he exhaled loudly before continuing: "The money's all gone. Women, you know. And children. It's all gone. The only thing left is the horse." Amadou Demba was one of the few in the village with a horse, although I wasn't sure why he had one or what his plans had been when he bought it.

"So why you not go back?" I asked him another day while lounging on my porch.

"Too old," he responded as he grabbed a pillow and reclined. "Besides," he continued with conviction, "the people there are crazy. Too much alcohol. They drink and then they don't know what they are doing."

He shook his head while taking a final long drag on his cigarette before flicking the stub all the way out into the sandy lane. After a brief pause, he added, "They lack morals there. You should see how the women dress." I self-consciously checked to make sure my body position and the lay of my dress was sufficiently modest. I knew it often wasn't as women frequently tugged at my pagne or suggested I shift positions to lay sideways. Now I was certain I probably appeared more like those loose Ivory Coast women than an appropriately modest Mauritanian one.

I liked Amadou Demba a lot. He was more open and curious than most of the villagers and had the experience of living abroad. Plus, he spoke reasonably good French. To seal the deal, one afternoon while we drank tea, he gruffly told the bothersome teenagers I still dealt with, and who were just then entering my compound, to leave and not come back. Much to my amazement, they reversed direction and never returned.

I also became acquainted with the son of my next-door neighbors, Harouna the fisherman and his wife Maimona. A mechanic about my age, their son Sarr lived most of the year in the northern coastal town of Nouadhibou. Shortly after I arrived in Civé, he returned home for an extended visit.

Almost all Sarr's age mates had left the village, and being a bit of an introvert, Sarr shunned large gatherings and noisy conversations. In other words, he didn't particularly fit in. Until he discovered my place, that is. Once he did, it became his refuge. Soon, each of his daily visits stretched a bit longer until we regularly spent large parts of the day together. Eventually, he let loose his complaints about village life.

"Everyone's business is your business here. There is no privacy. You can't even stroll into the bush without everyone knowing what you are doing and where you are doing it," he lamented. I had indeed found it awkward to stumble across someone squatting behind a thorny shrub or pass them, water-filled all-purpose *satala* (a large aluminum teapot) in hand, as they urgently heeded the call of nature.

Almost each evening, Sarr came to my house. On one especially cold one, I produced my black polyester sleeping bag. Sarr looked quizzical so I handed it to him. Curious, he opened it, then wrapped himself up in it.

"Wow. What is this?" he asked.

"A sack. A sack to sleep in," I responded.

"The American Sack. It's strange. It's amazing," he said while pinching its soft padding.

Each night from then on, Sarr got Kmart's American Sack. Once swaddled in it, he taught me Pulaar, learned English, drank tea, and brought up random topics for conversation.

"What do you think of African Americans?" he asked one night, a question I didn't know how to answer. The next night he was more specific. "Would Michael Jackson make more money if he were white?"

"Probably," I responded after considering his question. Sarr nodded knowingly.

A few days later he had a different topic: "When you marry, does the woman join her in-laws?"

"No, unless no money," I responded.

Sarr let my answer sink in before nodding his approval. "You live with no people, then! Black people must do everything in big groups," he added with a note of resignation, surprising me with his willingness to engage in such sweeping generalizations.

Another night, Sarr asked what happens to the *haŋaabe*, 'the crazy', the developmentally disabled. This question had particular relevance given how many visibly mad children and adults lived in the village. Like my old friend M'bu.

"It complicated," I said, considering how I could ever find words to answer this one.

"It is complicated," he agreed. "The choice is painful."

The topic immediately summoned to mind a teenaged girl with my last name of Wane, a daughter of my original parents in Rosso. This nameless girl was mute and so violent they kept her chained to a rail in a small, bare, and windowless cement cell off in the corner of their compound. The few occasions I caught glimpse of her left me sick and brokenhearted. The only time I saw her unshackled was the afternoon she emerged from her cell blinking and with matted hair. I was rudely staring her way when she caught sight of me across the courtyard. Straightaway she dashed to grab a nearby metal sat-ala, then charged me, repeatedly banging my head with it while emitting animal-like cries. Finally, some teenage boys managed to wrestle her back to her cage.

Yes indeed, a painful choice. Gut-wrenching in fact.

***

My social life also grew to include Tall and his young wife Djeinaba; outside of my daily Pulaar lessons, I began visiting them regularly. Tall was an invaluable resource, always seeming to know exactly what puzzled me.

"I bet you're wondering why those round Fulbe huts are set apart from the village," he asked one day. Usually he was right, but not this time, as those huts had not drawn my attention. Tall gave a slow account, which with time I more fully understood.

Centuries ago, the Fulbe herding caste, of which Djeinaba was a member, settled the Senegal River Valley and claimed ownership over much of the region's fertile waalo flats and upland dieri fields. Occasionally, empires to the east or Moor emirates to the north swooped in and chased the residents south. The last time that happened was in the 1800s when Moor emirates monopolized the region's lucrative gum tree trade with the French, trade which took place at posts along the river. The French at the time were holed up at an island sanctuary located where the Senegal River empties into the Atlantic.

Mid-19th century, under the new leadership of the devious and ambitious General Louis Faidherbe, the French made their move. Slowly but surely, they expanded east up the river by vanquishing the Moors, co-opting Pulaar leaders, threatening (and carrying out) violence, and skillfully fueling political divisions. Eventually they gained control over the entire Fuuta. Once these turbulent decades ended, the added security of decisive French control coaxed Fulbe clans from the south back across the river to reclaim their ancestors' dieri lands. Many settled north of Civé in places like Maghama, M'Bout, Monguel, and Lexieba. Fast forward several decades, and their descendants began suffering through the current drought. Starving, many headed south, such as when a few families from M'Bout settled in Civé. They arrived and built the Fulbe's characteristic round thatched huts, locating their homes slightly apart from the dense rectangular mud homes of Civé. It was these huts that Tall was drawing my attention to.

"So they like refugees?" I asked.

"Yes. Pulaar society is filled with refugees," Tall responded with a yawn while grabbing a pillow to recline.

On another afternoon, Tall asked if I knew that the Rapide had not passed by for days. I had by now abandoned hope that this daily messenger would bring news from Guisse about Cóndi Hiraande's broken shaft. I thus paid no attention to its schedule.

"No," I responded. "Why not?" As I asked, I envisioned the truck wedged upside-down, deep in one of the region's narrow gullies, having suffered the same fate as my neighbor's goat.

"There is cholera. Officials have shut down all transportation along the river. Last night, two people up on Civé Dow died." I recalled that while in Frogmore, we had all received a cholera vaccine, and then suffered through a night of flu-like symptoms. That misery, I now knew, was well worth it.

"I saw Deiko in the morning. She looked fine," said Djeinaba, shaking her head, then swallowing hard before looking away. "Now she is gone. May Allah forgive her."

In Civé, Allah is great, and there is no such thing as an unexpected death.

***

"Imagine. Even with cholera, you can't get people to add bleach to their water," Tall complained to me the next afternoon while rapidly fanning himself despite the cool weather. Tall was well-educated and often looked down on those who were not; in other words, pretty much everyone in the village.

Tall took pride in keeping himself informed, not just about events in Civé, but also of those beyond. He was the only one in the village who listened to the news from France, and during our afternoon sessions, he became like my own private newscaster.

"Israel just airlifted thousands of black Jews out of the Sudan," he notified me one afternoon.

"They do?" I asked.

"Yes."

Another day, Tall announced: "The Soviet leader died. Now they have a new one." I struggled to recall the name of that now-deceased leader of the Soviet Union. "Chernenko," Tall added, reading my silence.

A month into my stay, it was Tall who informed me that Mauritania's army had just pulled off a coup.

"He dead?" I asked with alarm. Only a month had passed since I had shaken hands with President Haidalla at the Presidential Palace.

"No, he was away in Burundi on business." Then Tall added with a shake of his head, "His buddy took advantage of his absence."

Two years later, Tall took a rare and somber walk out to my home to deliver heartbreaking news from my country. "Your spaceship exploded on takeoff. Everyone died. May Allah forgive them," he mournfully reported while putting an unusual hand on my shoulder. I stood wordless as horrific images passed through my brain. Silently watching him as he turned to head back down the gully, I glanced skyward, then wondered who exactly "everyone" was.

Whether good or bad, Tall always brought me the news.

Originally from Mali, Tall was a member of Pulaars' *Toorodɓe* or religious caste. He came to Mauritania to earn a teaching degree at the nation's sole university. He returned to Mali to marry a cousin, then took up his first teaching assignment in a village near Kaedi.

Several years later, with three children and a wife in Mali, he was posted to Civé. Upon his arrival, a Fulbe beauty in the village, Djeinaba Deh, asked Tall for French lessons. Eighteen-year-old Djeinaba had just returned from a year in Zaire visiting her sister. She wanted to go back but knew her opportunities would be limited without speaking French.

Tall eagerly agreed to Djeinaba's request, and as he explained to me with a knowing laugh and a twinkle in his eyes, Djeinaba listening nearby, "I only charged her half price."

"And even that was too much. I still can't speak French!" Djeinaba quickly retorted with false anger.

It didn't take long for Djeinaba to become Tall's second wife and bear him a son, and then another. During Pulaar lessons beneath their hangar, Djeinaba was always present, nursing or swaddling her newborn, playing with her toddler, or making us tea. She always took part in our conversations, often countering Tall's critical commentary on village life. Which was especially pointed when it came to Cóndi Hiraande.

"It's a waste of time," he often pronounced. "It takes them two hours to decide to meet at 9 a.m., and then at 9 a.m. no one shows up. And Doro Thioub as its leader?" he'd scoff. "*So goo bonii limmore aayiima.*"

Chapter 15

Djeinaba

While Tall was condescending toward about those in Civé, Djeinaba was charitable. She was after all, related to a large share of them. She also hailed from one of the two Fulbe clans that settled Civé in the late 1800s, essentially splitting between them the area's good farming and grazing lands. As such, her family remained relatively well off.

Djeinaba was smart, witty, and most importantly, she liked to hang out with me, partly I'm sure because of the novelty I presented. An older sister in Zaire, a younger brother in the Zambia, and a husband from Mali helped her cultivate a cosmopolitan identity. Our friendship now made her downright worldly.

Plus, I spiced up her life.

One day during a Pulaar lesson, I unknowingly said something humorous, and Djeinaba unsuccessfully suppressed a laugh. Tall ignored her and soldiered on.

"No, not *soolde, suundu,*" he corrected me. "*Suuuundu,*" he repeated, drawing out the u's, knowing that my ear did not distinguish between the short u's and long uu's of the Pulaar language.

"Suuuuundu," I carefully articulated. Tall nodded his approval and continued our discussion of the migrating birds that were beginning to depart, one signal that the hot season drew near.

An hour later, our lesson was up and Tall was off to negotiate the sale of his two baby goats. I lay on a matla as Djeinaba steeped our third cup of tea. She handed me my shot glass just as a dark starling flittered into the compound to peck at some rice grains near

Djeinaba's eroding mud stove.

"What's that?" Djeinaba asked me, directing my attention to the bird, a wide grin crossing her face.

"Soolde," I said with confidence.

With Tall gone, Djeinaba now burst into laughter. Clueless, I nonetheless joined in.

"No?" Drawing out the o's, I tried again. "Soooooooolde," trying my best to mimic Tall's intonation.

Djeinaba's amusement doubled. Her infant, who had been sound asleep, wailed. Djeinaba got up from the mat, then bent over to untie the pagne that secured him to her back.

I finished my tea and waited for Djeinaba to begin nursing Papis. Still giggling without knowing why, I poured Djeinaba what remained in the pot, and handed her the cup. She drank it slowly, smiling all the while, then *clack*, returned the glass to the metal tray. Turning to me, she rearranged her son, then mimicked the form of a certain male appendage with her hand.

"This is a soolde," she said, casting her gaze down at a hand held erect next to her baby's chubby buttocks. "That," she said pointing to the place where the starling had been, "that is a suundu." Then she burst out laughing until her eyes filled with tears.

That day sealed our friendship. While communication was slow going, Djeinaba was patient and kind. A gifted, natural teacher, she started walking me around the village to share facts about this compound and that, and to explain who was related to whom and how. Which was no small task to master. I once tried making a family tree of Djeinaba's kin, but a tree it definitely was not. In no time a jumbled spider web took shape, and I called it a day.

Our strolls through the village would typically wind up at her parents' compound up on Civé Dow, where we'd stroll in to see who was in. Spacious and clean, the Deh compound consisted of a single large freshly painted mustard yellow cement building with an artistic cinder block entryway. Out the back gate stood a carefully constructed large pen for their animals. When not out in the dieri, a dozen goats and several cows gathered there. You knew immediately if they were present or not, as the smell of manure and the tangy, sharp aroma of their urine was impossible to miss. I always made a point of walking over to this corral, as it was built just above the ragged cliffs that led down to the gully's sandy bottom. From this spot I could take in a bucolic view of Civé's eastern flanks: above us to the left were the round Fulbe huts inhabited by those refugees from M'Bout; down the gully and far off in the distance I could make out the top of my neem tree; and straight down the cliffs you could barely see a small segment of the soundless river and the never-ending activity on its banks.

Whenever the two of us dropped in, Djeinaba's younger sister Oumou would usher us over to thick matlas topped with embroidered pillows. Straightaway, a servant girl would be dispatched to bring us sweet milk, roasted peanuts, or a grilled corn cob, along with a fan and more pillows.

On one such occasion, Djeinaba's mother, who was a short handsome woman with a broad smile and dimpled cheeks, shortened our visit by handing Djeinaba a large bundle of bean leaves wrapped in the remains of a once colorful pagne.

"Take this to Kalidou so he can have haako tonight," she said.

Kalidou was Djeinaba's uncle. He lived in a plain mud hut almost directly across the gully from this compound, and adjacent to the round Fulbe huts. Haako, a delicious bean sauce that nearly everyone in the village ate each night, is made from bean leaves, dried fish, and peanuts, all stewed together into a sort of creamed spinach-like dish.

Djeinaba took the large bundle from her mom and placed it on her head. With me tagging along beside, we exited the back of the Deh compound, then carefully descended one side of the jagged ravine before climbing the other.

As we entered her uncle's airy compound, Djeinaba's young

cousin greeted us and took her load. A small woman whom I took to be Djeinaba's aunt asked if we could stay for tea. Before we could answer, a short, fit, bow-legged man with a scraggly beard entered, a jalo hanging limp from one shoulder. I immediately recognized this fellow from Becce.

"Fatou Wane," he called out to me in a loud jovial voice. "Welcome. Wane, Wane, Wane," he went on, vigorously shaking my hand. "Deh, Deh, Deh," I beamed back. I had liked this friendly man in the fields, and now that I knew he was Djeinaba's uncle, I liked him even more.

"Hey," Kalidou said suddenly while grinning and rubbing his hands together. "Have you some brothers? They are here." He settled his jalo into the crook of the compound's neem tree, scooped a large canful of water from an elevated calabash, then downed it quickly while awaiting my reply.

Puzzled, I responded, "I not hear you. Repeat yourself?"

"What do you mean Kaaw Kalidou?" interjected Djeinaba. "Her brothers?"

At this point Djeinaba's aunt, who had already spread open the bundle of bean leaves and was separating the leaves from their stalks, stifled a laugh. Something caught Djeinaba's eye, and she too began to chortle.

"Come," commanded Kalidou as he wiped his face dry with a sleeve. He then escorted me to the back of his hut where a small ravine separated it from a neighboring Fulbe compound located a mere stone's throw away. I spotted a large pen for goats built with thick branches, long strips of heavy bark, and thorny bramble.

"Brr brrrr brrrrrr." We heard someone fussing while directing goats into the pen.

"There," cried Kalidou.

And then I saw. Some ten yards beyond stood two pale-skinned teenagers, each with red hair and badly blotched skin. They did sort of look like they could be my brothers, except for their bare feet, baggy Aladdin-like pants covered by a tunic, and the sticks in their hands for guiding their herd. They were twin albinos.

The two teenagers looked our way. "Your sister," called out Kalidou, with a wave of both hands. A bit in shock, I waved meekly. The two unenthusiastically returned my greeting, then jiggled the wood gate to the pen closed before securing it shut with a fat branch.

As we turned back, Kalidou kept up his chuckle. I was silent, uncomfortably aware of how completely out of place I looked. As we re-entered the Deh's courtyard, Djeinaba slipped her hand into mine.

"Kaaw Kalidou," she called to her uncle, raising our joined hands for him to see. "Keyti is *my* sister, not *theirs*."

Kalidou stopped. His jaw slackened and his eyes widened. He rubbed his stubbly beard with both hands until a wide grin appeared.

"My niece," he exclaimed, turning back to place a friendly hand on my shoulder. "Let's go have tea." And like that, this jolly man from Becce was now my uncle.

While I was not an albino Pulaar, each day in Civé left me feeling like this place was home.

Or at least most days did.

Chapter 16

A Second Childhood

During my first months in Civé, inner turmoil brought to mind the time in my youth spent babysitting, especially the two-year olds, who were always the toughest clients. Now I understood why. Just when I thought I comprehended those around me, I realized I didn't. When I thought I could predict what came next, it didn't. I wanted to control my surroundings but couldn't. Like those toddlers I baby-sat, I often experienced deep frustration and confusion that only a good long shriek could cure.

Early on, I became acquainted with a woman by the name of Koumba Binta. Koumba was the vice president of a new hand-watered garden the village women had just initiated. Their plot lay beyond the last village homestead, and adjacent to a small grove of the short, thorny patouki trees, whose sap to the French in the 1800s was like liquid gold, feeding as it did Europe's rapidly growing fabric industry. So valuable was this Gum Arabic, used as dye fixative that the wealth earned from it—gained by boring holes into trees and then scraping off a sticky gum ball that gradually oozed out once the hot Harmattan winds arrived—gave power to the Moor emirate that controlled the region. But this product also accounted for its downfall, as it spurred France's eventual violent conquest of the region.

One of the first things I did in Civé was join this budding gardening group whose vegetables grew next to those historic trees. Vice President Koumba Binta helped me secure a king bed-sized plot, smack in the garden's center. Soon I had it seeded with lettuce, carrots, turnips, and mint.

Each afternoon I visited this garden and was shortly enjoying the cheerful cacophony and bustling activity of the women who filled it, even though I barely understood a word that passed. I quickly came to regret the gardening part of this enterprise, however, as keeping my young, thirsty plants from dying required fetching them tubs of river water each day.

After filling one tub up, I faced the daunting challenge of hoisting the forty-pound load up the bank on my head. During this climb, I sometimes became paralyzed, unable to move upward but incapable of discharging my load for fear of breaking my neck. After that, I'd reduce the water and try again, only to find that this bank was steeper than the one I was accustomed to. I slipped, lost a slipper, or worst of all lost hold of the tub and watched in dismay as the water cascaded to the ground. Once, to the merriment of all onlookers, my pagne came untied mid-climb and slipped down my legs. Fortunately, a sympathetic teenage girl came and tied it back on before guiding me up the steep embankment. When I reached the top, I was so thankful I wanted to hug this young lass, but instead just said, "*Ajaaraama.*" Thanks. Then we went our separate ways.

Despite such difficulties, I persisted with my garden. I tried to recall everything I'd learned in Frogmore about vegetables. Add sand to soil before planting carrots. A rule, I soon realized, that is much easier made than followed. Here in Civé, few could afford shovels or wheelbarrows, and carrying sand on your head is twice as hard as water. Plus, the soil was not the rich loam of Frogmore, but baked clay. I compromised on sand, and my carrots rebelled, eventually refusing to grow more than one inch downward.

It was through these daily afternoon appearances that I became enamored of Koumba Binta. She was a large and boisterous woman, full of personality. She waddled about the garden while bossing everyone around like a good-natured traffic cop. I admired her high spirits and humorous overbearance. She directed everyone's activities with a false fury which quickly gave way to a crooked smile if you played along. Soon I had singled her out for friendship, and frequently dropped in on her for greetings.

But one morning mid-way through that gardening season, Koumba Binta appeared at my home. Without much hesitation, she stood at my gate and, with a scowl, growled, "*Aan, a wadaaka barke.*"

I was pretty sure she had just pronounced me a person without Allah's blessing—a very serious insult. Not willing to trust my hearing, I listened further. Surely, she wasn't *really* insulting me? This must be some sort of a joke.

"What, my friend? I not hearing you," I replied, putting my letter aside and arising from my dinndeere.

She repeated herself, and this time there was no mistaking her words, no transition from feigned anger to crooked smile. I took note of her tone, her delivery, her body language. In case any doubt remained, she repeated her message yet a third time, spitting on the ground as she did. Then she elaborated: I spent too much time going to this house and that house; I talked with anyone and everyone I came across; and I gave gifts to whoever asked—a charge that was definitely not true. A good person, she hissed, sticks with her friends, and them only. In other words, I should stick with her.

Later that afternoon, I relayed this unsettling event as best I could to Tall. He and Djeinaba laughed, then he explained. "She's jealous. She thought she had you to herself. She probably thinks she'll get rich off of you."

Like the patouki trees of last century, I felt like others too might be considering boring holes into me to see what sort of precious substance might possibly ooze out if they sat patiently by.

For some time, I remained plagued by thoughts that others saw me as the promised manna that must be grabbed before others got it. I second guessed my impressions of others, as I couldn't trust my instincts. Useful in my own culture, yes, but somehow, my instincts didn't serve me here. I realized that what was *not* said was harder to understand then what was. My very partial understanding of the world around me left me contending with it the way I imagine a two-year-old does.

A second memorable instance occurred a few months later. It was afternoon, and I had just entered Djeinaba's compound. I found her alone on a matla in the shade, her infant son asleep by her side. To my shock, she was crying. I squatted beside her, struggling for words.

"Tall, he is healthy?" I finally asked leaning forward, realizing he wasn't around.

"No," she said wiping her eyes, a lone sob rocking her body. "No, no. He isn't well. He's… he's…" She buried her face to conceal a wail. I wasn't sure if I should stay or leave.

"I getting water," I said. Grabbing an empty cup askew on the ground, I began to rise.

"Tall wants a *lémbéyél*," she cried out as she blew her nose, grabbing the edge of my boubou as I rose.

I sat back down. Was Tall sick? Was this a word for a medical procedure?

"Tall wants a *lémbéyél*. *Lémbéyél*," she held up three fingers.

What the heck was she saying? Three *what*? Maybe he wants to move someplace. That wouldn't surprise me, he was so unhappy in Civé. Poor Djeinaba. All of her family here. I wondered where they would move to.

"Three moons you leaving?" I asked.

"No, no." She lay her son down and got up to fetch herself some water.

"*Jom suudu*," she said turning to face me, once again holding up three fingers. This time, I recognized the word for wife.

And then my jaw dropped, my eyebrows shot up. "Fadima, you,

and..."

"And *lémbéyél*," she finished for me with another wail. "Yes."

This news left me speechless. Tall wanted a *lémbéyél*, a third wife? Apparently, he was not satisfied with just Fadima in Mali and Djeinaba in Civé. How many conversations had I had with Tall about this practice of marrying many women? I found it so foreign, and Tall always bemoaned the practice, making clear his wish to rid himself of his first wife in Mali. He lauded Westerners for our 'advanced' culture and more humane treatment of women.

"Why do men need more than one wife? It's barbaric," he said several times. He criticized all the men in Civé who, once possessing an extra two cows, could think of nothing better than to exchange them for a pretty young bride.

"Pulaars can't take the road forward if they keep following old ones," I recalled him saying with disgust.

And now Tall was taking a third wife? That afternoon I too felt betrayed, although for different reasons then did his wife.

***

That afternoon in Djeinaba's compound, I realized I had misjudged the reasons for polygamy's persistence. Simply the threat of acquiring another wife gave men power over their wives; why should they relinquish this?

Civéans explained their penchant for multiple wives as Islamic in origin. The same reason given for removing part of young girls' genitalia. Yet both pre-date Islam. Like other expanding religions, Islam's doctrines proved nimble enough to incorporate many of their converts' cultural practices and spiritual beliefs. Nowadays, Islam in West Africa reflects many of the region's longstanding cultural and fetishistic practices and beliefs. Many West African Muslims venerate spiritual leaders who they consider to be saints and soothsayers, a practice quite taboo in mainstream Islam. They rely on good luck charms for almost every life event, and religious scholars (called

Marabouts) double as fortune tellers, healers, and the producers of those charms. Islamic purists have long found West Africa's 'Islamic' practices heretical. Bloody wars, both present and past, have been launched under the guise of converting West Africa's inhabitants to the true Islam.

The precise origin of the practice of cutting young girls' genitalia is a bit hazy. Nowhere in the Koran is it mentioned, nor is it practiced in most of the Islamic world. References to the procedure have been found in ancient Egypt, Greece, and Rome. Probably the real question is why this practice continues in Christian, Islamic, and animist pockets of Africa.

I rarely discussed this topic with anyone in Civé, partly because I found the subject an awkward one. When I did, though, I heard the same response: "black women are not like white women," followed by "trust me." Even though I didn't. A European-educated acquaintance of mine who lived in Kaedi swore he would never allow his young daughter to undergo the procedure. Yet one day while in Nouakchott on business, his mother took matters into her own hands. He later said he was shocked the deed was done without his permission. But my experience with Tall and Koumba Binta left me unsure whose word I could trust.

Chapter 17

The Castes

In helping to convert the village to progressive, capital-intensive agriculture, I was a modernizer. Yet the whisperings of the region's past were everywhere, and I sometimes wondered how this project I was promoting squared with that past.

My first doubts over this role of mine were raised after an evening spent with my next-door neighbor Sarr. It was a cold winter evening and a stiff, sandy wind had driven us inside. Around 9 p.m. a bowl of couscous topped with haako arrived and we settled in to eat. After we'd washed our hands, I scooted my lantern now swarming with tiny flying objects closer to the bowl's contents. Then amidst deep shadows, we ate from the common bowl until the lantern's dim glow showed no haako remained. Sarr poured a small bowlful of milk still warm from the cow over the remaining couscous, and before long we had consumed the last of our tasty two-course dinner.

Just then, a voice hollered through the dark. "Konk, Konk!" The motor pumpist Amadou Demba announced his arrival. "May we pass the evening in peace," he continued. "Ah! I'm in time for tea. I was hoping so," he chuckled as he passed through my open front door. Before plopping down, he spread wide a new purple boubou he'd purchased at the tail end of a week in Kaedi selling onions. Smoothing out the back of his robe, he laid down on the second of my two matlas. Positioning a pillow beneath his head, Amadou Demba feigned a shiver. "Hand me a blanket. I'm freezing.

It's like America here," he said laughing, as he unwound the turban on his head.

"It gets colder in Nouadhibou," said Sarr, referencing the northern coastal town where he worked.

Sarr and Amadou Demba fell to comparing notes on life in Nouadhibou and Daloa, the Ivorian town where Amadou Demba had worked as a corner merchant.

"Amadou Demba," I interrupted, wanting to change the topic. I nestled the first pot of water amid some scattered hot coals. "You here when cooperative start? How it start?"

By the time a large block of sugar had melted into lowwol, Amadou Demba and Sarr had outlined for me the origin of Cóndi Hiraande.

A decade earlier, Civé had been selected to receive one of the river valley's first World Bank-financed irrigated perimeters. Soon SONADER tractors arrived, and Cóndi Hiraande was mapped onto the clay waalo lands that lay upstream. These thirty hectares had previously been owned by—or better said claimed by—Samba Ba, my 'father' who lived across the lane and now spent his final days in a thin hammock.

In Pulaar, Cóndi Hiraande translates into "flour for dinner." It generally refers to the beloved couscous, a staple in the Pulaar diet. 'Cóndi hiraande' is so treasured that it is occasionally used as a term of endearment. Labelling the fields this might have reflected the hope that during this wretched drought, the new perimeter would provide residents with the one thing dearest to their hearts: food.

When SONADER first came to Civé to discuss building a perimeter, Samba Ba was the village's official "chief" by virtue of his descent from the Fulbe clan that settled Civé and established themselves as its leaders. Now well into his eighties, Samba was toothless, all skin and bones and bent over with age, as poor and desperate as anyone else in the village. When SONADER came to discuss converting his extensive waalo flats into an irrigated rice perimeter, he agreed.

"Why he do that?" I asked, wondering why my father had so readily handed his land over to SONADER.

"He was starving," Sarr explained. "Of course, he agreed. No choice was left him. No choice was left anyone." And thus began a lesson on Civé's castes.

I came to understand that the original inhabitants of the village who arrived in the late 1800s—the grandparents of Samba Ba, Doro Thioub, and Djeinaba's parents—built their homes on Civé Dow, or upper Civé.

"But what about Civé Less?" I asked.

Just down the slope from Civé Dow lived many members of Becce: Amadou Demba, Kebe, Mamadou Konaté, and the town crier Ballal.

"Ah!" Amadou Demba chortled as he leaned over to grab the woven fan by my side. "That's where the Bambara live." He laughed and began fanning the waning charcoal.

Sarr explained. In the late 1800s and early 1900s the French were assaulting African empires to the east as they expanded their colonial enterprise from the recently conquered Senegal River basin east to the Niger River. Decades of political intrigue and violence left that region in complete chaos and social disarray. Many residents from the 'land of the Bambara' fled these troubled lands for the security of the fertile Fuuta where the region's political elite welcomed their labor.

More refugees! I thought.

Whether ethnically Bambara, Mandinka, Mande or Wolof, these newcomers were outsiders. And typically, heathens. To join Pulaar society, each needed a family sponsor to provide them with protection and access to land in exchange for their servitude. As a group, they were labeled *The Bambara*, a term that in Pulaar society continues to designate its slave caste.

"And you, you from Mali?" I asked Amadou Demba.

"No, but lots from Becce are. Mamadou Konaté, Ballal, ..."

Sarr broke in: "You aren't from Mali? Where then?"

"Guinea. My grandparents spoke Mande," he explained. "But I'm still a Bambara!" he added.

Civé's new "Bambara" population built homes within the fenced-off area of Civé Less. In addition to this distinct neighborhood, they received designated spots for burying their dead, performing their rituals, and gathering water. They also gained access to fertile river-front farmland west of Civé along with some dieri lands behind the village for forage and growing millet.

With the passage of time, Civé's Bambara began producing talismen written in Arabic, and then encased in leather amulets. More time still and Allah replaced Pemba and Faro, they faced Mecca to pray, and soon had their own mosque. A few decades on, and all remnants of the fence between Civé Less and Civé Dow disappeared, as did all traces of Civé's multi-cultural and multi-lingual past.

This amalgam of assorted ethnic groups—Fulbe, Bambara, Wolof, Mande, and others—are today collectively referred to as Haal-Pulaaren ('speakers of Pulaar'), or Pulaars for short. To be Pulaar in other words, is a bit like being American, as it refers to membership in a society rather than an ethnic group.

Sarr continued to explain that Civé also had a few families that, like his, were members of the fishing caste.

"Any other caste here?"

"Yes," Sarr laughed. "Toorodɓe."

"Who?"

He grinned. "Why you! Wane. And, Tall. And of course, the Imam Thierno Ly."

In Pulaar society, the Toorodɓe, the region's religious caste, are nobles. Several centuries earlier, the Fuuta's residents began converting to Islam. In the noteworthy year of 1776, some Islamic scholars managed a religiously inspired coup, pushing the Fulbe dynasty that had controlled the Fuuta for centuries out to the Fuuta's far eastern reaches. The new Toorodɓe theocracy—although one more in name than in practice—built mosques and Koranic schools throughout the Fuuta, and vaulted spiritual leaders to the top of the region's social hierarchy. Today both Fulɓe and Toorodɓe (like Tall and my Rosso family) constitute Pulaar's noble class. This was why as a Fulɓe, Djeinaba could marry my instructor Tall. And why the two of them laughed at my last name, which apparently marked me not just as a member of this elite religious caste, but one issuing from a noteworthy royal clan to the west.

"You are a noble and I am a slave," finished Amadou Demba with a chuckle. "That's why I should make the tea, not you."

With the second pot of tea now brewing, I steered the conversation back to the topic of Cóndi Hiraande's beginnings, back when Samba Ba had relinquished control over his mudflats.

"But he was still the master of the land. The farmers owed him a tribute," explained Sarr, before adding: "At least that is what he said."

Amadou Demba sat up from his prone position as I handed him *saani*, the second cup of tea. He drew a long loud sip, expressed satisfaction, and then snickered. "Go into Samba's back room," he said, his outstretched arm pointing beyond my doorway. "You'll see. There is a BIG mountain of rice there. Those of us at Becce, we did that too."

"Give him rice?" I asked.

"Yes. After each harvest." Even in the dark shadows of my room, I could make out his disapproving nod. Returning his tea glass to my platter, Sarr indicated his displeasure as well.

"It wasn't fair. Everyone had to give up a sack of rice. The hearts of many turned against them," Sarr chimed in as he lay back down and pulled his sleeping bag over his shoulders. "Times had changed. Mamadou did a good thing."

I wiggled the third tea pot deep into the dwindling coals.

"What he do?" I asked.

"Mamadou wouldn't pay. There was a big fight. Everyone picked a side. Those who didn't pay Samba Ba, they joined Mamadou and went to look for new land."

"Yep," continued Amadou Demba. "They went out to Becce. A lot of Bambara like me followed Mamadou."

In this act, I now understood, the men of Becce had rebelled against the region's social hierarchy and traditional land tenure rules. But on those distant waalo lands located half-way to Matam grew a thick assortment of thorn filled chulucki, murotoki, and dounoube trees.

"It was a real jungle," commented Sarr with a laugh. For centuries the land there had been left uncultivated, and trees had thrived. The men from Becce felled them all with simple tools, and eventually built a twenty-four-hectare rice perimeter amid the stumps.

"But not all the trees went," stated Amadou Demba. "We left Baaba Njiia!"

This was the name of the single handsome dounoube tree under which Becce conducted its business in the fields. Literally, Baaba Njiia means 'the father will see.'

"Why Baaba Njiia? What that mean?" I asked Amadou Demba.

"There were so many trees out there. It was dangerous, people didn't like walking through the forest. Wild animals and spirits! Some trees, like Baaba Njiia, watched over us when we did. We kept one."

"Really? And dangerous animals?" I was doubtful. Aside from the occasional *liwoogu*, manatee, or *yahre*, scorpion, what menace could there be in these parts?

"Ahh. But there were hippos, crocodiles, lions, hyenas, and elephants," Amadou Demba continued. "It *was* dangerous. And cattle and goats on the dieri? Not like today. When I was a boy, herders had to actually watch their animals, not nap."

True, an extensive dry stretch of waalo land not far from Becce was named *Wendu Nooro*, but I hadn't realized that Nooro meant crocodile in Pulaar. Wendu Nooro means Crocodile Lake. This body dried up long ago, and with it the region's last crocodiles. But the terror of these creatures remained in the tales told by village elders. Later I learned that some distance downstream lay a small islet. A century earlier French scouts had landed on it and named it 'The Isle of Ivory' after discovering elephant tusks there.

"And my grandfather once spotted a lion outside of Selibaby," continued a wide-eyed Sarr, referring to an inland town some 100 miles upstream. A few months after this exchange, a wildlife expert in Nouakchott confirmed with me that Mauritania's last lion had been killed in that region a few years earlier. The last of West Africa's remaining lions are now protected in a Senegalese game park 150 miles south of Civé.

Aside from shade and a convenient gathering place, the tree Baaba Njiia, I now understood, was like the cooperative's good luck charm. And from what I could tell, it worked.

Sarr now posed a question to Amadou Demba. "When did you start growing vegetables?"

"Ahh." Amadou Demba sat up, then picked up my fan to wave it over the last remnants of the coals until small green flames flared around my tilted teapot.

"Third year. That's when we made lots of money."

Some years earlier, international organizations funded a gigantic dam and irrigation scheme along the Gorgol River seventy miles to the northwest. Civé's first Peace Corps volunteer Tom helped arrange for Becce to provide the tubaak engineers there with fresh vegetables. To do so, the cooperative had to extend its land. Jalos out and heads down, the men dug an extension out of the claypan, leveling several hectares of it and molding a mile of irrigation canals, all by hand.

"That's why we call the cooperative Becce," concluded Amadou Demba, proudly thumping his chest. This feat of strength, he was telling me, is why the farmers call their cooperative, *Becce*, the Pulaar word for chest.

The tea now boiling, Amadou Demba picked my pot off the coals, then quickly placed it on the metal platter holding our three shot glasses. "Hot," he exclaimed, snapping his fingers.

Irrigated vegetables turned out to be a huge success. Lunch bowls were fuller and more varied, and onions became a welcome cash crop.

"See this new purple boubou? Vegetables," Amadou Demba said with pride. "Also, my haircut," he added, turning his freshly shaven head toward the lantern's glow.

Best of all, those engineers paid sky high prices for Becce's leeks, cauliflower, and squash. Each Sunday morning, a Land Rover descended on the awaiting farmers; soon freshly harvested vegetables were exchanged for a fat stack of bills.

"The tubaaks made us rich," I'd heard from more than one Becce member, although until now I had never quite understood their meaning.

It must have seemed to those men of Becce that with Mamadou's leadership, anything was possible.

"Cóndi Hiraande?" I was still trying to figure them out. "What about it?"

"Good luck there. It is old men, women, and children," was Amadou Demba's final pronouncement. After a moment's reflection, he added, "But Becce. Now we want fruit. Mangos and bananas."

Civé was more complicated than I realized. Castes, immigrants from the east, refugees from the north, fault lines within, and a relatively short history. And irrigated agriculture was ushering in a host of new conflicts.

Maybe fruit trees could be a good idea, I thought as I dropped a large chunk of sugar into my teapot's open top, watching through the shadowy light as the lump slowly melted into our final round of tea. Out of that top arose a sweet syrupy scent, one oddly smelling of mangos.

Chapter 18

A Wedding in Ceeɗu

As the month of February ended, in blew the desiccating winds of *Ceeɗu*, the dreaded hot season. Each day the river withered; upstream it sank completely into its bed, becoming an international road across which bicycles, camels, and donkeys travelled. At night, the synchronized chirping of crickets dulled, no longer lulling me to sleep. Sadly, one night their singing halted altogether, and I realized I missed them.

Mornings lost their chill, and the daytime air became dustier and hotter, taking on the smell of dirt mixed with the odd sweet-sour odor of decomposing animal flesh. In the shimmering distance, land and sky merged into one. And each day, more Fulɓe women balancing large empty gourds on their heads descended from the north as their inland water sources shriveled. By late-February, bare-foot Haratin, the "Black Moors," began guiding large herds of camels through a ragged gully just beyond Cóndi Hiraande.

"They're early," mumbled the blue capped Kebe one morning as we awaited their dusty passage while making our way to Becce. I noted his worried tone and gave him a quizzical look.

"It's getting crowded," he responded before taking off his knit hat. "And hot! Let's go."

Those camels arrived while the village's pregnant cows, donkeys, and goats delivered their progeny; to my deep dismay, the stillborn among them found their final resting place in the craggy cliffs below my bluff. For several weeks, the night breezes delivered pungent odors bedside, dashing any hope I might have for a good night's sleep.

One evening in early March, the croaking frogs fell silent. "Gone," pronounced Amadou Demba as he sipped tea. As if to underscore this, he took a final drag on his cigarette, taking his stump down to the filter before crushing it into my cement floor.

Then he added: "One more week and the birds will fly toward the setting sun." And he was right. In fact, with the arrival of March, nearly all plant life had been sucked dry of life.

One day I awoke to find the donkeys scattered throughout the village hobbling about, their legs tied together.

"They eat too much," Amadou Demba explained, then added with a grin, "They don't like to share."

Then, with full force, Ceeɗu hit. By eleven in the morning, the sky was ablaze with an angry haze, the air almost unbearably hot. By nightfall, my voice was hoarse, my throat sore, and my head ached from the day-long intake of hot, sandy air. Each morning, I doubled the amount of water I hauled to my hut, and rarely did three hours pass before I battled the furnace-like airs to find momentary relief prone in the stagnant river. With each hour the temperature climbed, finally peaking when the sun lay low on the horizon, its wrathful glare at last blinking.

And then the merciful night arrived when temperatures cooled to the 90s and villagers arose from the dead. On nights when the moon was full, the village turned festive as the shouts and games of young boys coursed through its lanes, their long shadows bouncing off huts and bushes until the village muezzin called residents to the day's first prayer.

As Ceeɗu bore down, my trips to the field dwindled. Instead, I spent as much time as I could motionless. Nights brought male friends over for tea and talk. Several times my mom popped over to see who was visiting, as I'm sure her status as my guardian put her in a quandary. But with time she accepted my oddities, allowing men to visit, and me to sleep each night under the wide-open sky, hoping to catch a chance odor-free breeze.

***

During the heat of the day, I frequently found myself prone next to Djeinaba at her place. After one long afternoon so engaged, I was drifting off when Djeinaba slowly rolled over to announce a surprise.

"Next week, you can help with a wedding!"

Picking up a nearby fan, I raised my eyebrows. "Not your own," she laughed. Djeinaba knew I was weary of the continual parade of marriage proposals that came my way.

"Aissata and Elimane's wedding. I am helping to prepare the meal. You can help too."

Aissata was a teenage girl in the village who was newly engaged to the village nurse, Elimane.

"What we help?" I asked.

"We cook," she said with enthusiasm as she poured some water over a rag and wiped down her sleeping baby's body.

"All day? But heat? Too hot?" I found her news alarming.

"Oh, it's not so hot yet," she reported. My heart sank with news that the worst still lay ahead.

While the novelty of participating in such an event was too tempting to pass up, I knew I had a problem: I didn't have anything to wear. Whenever I attended any event where Pulaars dressed up, I felt sure I looked like a person at church showing up in shorts and a T-shirt. I wasn't even sure what 'dressing up' meant. Pulaars' formal wear was like something out of Victorian England, with too many layers in orders I didn't understand, and mixtures of cloth I'd never get right. Plus, their formal wear would take several months of my income to buy. I always opted for modest boubous with simple pagnes; practical, yes, but completely lacking Pulaars' keen eye for style, texture, and flash.

Djeinaba appeared to have anticipated my dilemma. "I will dress you," she responded to my hesitation. As she picked up her crying son, I noted red bumps covering his chubby body. "It's the heat," she said, as she pulled aside her boubou to feed him.

It seemed Djeinaba's son Papis and I were the only two this baking heat bothered.

***

Late morning the following week, the wedding day arrived. I entered Djeinaba's compound and found her in the company of a younger sister and a cousin. All three were richly dressed in fine cloth with matching headscarves and gold jewelry. Their fingertips and palms were dyed deep purple, their hair was freshly braided into cornrows, and their lips were painted red.

"This way!" Djeinaba greeted me jovially, then escorted me into her dark bedroom. By the side of the bed, a small simple clay pot released a thin bead of smoke which filled the room with its earthy but spicy smell. She cracked open a back shutter so that light might reveal the neat line of clothes before me.

"You'll look good in this," she said with a big smile, then disappeared.

I mulled over the outfit before me. Then, slowly I slipped off my clothes and put on a small white underpagne. Over that came a full-length indigo pagne with white geometric patterns made from panels of hand-woven thick, coarse fabric. It was gorgeous. I knew this armor-like fabric and the dye it contained was highly prized, but putting it on made me feel like a knight dressing for battle. Once tied on, a hot gust of wind blew in through the open shutter, and I looked wistfully at my thin cotton pagne laying lifeless on Djeinaba's bed. I sighed, but it wasn't over yet.

After that gorgeous but suffocating pagne came a long 'grand boubou' made of seven yards of fabric, enough to clothe an entire family and then some. The bottom of the boubou touched the ground, and the arms extended to my fingernails, its floppy arm-holes extending five feet in diameter. This cloth, too, was made of thick damask with a rich pattern woven into it. The top was embroidered along the neck with intricately designed small circles, topped with some straight piping forming a v-shaped pattern down its front. It was elegant and exquisite, the nicest thing I had ever worn. I loved it, except that it imprisoned me with its smothering weight. I cast one final longing glance at my crumpled clothes lying on her bed, checked my watch, and after making some final adjustments, closed the shutter and exited Djeinaba's room.

"Heyoh, heeeyohhh, heeeeyoohhhhh, heyoh!" hooted the three women as I appeared. "Look at this true Pulaar!"

Djeinaba's sister helped me tie on a matching headscarf then added some color to my plain lips.

"Ready!" she exclaimed, then grabbed my camara. "We'll take lots of pictures today!"

Off the four of us went, and shortly we entered a small compound adjacent to Civé's one-room health center. There a few of the groom's friends had begun to gather. Mounds of potatoes, liters of cooking oil, a burlap sack filled with rice, and a large platter full of various spices and sauces soon arrived.

Across the compound, the young men started a card game while we began our task. Someone handed me a short stool and a dullish knife, and I set up beneath a neem tree to peel what seemed like an endless supply of misshapen potatoes. Amid swirling hot winds, Djeinaba disappeared. I felt completely wilted and short of breath when thirty minutes later she returned trailed by a half-dozen smiling girls bearing a wide range of metal platters, bowls, ladles, ground clothes, utensils, and three very large cast iron pots. Just then, the Becce member Ballal, who also doubled as the town crier, made a dramatic entry. In a saucy but lyrical voice he sang out greetings to all. The men across the way quickly laid down their cards and arose from their matlas to head our way.

A loud *bleat* drew my attention to a grey goat with spindly legs staked to a pole behind me. The goat was now backing away as the men approached. The executioners untied her and dragged her by leash just beyond the compound's fence, at which point two of them wrestled her to the ground while Ballal uttered a quick prayer before slitting her throat, the blood from her nearly severed head draining out into the dirty sand. Within minutes that goat hung lifeless from a tree, the eyes in its dismembered head still registering terror. Working quickly, deftly, and skillfully, Ballal soon had its grey skin and head separated from the meat. A few minutes more and platters of glistening wet, red chunks of goat lay before us.

During this beheading, Macho's last moments appeared before me, as did our trainer's instructions, knife in hand, that we were to get used to what we were about to see. *Neil, I failed that lesson. I cannot possibly manage even a single bite of the meal we are preparing.*

Then, for one long, exhausting day we worked. We hauled around huge tubs of rice, fried meat, grilled potatoes, and prepared the yogurt-like drink *tufam* from the sour milk Fulbe women brought to Civé to exchange for rice. We cooked over large scorching open fires while my body remained on the verge of a panic attack.

Sometime during our cooking activities, the bride, surrounded by a dozen young girls, arrived. They all retreated to the opposite side of the compound to spend hours tying heavy gold earrings on each other using bright thick red thread. The girls talked, ate peanuts, drank tea and tufam, and engaged in teasing banter with the nearby men.

It was only then that I noticed something: there were no parents around, nor even any other adults. In fact, I appeared to be the oldest one around.

"Djeinaba." I got her attention. "Where parents of Aissata?" I asked in a tired voice.

"Parents? Oh, at home."

I was befuddled. "Today is not their day," she continued.

"But wedding of daughter. Not come?" I felt faint and disoriented, and my heart began pounding even more.

"Oh." Djeinaba now seemed to understand. "Today is not the wedding. It's a party. The ceremony is tomorrow."

"Oh." My heart sank. I prayed I hadn't also agreed to cook for the *real* wedding.

Mid-afternoon, our meal was finally ready. With temperatures still rising, I was utterly spent. I wanted to keel over, but I managed to help serve the guests now gathering on straw mats. To each group we delivered a bowl piled high with rice, fried potatoes, and succulent, spicy and oily goat cooked to perfection; even I thought it looked delicious and knew from its scrumptious smell that it would be.

Djeinaba prepared a final bowl for the four chefs, topping it off with a generous portion of the delicious layer of rice that caramelizes in the pot's oily bottom. A quick blessing, and we dug in. The dish tasted even better than it smelled, and for a brief moment my deep distress retreated.

"It delicious," I pronounced, the others nodding their agreement as each woman tossed pieces of meat around the bowl to the others. Djeinaba picked up an especially large hunk of goat and held one end while I pulled at the other.

Hello Macho, I thought to myself as I eyed my half before savoring it.

Next came countless pots of tea. By now the temporary lift in my spirits had vanished. I was so hot that all I could think of was wobbling to the river, stripping off my clothes, and lying face up in the water until the sun sank. I looked at the huge pile of dishes off to the side.

"Djeinaba. I wash dishes?" I asked.

"No. Not yet," she replied. "The groom must arrive."

She then explained that it was time for the friends of the

bride—about a dozen of us—to gather in a small bare room behind where the men played cards. Our job was to keep the bride company until her groom arrived. I looked at the room to which we were headed, and terror struck: A tin roof. Why would anyone voluntarily imprison themselves in that hot house? But imprison themselves they did. Unwillingly I trailed the line of people stuffing themselves into this box; in the center of it, the veiled bride sat on the floor. The hot room turned into an oven as each body filled it. Yet I seemed to be the only one not in the best of spirits, as others itched with anticipation for the impending arrival of Aissata's soon-to-be husband.

Several hours earlier, Djeinaba had pulled me aside to announce that I had been selected to be the guest of honor at this event. That meant I had the distinction of announcing the groom's arrival. For this I needed to remain positioned at the door so that I could see him approach; when he did, I was loudly to proclaim his appearance.

"You are lucky," she told me. "It is the bride's best friend who usually does this. But today it will be you."

I was accustomed to complying with odd requests, so I told Djeinaba I was delighted with this honor. Upon the groom's entry, she instructed me, I was to belt out my greeting, "*O arii, o arii, o arii kooy.*" Which translates into 'he's arrived, he's arrived, he's *really* arrived.'

By now I was collapsing with the heat, and with each breath the hot air filling my lungs sent an alarm ringing through my body. I could think of nothing but the stagnant remains of the river a mere 100 yards away and could not understand why this entire party was not taking place in the middle of it. Now *that* would be something to celebrate.

To my dismay, the groom did not come for what seemed like an eternity.

"When he come?" I finally asked a young teenager next to me.

"Soon," she said, looking as fresh and cool as one of the water lilies that occasionally spring up overnight when standing water is present. I, by contrast, looked and felt like whatever was left of those flowers now. I leaned back against the mud wall and closed my eyes, knowing that 'soon' might mean three hours. The young woman then tapped my shoulder and handed me a fan, then continued her animated conversation with her neighbors. I fanned myself while feeling my heart flutter, as if it were faltering, and imagined that this was its final effort to keep me alive before giving up and letting me keel over. *Take me to the hospital,* I practiced silently in Pulaar, hoping I'd remember it even in my soon-to-be comatose state.

Just then, someone tugged on my arm. I opened my eyes and, looking through the door's threshold, saw the groom Elimane approach. *Praise be to Allah,* I thought, perking up.

Djeinaba had explained that it was essential that both the bride and groom hear my greeting. I practiced it once more in my head, thinking that all that lay between me and a soak in the river was my successful completion of this honored role. I summoned all my strength so that I could play it well.

Djeinaba queued my performance. "Silent talk. Silent talk," she called out.

A brief pause for dramatic effect, and I cried out my part, "O arii, O arii, O arii kooy." I hoped my raspy, tired voice had enough volume and enthusiasm to do the trick.

Silence.

Then everyone burst out laughing. I turned to those in the room, stunned. Had I said it wrong? Was my accent so terrible? Laughter wasn't the response I had expected. Then chaos broke out when in dramatic fashion, Elimane whisked away his giggling bride. Djeinaba and the other two sous-chefs pulled me outside; surrounding me, they doubled over in laughter. I understood nothing.

Seeing my complete incomprehension, Djeinaba grabbed my hand while covering her mouth with the other. Soon all three were in deep hysterics, as was everyone else now spilling out of the room.

Dizzy and disoriented, I had not the energy nor inclination to figure out what exactly was going on.

Then it hit me. I had been had. My 'arrival announcement' was no 'greeting to welcome the groom.' I did not know exactly what I had just said, but I was now certain it was raunchy.

"That wedding party is now a memory for all," Djeinaba called. Everyone once again fell to such deep laughter that no one could talk.

Completely worn out and too tired to think, my only response was a weary, defeated look. Then without a word, I turned to go.

I waddled through the gate and made my way down to the riverbank, suffering all the way under the weight of that beastly outfit and the heat of that ghastly day. Arriving at the river's edge, as swiftly as I could in that oven-hot air, I peeled off layer after layer of clothes until all that was left was the simple white underpagne. Feeling unusually exposed, I crossed my arms over my bare chest, waded into the muddy water, and was soon overcome by the relief brought by its icy ninety-degree coolness. When the river reached my thighs, I toppled over, completely drained of energy and irritated anew by the shiver now passing through my body. I turned over onto my back and blankly observed the hobbled donkeys on the banks, vaguely aware of some chatter downstream. My gaze returned to the mud huts lining the banks above. There at the top stood Djeinaba with the other two. They waved, their lingering merriment still evident in their body language.

I sank under the stagnant water for a moment, feeling the deep relief of a relaxed body and the release from fear that my heart was about to fail. Without moving a muscle, I floated up, then gazed past my knees to where I spotted the three women, arms at their sides, still looking my way, their glee less evident now. I considered them a moment, then a slight smile crossed my face, followed by a sigh. I realized they had just pulled off a pretty funny prank. My sister would have appreciated it, as she too enjoyed taking advantage of my gullibility.

Then it hit me: Djeinaba reminded me of my younger sister. I summoned the energy to wave to the three striking beauties lighting up the parched, hazy bank. I hoped they realized that I too enjoyed a practical joke, even if I wound up the butt of it. I closed my eyes and let my body slowly sink below the surface, my waving hand the last part of me to submerge into the muddy depths.

Later that evening, I lay beneath my neem tree, a scarf hopelessly attempting to keep the smell of decomposing flesh from the nearby cliff at bay. I began a letter to my sister. As I did, I flipped through my calendar to note the date. For some reason, the day's date was circled. I thought for a minute, then recalled my personal commitment to remain in Civé at least six months. As this milestone sunk in, I pondered it.

Then I flipped ahead six months and circled that date. With that, I began to write my sister about this interminably long and distressful day that oddly enough helped steel me for more.

As Pulaars say, 'sometimes it takes the day to appreciate the night.' In my case, I'd reverse that order.

Photographs

Wourri Kebe and Djeinaba's younger sister Ramata under my neem tree, displaying the tablecloth made for St. Christopher's Church.

Sadyo Konate at Becce, 2012. Mango trees in background.

Djeinaba and my son Ben on Dow Hayre, Civé in the background.
2012.

Me with Sarr and his sister and son.

Tall between his wives Djeinaba (l) and Fadima (r) with various children. Mamadou Konate on right. Taken in Tall and Djeinaba's compound.

Koumba Djourbil, my mom's sister and head of the gardening group, atop Mr. Lamborghini.

Me with Sarr's wife Athia after transplanting rice shoots in my plot at Cóndi Hiraande.

Steve Hilbert sets the first brick for the women's center. Kebe on left, Sala Ba third from left, Mamadou second from right.

The Women's Center is now open for business! Women are tie-dying.

The rice warehouse is full! Kebe is second from left, Mamadou second from right.

Under my neem tree wearing CRS t-shirts from Steve Hilbert. With Kebe and Mamadou (seated).

Becce farmers. Mamoudou Bayal, Kebe, Mamadou Aissata, and Amadou Demba.

Juulde Korka, praying on a dry river bed. Thierno Li in front, women in foreground.

Awaiting the President of Mauritania's arrival. The male village elders sit below the Mauritanian flag. Dancing girls in foreground.

Souleyman Konaté, visiting Civé from Nouakchott, takes a trip out to Becce to see the bananas.

part two
SAANI

Chapter 19

A Geography Lesson

It was hard to convey to those back home just how miserably hot it was in Civé. Attempting to do so, one day I wrote a friend: "Imagine a humid 100 degree day. Then put on a fur coat, gloves, and a knit hat. Now run! Uphill!"

A bit of hyperbole on my part to solicit sympathy, no doubt. But during the hottest summer afternoons of my youth, I regularly spent two hours in tropical heat running intervals at track practice. The stress of those afternoons was nothing compared with the panic and anxiety of my first Ceeɗu. Some days were so awful I spent hours considering if a mere lift of the hand to satisfy an itch was worth the effort. Usually, it wasn't. At night cows moaned, goats bleated, and donkeys brayed, all of us finally able to summon the energy to complain.

During those long sweltering days, I looked for low-effort activities. One day, my adoptive mother Taanooy suggested one; it was time for me to learn the art of cow milking. Sitting on a stool next to me, an irritated cow by our side, she soon was stupefied by my inability to wring anything from her cow's udder.

"It dry, it dry," I protested. But she just walked off clucking.

The following day I brought her a round pot of Nestle milk powder. "Tubaak milk," she called it dismissively as she took it from me while issuing another round of clucking.

One of my most common pastimes was writing letters home. My mom was my best correspondent, always writing me once or twice a week. Without fail at the end of each, she asked if I was sure there wasn't anything she could send. I always wrote back that no, there really wasn't. Until Ceeɗu hit.

'Send a milk tank full of cold lemonade,' I wrote one sleepless night after yet another stumble down to the stagnant black river.

A month later, over a warm beer in Matam, Senegal, I sifted through a large stack of letters sent to my mailbox there. One from my mom was mysteriously packaged in a thick white envelop rather than the pre-stamped blue international ones she favored. I opened it and out plopped several packets of lemonade-flavored Crystal Light.

Early next morning, I filled my canteen, sprinkled in some of that yellow powder, then set off for Civé. Before crossing back into Mauritania, I had become swept up by the wonders of Crystal Light. Delicious. Maybe even better than beer. Soon I was sharing the powder with friends in Civé, and what mom figured was a month's supply was gone in days.

'More Crystal Light,' I wrote. And soon a steady supply came my way: fruit punch, peach-mango, iced tea, wild berry, and of course the old standby, lemonade.

Upon any return from Matam, now the greetings of others included a new twist. "How is your peace? How was the journey? Did the road treat you well? How is your mother? *How is your crisselit?*"

Crystal Light, it turned out, was even a bigger hit than were the new can openers and potato peelers now circulating about the village.

Shortly thereafter, I sent my mom a second request. Its origin lay in an exchange I had with some kids during yet another blistering afternoon. I had finished lunch with the Bas across the lane and found it too hot to walk the few dozen paces home. So, I remained sprawled face up atop one of their wooden dinndeeres, arms splayed out. A pre-adolescent granddaughter of my neene Taanooy came over to ask if she could braid my hair.

"Why not?" I responded.

The adults in the compound had long ago passed out and were now lying under shade structures some distance away. The compound's kids perked up with my response, giggled, and gathered around; one trotted off to collect the necessary supplies of a comb and a spot of oil. Mari, a cheerful girl with an open and endearing spirit, sat up and patted her lap. I scooted over to place my head in it. A gaggle of intrigued kids quickly surrounded us, commenting on every detail as the procedure began. Mari's twin sister retrieved a straw fan from the matla of a sleeping adult and waved it over me as Mari set to work. Under the intense observation of all, the youngster began weaving my hair into braids tethered to my scalp. Periodic words of advice ushered forth from the watchful crowd, followed by squabbling over whose turn it was to fan me or to hand Mari the comb.

After a while, I became aware that the three-hour lunch break was drawing to a close, and that the completion of my new hairdo might interfere with the kids' afternoon classes. I interrupted the mostly incomprehensible chatter around me to ask Mari what she was learning in school.

"We're learning about Mauritania," Mari responded.

"What are you learn?" I inquired.

I was curious to know what exactly they were learning about their nation. Everyone loved to talk with me about how far away America was, and how long it would take to get there. Since I was from Hawai'i, it was hard to explain that I could get home by either going toward the rising sun or toward where it sets. Either direction, it took many miles, hills, rivers, and oceans.

"It doesn't matter which way! Ha!" exclaimed more than one person while shaking their head in disbelief at yet another bit of tubaak nonsense.

So, I asked Mari: "Do you see map Mauritania? Map Africa?"

Mari's twin Maimona replied that they were learning about each of Mauritania's thirteen regions. The other kids leaned in as Maimona pulled out her school notebook where each day's lesson had been dutifully inscribed. She read from the book in halting French, "Mauritania has thirteen regions, subdivided into forty-four departments."

I slowly lifted my head out of Mari's lap and looked over at Maimona's notebook, then repeated my question. "You see map Mauritania?"

"No," she responded.

"Your teacher, he has book?" I asked further.

"Yes, he writes on the chalkboard. We copy everything into our notebook."

"Maimona," I inquired, sitting up, all the kids now giggling over the cornrows that ran halfway across my head. "You say, 'I'm going to the river' in French?"

Maimona said, "I." She struggled for a minute, the kids silent as they watched her. She never arrived at the verb 'to go.' She was not even sure what the French word for river was, when so many conversations in the village referenced it—the ease of getting to Senegal, the difficulty of getting mud out of clothes, the size of fish in the lunch bowl, and the precise location of the motor pump.

"*Je vais au fleuve*," I said.

For the next five minutes the kids practiced this sentence, correcting anyone who got it wrong. Meanwhile, I admired Mari's work in the two-inch dull mirror handed to me by my young hairdresser. With the adults now stirring, the older kids finally made a move to return to the schoolroom on the opposite side of town.

After this experience, I struck on the idea of asking mom to send me a world map. Among other things, I could show others why it didn't matter which way I traveled to get home.

It didn't take long for my request to arrive and straightaway I had a large colorful map tacked to my front room wall. I stood back to admire my new home decor. Now I'd get people to talk about something other than the dead camel on the road to Tokomadji that blocked the daily Rapide. Or the locusts that ate the village's rice and cabbage. Or the rains that in bygone years were so plentiful that the river ran white with dumped milk. We'd compare the Nile with the Senegal, the Gobi with the Sahara; we'd contrast the height of Mount Everest with the red laterite outcroppings of Dow Hayre. This map would be a hit.

Except that it wasn't. Not a single person showed interest. Well, initially they did, and several visitors even expressed awe at indeed how far away America was before acknowledging that Hawai'i lay halfway around the world.

"You speak the truth," they assured me. Then eyeing my cold tea pot lying on a metal tray in the corner, they'd change the topic.

I was perplexed. Anything new almost always merited a long discussion. Why not my map?

***

By this time, Mamadou Konaté and I had become friendly with one another. He was less obviously aloof and had started to note my presence. A few days after Elimane and Aissata's wedding, for instance, I was at Becce observing the final irrigation of the barely surviving eggplants, peppers, and cassava. Mamadou found me standing in waist-deep canal water, supposedly helping a farmer locate the rag used to regulate the water flow into his plot. In truth, I was just cooling off.

"How do you like Pulaar weddings?" Mamadou asked, while peering down at me, his long partially covered calves about three feet from my head. Surprised at the question, I looked up at his blotted image against the glaring sky. He became distracted by something, and off he trotted, yelling at some farmers who were sprinkling white powder with their bare hands on their bug-infested eggplants. After a few steps, he turned and called back, "Keeeytiiii.

Don't let them powder into the wind!"

Occasionally Mamadou even dropped in on me. It was Mamadou Konaté, in fact, who was the first and only person to show real interest in my map. Early one morning after I'd hung up that prized but underappreciated possession, he filled my doorway as I gathered dirty dishes from the night before.

"What's that?" he asked with a perplexed look, as he peered at my map from the doorway.

"A map all the land," I responded as I emptied used tea leaves onto a platter, ready to deliver the limp mound to the Ba's goats.

Mamadou entered, approached the map, and squinted. "Where's Mauritania?" he asked after a moment's inspection.

I placed the platter on the ground. "Here. And Civé here." I'd already made a red dot to mark Civé's approximate location on the map. A few farmers heading for the fields called out greetings to me, and I went outside to return them; we all agreed it was going to be a hot day and it was good they were getting an early start.

"Where's France?" Mamadou persisted.

I re-entered my hut and pointed it out. Like many in the Fuuta, Mamadou had a personal connection with France, as his younger brother had moved there a decade earlier and remained there still. Mamadou looked to where I pointed, then indicated the English Channel asking, "What country is this?"

I paused, trying to recall the word, but couldn't. "Big, big river," I said, spreading my arms.

He paused, considering my response. "*Geech*?" he asked.

"Yes, yes, the ocean. That's the ocean," I responded.

I was mystified by this exchange. Mamadou was interested in my map, but clueless. I looked at him as he leaned toward it, and then puzzled, turned to examine what it was that confused him. Very slowly it dawned on me that he had never before seen a map.

"You know where water and where land?" I asked.

"No," he answered, turning to look down at me with an

inquisitive look.

Finally, a geography lesson. Stretching my vocabulary, I explained the lines on the map and the meaning of the different colors. In the process, I came to a clarifying realization. My map of the world looked as incomprehensible to Civéans as the arch-shaped wood boards carried around by Civé's young chanting *fósinaaji* did to me, covered as they were in Arabic verses from the Koran.

I finally understood why everyone had turned my planned conversation about the Nile into a discussion of the clouds forming in the sky and what that foretold about the upcoming raining season. I had been stumped by this. Now, at least, I figured it out. Yet one more reminder that even though, like me, the villagers loved Crystal Light, our worlds often remained mutually incomprehensible.

***

Misunderstanding comes with the territory, I suppose. One reason for our different perspectives is the limited exposure those in Civé had to life beyond their river valley. While the local elementary school (which many children didn't even attend) left most illiterate, very few progressed beyond it, as doing so required a move to Kaedi. Perhaps more to the point, educating kids was pricey; if they were in school, they weren't available to work in the fields, escort cattle out to the dieri, lug water up from the river, or scour the countryside for a day's worth of firewood. And to what end? Jobs in urban centers were few and far between, especially for those not connected to any of the Moor-dominated levers of power.

Many teachers I came to know believed that the enterprise of education was a bit pointless. My Pulaar instructor Tall, whose day job was teaching in one of Civé's two mud classrooms, stayed home if it was too hot, his back hurt, or an out-of-town visitor arrived. In other words, often. If one boy proved especially smart, a family with means might invest in sending him to Kaedi for middle school, and perhaps even Nouakchott for high school. With luck, that investment would land him a job with the government, or in the fishing or iron industries to the north. But you wouldn't make such an investment with all your kids, any more than in the U.S. you'd invest all of your money in real estate.

The educational system thus left most villagers with a limited understanding of the world beyond the Fuuta. But lack of worldliness did not mean Civé fell short on residents who were smart, wise, or thoughtful. I had come to appreciate that those traits were as common in Civé as they were in my own land.

Chapter 20

Painting the Moon

That long miserable Ceeɗu dragged on and on. During it, the chain-smoking motor pumpist Amadou Demba became my best friend, so close of a friend, in fact, that many jokingly referred to me as his wife. "Hey, it's Amadou Demba's jom suudu," became a common refrain.

By this time, I knew that a sterling reputation was part of the ticket to working in Civé. So, I was super cautious, never completely sure where a host of landmines might lie in the village landscape. Besides, I couldn't imagine the unknown complexities a village romance would bring, and my life in Civé was already filled with enough anxieties to keep me perpetually off balance. So, anyone who approached me with overtures of romance—and thankfully Amadou Demba was never one—left disappointed.

Word traveled, and soon all suggestions came to a halt, as did eventually any reference to me being Amadou Demba's jom suudu. I paid for this, though, as I often longed for something more than laughter, friendship, and novelty. I hadn't left anyone back home, yet I waited with anticipation for a letter from a beau of sorts I had inopportunely met months before Frogmore—although his letters stopped once he haltingly wrote of his recent engagement. I didn't know him that well, but once his letter slipped noiselessly from my hand, I felt as a tightrope walker might if the net below suddenly disappeared.

At any rate, I was not Amadou Demba's 'wife,' and eventually everyone figured this out. But Amadou Demba was a really sweet, hard-working, and good-tempered man with a terrific sense of humor. I valued our friendship immensely. After a satisfying meal and tea, Amadou Demba loved nothing more than a good laugh.

But Amadou Demba did not manage his money well. He smoked up a storm, which ate up so much of his money that he had none left for medicine when his delightful young baby daughter Mairam fell ill. Two days later, the women wailed as the men buried her.

Like many others in the village, Amadou Demba spent every cent that came his way on fine clothes, meat, a bit of macaroni, and the sweet-sour milk drink called tufam. And when a birth, or *Eid*, or some other celebratory event occurred, he spent money he didn't have. These periodic extravaganzas left Amadou Demba perpetually poor. So, when he wanted the luxury of tea, he wandered up to my place, made himself comfortable, and either eyed my teapot, or simply announced that he would prepare tea for all present.

That Ceeɗu, Amadou Demba came almost every night, often in the company of other Becce members. By now I had become known for my close association with the village men. I arrived in the village like an orphan, and it seemed the families of Becce had chosen to foster me. An odd family it was, but I came to appreciate those long hours together drinking tea, listening to music, and searching for some entertaining topic to kick about.

One evening Amadou Demba arrived with Mamadou Konaté's handsome younger brother Sadyo Konaté, a short, squat man with a big grin named Kalidou Mbu, and the blue stocking-capped treasurer of Becce, Kebe, a man I still adored. In fact, if I were ever to become anyone's wife, the gregarious Kebe would have been my early choice. The quiet and thoughtful Sadyo Konaté would have been my later more considered one. But I digress.

My four guests that night were all Becce stalwarts, all a few years older than me. Sadyo Konaté was a quiet, reflective man who appeared accustomed to living in the shadows of his charismatic, gregarious, and articulate older brother Mamadou. He was also a gentle soul I could always count on, like when a few months later he quietly came to my aid when my rice plot at Cóndi Hiraande nearly flooded after I botched the location of my irrigation pipe. An hour later, my rice rescued, he simply said, "There," smiled and silently returned to his own affairs.

That evening, the five of us lay on matlas near my neem tree talking of nothing in particular. I had never before lived a life where hour-after-hour, day-after-day was spent 'shooting the breeze.' But such was about all you could aspire to during Ceeɗu. Whether during those blistering hours when the sun was out, or evenings when you could enjoy a brief lull, I came to appreciate an entertaining storyteller, or a good practical joke played on some unsuspecting soul.

That evening we lay in the open enjoying a warm breeze. Kalidou discussed his planned trip the next day to Matam. Amadou Demba mentioned that his neighbor's goat had gotten into a bag of fertilizer and died. Kebe heard that onions were fetching eighty ouguiyas/kilo in Kaedi. All mentioned the increasing presence of Haratin in the area, some watering camels, some not. I didn't know why, but any mention of Moor sightings always left me with a sense of foreboding.

"They're looking for land," Sadyo said, and everyone murmured their assent.

The tea simmered away on the side while Baaba Maal played softly in the background, the musician's stirring Pulaar lyrics and spare musical accompaniment piercing that warm, clear night air.

Next to me, Amadou Demba was making tea. He sat up to steep saani, tasting it to make sure the sugar was exact. Across from me Sadyo lay silent, gazing up at the full moon climbing in the sky while chasing away the deep shadows around us.

Sadyo finally asked the question he'd been mulling over.

"Americans visited the moon, truthfully?"

I let his question sink in as the others awaited my response. After a bit I answered. "Yes, many time we travel. Five time." I guessed at the exact number.

After a moment's reflection, Kalidou sat up to announce somewhat matter of factly, "There's no rice there!" We laughed, all eyes now gazing at the bright, awe-inspiring moon above us. Kalidou, I imagined, was wondering exactly what it was that drew Americans so far away from our home.

"In America, we say the moon is cheese. A ball of cheese," I added.

Everyone laughed, but since none of my guests had ever seen cheese before, they probably didn't get the connection. I wasn't even sure I did, so I left it at that.

Still, Kalidou followed up, "Well, did they taste it?"

Our laughter was followed by silence as Amadou Demba handed us our teacups. Sadyo propped himself up to take his, and then revisited his original question in his characteristic quiet and understated manner. "So, Americans sent a pirogue to where the moon lives. There is no rice. There is no cheese. So. Why didn't they paint it? You know, so we can see?"

The other three men turned expectantly to me, awaiting my response. Completely flummoxed, I asked him to repeat his question. In earnest, he repeated it more slowly. Then it sunk in, and I burst out laughing. The others quickly joined in and started to select the best color for the task. Blue. Green.

"Or what about stripes," suggested Kebe as howling once again filled the air, drowning out both Baaba Maal and the loud moans emanating from the Ba's pens across the lane.

Sadyo's question was a difficult one: these trips, he was asking, what was in it for us here on earth? Why was there no sign left behind to show us why those trips mattered? With the stark nature of his question, for which I had no answer, the two worlds

I straddled drifted further and more uncomfortably apart. How do you explain to people in Civé why we sent people to the moon, a place where there is neither cheese nor rice, and when they left no color to entertain the folks back home?

Sadyo's inquiry was memorable in part because we all enjoyed so much merriment over it; not just that night, but in the days to follow. In fact, soon the entire village was hooting over our exchange. But for me it was memorable for another reason: I wished I had a good answer to Sadyo's question. Here where babies die because parents like Amadou Demba lack a dollar, where kids can't attend decent schools, and where people starve because the rains fall a few inches short: Why *did* my people think it a good idea to send a ship out to where the moon lives?

And why did it send me here when there was nothing that I could do about any of these wrenching problems? My growing bond with the residents of Civé sometimes left me feeling more rudderless than ever.

Chapter 21

Koorka and Ceeɗu

Djeinaba had been right: the first days of Ceeɗu were mild compared with the ones that followed. By May, all my movements were
deliberately sluggish, and all my plans centered on the precise location of that blasted ball of fire in the smoky sky. Activities shrank to
the bare necessities. Each dawn, a stream of young girls, followed
by Mamadou's eighty-plus-year-old mother Koumba, headed to the
dieri to pluck whatever wild *ulo* might still be growing, or scavenge
a few thilouki branches to serve as fuel. A few others might head to
Becce to pull up cassava roots to add to that day's bland lunch bowl.
But whoever headed out was back before the sun looked down on
her head. If not, she had no choice but to find a tree to rest beneath
until the sun looked in her eyes.

"When it end?" I asked Tall one day as he lay nearly passed out
on a matla beside me.

He mumbled something I couldn't make out, and Djeinaba
magnanimously leaned over to fan me. "Soon, if Allah wills it," she
said with a soft hoarse voice. *Please Allah,* I prayed.

Eventually, eventually, I became accustomed to the furnace-like
winds and oven-hot air and could think of something other than
the sun's departure beneath Senegal's flat glimmering savannah.
But whenever anyone sniffed the air, gazed upward at the sky, or
scanned the east for signs of approaching moisture, my hopes rose.

It was around this time that I became hooked on the idea of
bringing fruit trees to Civé. This idea had been one stored in the

back of my head, originally placed there by Mamadou during that morning on my porch one week into my stay, and later nudged forward by talks with Amadou Demba and Kebe. But I'd also stashed this suggestion alongside a clutter of others, like filling the village with mud stoves, growing strawberries, or replacing Doro Thioub with the silent but capable Sadyo Konaté, the man who wondered why ships sailed out to where the moon lived. In other words, projects not well-vetted in the real world.

Midway through Ceeɗu, though, the Peace Corps had its annual training for volunteers at Mauritania's National Agriculture School in Kaedi. There, the ten of us remaining from my Frogmore group joined up with eight from the previous year, and for a week we camped out in tents pitched on the grounds of this old cinderblock French colonial-style school. Mornings, we listened to agricultural lessons, and during long harsh afternoons we slept, played cards, or doused one another with small buckets of water.

Those morning sessions covered a wide array of topics, including how to grow rice hydroponically. I found it amusing to consider the prospect of convincing Cóndi Hiraande members to scrap their current rice cultivation practices for ones requiring no soil. Luckily, though, not all sessions were so academic. Two days were spent at an agricultural research station located a few miles out of town. There grew Mauritania's only banana, mango, lime, guava, and grapefruit orchards, and we learned about growing them under severe weather constraints.

The station's agronomists conveyed to us their excitement over Mauritania's untapped potential for growing fruit. I eagerly took it in. Of course, who wouldn't be excited? The presence of gigantic mango trees which provided a shady oasis from Kaedi's mind-numbing heat and a barrier against the Sahara's scorching winds had instant appeal.

After Kaedi, we headed north to learn about vegetable growing in oasis communities, made possible with the aid of a clever donkey-powered irrigation scheme. Then, on we continued to Nouakchott for a few days of drinking beer, eating pizza, and playing bridge in the air-conditioned comfort of Nouakchott's American Club.

While passing through Kaedi on my way to Civé, I found I couldn't shake the memory of those tall, stately mango trees. So before continuing to Civé, I paid a dollar and hitched a ride on a two-wheeled rail-less wooden cart pulled by an aging donkey, a mode of transportation called a *charet* in French. After a bumpy forty-five-minute ride, I arrived at the research station. A worker I recognized was sitting at a desk under a sprawling mango tree and I approached him. Shortly two other workers joined us. A quick order for tea went out as we gathered amidst protruding mango roots to discuss how to bring mango trees to Civé. I took detailed notes on costs and logistics. By the end of our conference, the workers had convinced me that it was possible to plant the nation's first orchard in Civé, with the essential caveat, "If Allah wills it."

I tucked my notebook into my backpack, bid everyone a day of peace, and under a burning mid-day sun, returned to Kaedi and then onward to Civé.

A second occurrence cemented my interest in fruit trees; the confluence of the hot season Ceeɗu with Ramadan, called *Koorka* in Pulaar. Ramadan is the ninth and holiest month in the Islamic year, one where Muslims refrain from eating, drinking, smoking, and sex between dawn and dusk.

When Koorka falls during Ceeɗu as it did in 1985, Ramadan proceeds from being immensely challenging to downright lethal. I still can't comprehend the willpower required to forgo water during Ceeɗu. Out of solidarity, on Koorka's first day I too fasted. Or began to I should say. By mid-morning, the alarm of having a mouth sucked dry of saliva sent me fleeing to my calabash, and in record time I downed two quarts from it. From then on, I never again attempted to skip drinking, although out of respect—and lack of good options—I never ate while the sun was up. It was because of this half-hearted attempt to fast that I earned the moniker 'half-faster' from my mother, a common term used to describe the fasting practices of small children.

"Hey half-faster," Taanooy would call after me with a wave as I headed to the village.

"That me," I'd call back returning her wave. "I your half-fasting tubaak." Taanooy always chuckled at that and nodded her approval.

During those long quiet days of Koorka, I caught up on correspondence, recorded my notes, read, and made hourly trips to the river. For long stretches of each day, I mimicked what others did and lay motionless below a wet sheet; an African air conditioner, as Kebe liked to call it.

I found the villagers' endless reserves of willpower simply extraordinary to behold. Each morning at 4 a.m., they awoke to the town crier Ballal's raspy, bellowing calls as he wound through the village informing all that it was time to rise, pray, eat, and drink before day broke. Up people got, often only hours after lying down. In the dark, women hastily built fires, then cooked a thick rice porridge served with the midnight bread of the village baker Alasanne. All was eaten, then chased down with as much water as the stomach could hold. And then more, the last gulps sliding down as the first signs of daybreak appeared above Dow Hayre's rocky outcropping. If work took you to the fields, out you headed before that drowsy sun awoke.

One morning a week into Koorka, I noticed Mamadou Konaté in the distance, seemingly returning from Becce. At first, I didn't recognize him, as an unfamiliar large umbrella obscured his figure. But soon his long, purposeful gait, with a bounce mid-step, gave him away.

Shortly Mamadou entered my compound, his boubou completely wet. It was then that I realized he'd made a pit stop at the river. Once on my porch, he closed his umbrella. It was clear he was spent and intended to stay. I stood a bit dumbfounded with tub, clothes, and a bar of soap in hand, ready to head to the river to wash clothes and sit in the river. I set my tub down, retrieved my matla and a pillow and placed it on my dinndeere.

Without a word, Mamadou slowly removed his headdress, lay down, then carefully and completely wrapped himself up in his boubou and turban to protect his skin from the desiccating winds. His clothes now completely dry, a light breeze rippling over them, he soon fell fast asleep. Shortly the entire village would be in a similar trance-like state, ensconced in their own cocoon as if stung and preserved by some paralyzing insect.

Within a few days, it was apparent that Mamadou had selected my veranda as the perfect spot to wait out the sun. And, in fact, it was. Perched several dozen feet above the river, it was protected from wind blasts but subject to a breeze; far from his house, it provided respite from his family's demands; and housing a family of one, it lacked noisy kids, roaming animals, clattering pots, and crying babies.

And thus, each morning that Koorka, out came my matla for Mamadou. And nearly every day, whether I was home or not, he came. Whether returning from the river, a visit to Djeinaba's, or a tour of the village, I was sure to find Mamadou on my porch sleeping, praying, resting, or just thinking.

Up until that month, Mamadou and I had not spent much time together; and what time we did always involved work. After our agricultural training in Kaedi, I had handed him a small bag of high-yielding rice seeds given to me by a researcher. A month before that, the two of us had planted a nursery with some fast-growing tree seeds. Another time we discussed where he might purchase seeds for the Violet de Galmi onions he prized.

Yet I remained wary of Mamadou. He was a powerful man, and I tended to shrink in his presence. I was not sure I wanted to be under his sway. Besides, my limited language skills meant I hung out with those with patience and time to kill. Mamadou had neither.

But this formal relationship was about to change. Like a sleepless person in the middle of the night, Mamadou wanted to talk while lying on my porch, as conversation seemed to hasten the slow passage of time.

To my utter astonishment, one afternoon Mamadou awoke from his daze and began talking of Allah. By now I could talk intelligently about motor pump parts, the dozen or two features of a good round of tea, and the various stages that turnips go through from seed to a marketable product. But talking about faith, the hereafter, holy texts, and submission to God's will left me speechless. At the age of thirteen, I had learned about the Trinity and Holy Scriptures while studying for my Confirmation. I'd even memorized passages out of the *Book of Common Prayer*. All that seemed so long ago, and I hadn't really given that material another thought once the local bishop blessed us.

These religious conversations for me were slow, tedious, and exhausting. But Mamadou persisted each afternoon until roughly 7:12 p.m., when neighboring compounds began stirring to life. After glancing at his watch, Mamadou would slowly rise then disappear down the gully. Once home, he along with everyone else praised Allah, then urgently downed a mammoth tomato-paste can full of water, followed by a second. After that came a bitter bite of the date look-alike fruit from the murotoki tree. And finally, all who could consumed large quantities of a hot sweet drink made from the spicy leaves of the kinkeliba bush.

"Hot? Why hot?" I asked Amadou one day out of curiosity.

"It helps to stretch the stomach," he explained. "You can eat more after drinking it."

But until 7:12 p.m. arrived, Mamadou lay on my dinndeere talking of Allah.

Koorka's moon grew rounder, and each day my religious

vocabulary expanded. I even began to warm a bit to this topic of God, and I challenged Mamadou. What god would want people to suffer so much? The month of Koorka took up an entire moon. Could people in Civé afford to spend an entire moon without working? People must die from this daily ritual.

In fact, I was certain my 'father' across the lane died a bit each day. Every morning Samba's voice was weaker, his thin face more skeletal, and the effort to arise from his hammock more insurmountable. "You can fast Saudi Arabia. It have air conditioning, servants, and oil that turn to money," I said. "But Civé too hot, empty stomachs, and rainless skies."

One day I asked: "What god do this? Think Koorka a good thing for people?"

I surprised myself by issuing such a blunt challenge, but each day my unspoken alarm over the effect fasting had on villagers grew. People were listless, weak, and complained of throbbing headaches. Many suffered through violent bouts of coughing.

For someone who probably had never discussed religion with another not of his faith, I found Mamadou to be remarkably reflective. He always had answers at the ready.

"It… challenge… Allah… convictions. Allah… dedication. Life on earth… Approach Allah… submission." Only a few words made sense, but I could string them together.

I respected Mamadou for hearing my challenges. And I really admired everyone for their other worldly demonstration of self-discipline and unwavering faith. In fact, such displays of devotion left me feeling shallow, embarrassed by my near-complete and singular focus on food, water, and the air temperature. I could not imagine ever having such convictions that I'd willingly suffer as much as those in Civé did that month. They felt something I did not, and I was envious of their certitude and clarity of purpose.

One moon leaves plenty of time for discussing topics other than religion. Mamadou also took keen interest in detailing the village's problems to me. For instance, one afternoon he described the widespread problem of diarrhea, especially among newborns, and of the cholera that periodically struck.

"We need a well," Mamadou concluded.

That was obvious to anyone. During Ceeɗu, the river consisted of stagnant pools of festering water increasingly crowded by the dung of large migrating camel herds. To get water, you first had to locate a brown pool to wade into. Next you swept away the floating camel dung with one arm while quickly dipping your tub into the water before the morsels bobbed back into your path. I offered my bleach to anyone who wanted it. But no one liked the taste. While I doubled my usage, they politely declined it. Diarrhea swept away the lives of so many babies that after six I stopped counting. Still, it seemed people in Civé wanted a well as much as they wanted bleach added to their water.

"Why Civé not dig one well?" I pondered aloud. But I already knew the answer. "The money is painful," Mamadou replied. "And it's different."

I nodded my understanding. I could see how different it would be for villagers to visit some central well rather than the riverbank closest to their home. Plus, the river offered one-stop shopping: bathing, scouring dishes, scrubbing callouses, washing babies, cleaning clothes, and gathering water. And, of course, the village glue of gossip.

Mamadou not only honed in on Civé's problems, he offered solutions.

"Women need work, they need to not always ask men for money," he grumbled one day, a bit out of the blue. I agreed, but his observation surprised me given what I'd seen of his household; he did, after all, have two obedient wives, and there was no question who held authority, power, and the purse strings in his household.

Then he continued: "Women need to organize into a cooperative, so they could earn some money. They need something like

Becce."

I filed all of his ideas away, saying vaguely that I would look into them.

After one such conversation, Mamadou grunted and mumbled something before springing up with the realization that the day's third prayer had arrived. I handed him a satala for water and fetched my novel. He performed his ablutions then set up beneath my tree to face Mecca. There he stood, knelt, and rocked forward to the ground, while reciting a portion of the Koran repeated twice daily by all the region's Sufi adherents.

Sufi Muslims believe that their spiritual leaders can communicate with Allah or the Prophet Mohammed. In the Sufi sect common in the Fuuta, the Tidjiani Brotherhood, the guiding saint is the eighteenth-century Algerian Sheikh Ahmed Tidjiane. Members of the Tidjiani Brotherhood believe that the Prophet Mohammed revealed numerous litanies (called wirds) to him. In seemingly endless recitations, Tidjianists repeat these wirds twice daily. Sitting aside praying Tidjianis and hearing their quietly hummed long supplications, had an oddly soothing effect on me.

His recitations over, Mamadou rose, returned to his matla, and began discussing cooperative members' need for credit. Affordable credit, he claimed, was crucial because the high cost of credit kept everyone poor. He mentioned some sort of a store. It was complicated, and I didn't understand everything. Woozy with the heat, I fell asleep. That night I recorded what I remembered of our conversation.

The third week of Koorka, the moon now thankfully waning, Mamadou once again turned to the problem of cash flow.

"We need something for cash. We eat our rice and vegetables. We eat our animals. But people need cash...."

"...to buy medicine," I finished, more to myself. Once again, the image of Amadou Demba's infant daughter appeared before me. It had only been a few months since Mairam had suffered through two days of flu-like symptoms before, cradled on her parents' bed, she breathed her last.

Mamadou ruminated. He picked up my novel and flipped through the pages, studying it carefully. He pursed his lips and pushed back his turban.

"An orchard. We need an orchard. Fruit have vitamins, yes?"

"Yes. Yes, they healthy," I replied.

Suddenly I realized I knew about fruit trees. I knew where they were, how to get them, and what they cost.

"Wait," I said, and retreated into my hut. I passed into my second room. With the help of a flashlight, I located the budget I'd drawn up with the field workers the morning we spent beneath their mango tree.

"Here. Plan fruit trees," I said while emerging from inside, handing Mamadou some papers.

Mamadou had nodded off, but my words awoke him. Propping himself up, he reached over to take the papers from me. The words, the numbers, the few drawings, he studied them all. While he couldn't read, he looked them over as if their meaning were sinking in.

"If have land, trees grow here. Mangos blossom best. You need good land. Good water," I explained.

"We have all that." He turned over one of my sheets and saw some drawings. "What's this?"

"Wind blocks. Fruit trees don't birth if too hard wind. Wind blocks stop too hard wind." I pointed to the lines on my drawing signifying heavy winds.

"Wind is a problem. What else?"

"Nematodes. Fruit trees need white powder."

I knew any specialized products requiring careful application would create problems. Farming in this region had long entailed dropping seeds into holes, praying for rain, and if they came, keeping hungry animals at bay. Growing fruit trees required the care and precision of rice, a crop that cooperatives up and down the river grew about as successfully as did Cóndi Hiraande.

Mamadou returned to the drawings, then turned to another sheet containing a column of numbers.

"That," I said, pointing to a large number at the bottom, "that cost of one mango hectare."

It was a monumental sum, I thought, but Mamadou didn't flinch. He nodded, thinking.

"Lots of nematodes at Becce. But we have land. We can learn." He paused. "This can move us forward. OK. Let's do it."

"OK," I said, not exactly sure what I had just agreed to. "I look for funders in Nouakchott," I added with more certainty than I felt.

Ever since we met in SONADER's Kaedi headquarters, I viewed Mamadou as bossy or intimidating, often both. I steered clear of him. But as Koorka lengthened, I came to think of him a bit like my stern high school track coach, Miss Reid, who somedays struggled to keep us focused on the day's workout. Behind her back we grumbled, but deep down we all respected her. Especially during my sophomore year when, against all odds, our team placed second at the state championship. Mamadou had much in common with Miss Reid, I decided.

The following night, a shrinking slice of the moon rose deep into another hot night. I wrote to friends and family back home that fruit trees were coming to Civé. For the first time, I neglected all mention of the blasted heat.

Chapter 22

N'dungu

The transition from the final flicker of Koorka's moon to the glimpse of a new one was just jolting. *Juulde Koorka—Eid Al-Fitr* in Arabic—started piously with the village men gathering on the dry sandy river bottom, joined at a respectful distance behind by the women elders. I stood in my backyard some fifty yards above the still river and praying villagers, observing the rites, and watching as a herd of goats wandered among them. Looking across to the flat stretch of Senegal beyond, I could see the smoky air promised yet another stifling hot day.

For an hour, Civé's religious leader, the revered iman Thierno Ly, led the crowd in prayer. Finally, the rhythmic praying and hum-like chanting ended, and in good cheer all headed up the banks. At that exact moment, all hell broke loose. Sheep and goat were slaughtered while women and girls converted their water buckets and pots into drums to accompany the festive music now blaring from fully charged radios.

Straightaway, women and men emerged from their homes to stroll about dressed in their finest. The women's skin glowed from shea butter, and, in an astonishing display of wealth, their bodies shone with more gold than I'd ever seen. Along with cattle, gold was how Pulaars held wealth, and on this day out it all came from locked trunks. The elders among them wore necklaces anchored by a large plum-sized gold rock with earrings to match. Many also had feet stained black from manioc-infused henna, and almost all the women elders had covered their heads with new gauze veils, lending a conservative touch to the day's otherwise celebratory air.

Meanwhile, girls paraded by with hands stamped with intricate bright orange geometric motifs. To achieve this, the day before they had designed patterns on their hands with thin decorative tape, slathered henna paste over it, then using socks as mittens, had sat immobilized for half the day. The results were hands stunningly tattooed orange. Other girls showed off tightly braided cornrows, and on rare occasion, a spot of lipstick or a coat of bright red nail polish.

Not to be outdone, the older men bore new elegant boubous, some of which were trimmed with rich thick gold embroidered patterns. Younger men sported colorful two-piece baggy outfits that looked all the world to me like pajamas. Mid-day while myself parading the lanes, I halted speechless as two young men in such new digs passed by. One wore an outfit made of fabric stamped with large 100-dollar bills, a sideways Benjamin Franklin gazing out at me. The attire of the second loudly projected portraits of President Mobutu of Zaire, complete with his leopard skin hat. In one way or another, everything contributed to the day's celebratory and bewildering air.

When and how all this organizing, purchasing, and preparations had taken place threw me, as I had mistakenly thought that everyone in the village had spent the last few weeks (as I had) half dead. All day long, villagers wandered from hut-to-hut, partaking of the good cheer, laughter, water, and food, all of which were now in abundance. Kids sucked on candy, and everyone ate meat, meat, and more meat, in most cases more than they'd consumed since the river began its retreat. Of course, this also meant that the day's festivities would soon be paid for with a prolonged bout of diarrhea. But on this day, that cost seemed both distant and minor. So, ate they all did. And in a disoriented state, so too did I, something I too eventually would pay for.

Around six that evening, with temperatures still over 100, a large posse of teenage boys began a game of soccer. Becce's treasurer Kebe dug out a whistle, put on a fresh white tunic, pulled on a rare pair of tennis shoes, and was soon trotting out to serve as the game's stern but dapper referee.

"Take my picture," he instructed, flashing his charming white smile for the camera. I did. Then the shrill of that finely polished whistle signaled *Game On.*

***

Finally, finally, the blessed rains arrived. It was early July, and I was out at Becce ferrying rice seedlings from a nursery bed to Amadou Demba's flooded field. All night and into the day the clouds had been gathering while in the distance thunder rumbled. Then mid-day a lightning flash bolted across the sky. Stiff winds followed, carrying first moisture and then rain.

Finally, the clouds let loose. Down it came, the large dense drops quickly soaking even those who had taken refuge under Baaba Njiia's wide leafy umbrella. A few farmers immediately packed up and headed back home, but most of us continued our work shuttling back and forth between nursery and field, transplanting those rice shoots.

At first, the rain left me giddy, like the first snow of winter. The initial drops were cool and as welcome as a breeze. Soon though, the drops grew to pebbles and the breeze transformed into howling winds. Completely soaked, I began to shiver, and did what I could to protect myself from that punishing assault from above. Together with others, I began running along the slippery canal banks to ferry our seedlings from nursery to plot, nursery to plot as quickly as possible. Clenching a handful of tiny green stalks, with jaw chattering, I plunged into Amadou Demba's swamped field and as rapidly as I could drove the roots of each seedling into the soft, muddy bottom, each stalk a palm width apart. I did my best to eyeball the distance to make sure it was right; after all, as a SONADER official, this was the precision I was expected to enforce. Yet the pelting rain and my blurred vision made it impossible to tell, and soon I no longer cared about anything but finishing.

After an hour, Amadou Demba shouted that we should pack it in. I picked up my drenched backpack and note pad and joined a stream of others stumbling toward the perimeter's western gate. Tagging along behind a large group, I found we were following a circuitous route home. I followed blindly, not asking why. But soon I saw; the gullies we usually traversed were raging with water. Circumventing them required sloshing knee-high through wide lakes that stretched as far as the eye could see. Halfway home, the large heavy drops lightened a bit, and thick vapors from the muggy earth began drifting skyward. Still, I could not remember ever being so cold, nor ever seeing so much rain. Even the tropical storms of Hawai'i that turned streets into rivers did not let loose the torrential downpour of that day.

We reached the outskirts of Civé and I peeled off from the group, waving to Amadou Demba's wife and nieces, all of them now in clothes shrink-wrapped to their bodies. I entered my house and in a rare moment of privacy, closed my front door. In the space of a minute, I stripped off my soggy clothes, donned my one sweatshirt, put on a dry pagne, and in the darkness of my room wrapped myself up in my sleeping bag and collapsed shivering on my matla. And there I lay shuddering until a few minutes later when drifting away, images of hot chocolate and marshmallows arose from nowhere.

And thus arrived my first experience of the Fuuta's third and final season, *N'dungu.*

***

A few days after that deluge, a steady stream of families began trekking to upland dieri fields carrying their *luugal,* a large pencil-like contraption used for jabbing holes in the ground; kids followed them lugging large gourds full of sorghum, millet, bean, and melon seeds. Meanwhile, the river continued to surge, some days doubling in size. If it no longer was raining here, it certainly was in the river's headwater countries of Guinea, Mali, and Senegal.

Immediately the river had been transformed from a series of isolated stagnant pools into a dangerously gushing one. And it was filthy. While thankfully camel dung no longer dotted its surface, it now ran red with mud. And on its surface floated the bodies of cows, goats, donkeys, and camels that had either died on the banks or been left to rot in steep crevasses leading down to the river. The river was also thick with the garbage of the basin's residents, as the river's banks served as each village's dump. Tumbling in the water, these carcasses and piles of debris flushed by, twisting, turning, and flipping as the river briskly carried them the 300 miles out to the Atlantic Ocean.

N'dungu ushered in the busiest time of the year. Before it arrived, the rice nursery had been prepared, the soil in the perimeter broken up, the plots flooded, and the fields leveled. Once the rice seedlings had been transplanted, the work continued; weeding, irrigating, fertilizing, monitoring each plot's water level, and repairing the canals and diggettes surrounding each farmer's plot. There were also the rain-fed crops out in the dieri to tend to, and the few spare animals to fatten up. If Ceeɗu passed in slow motion, jam packed as it was with work, N'dungu sped by.

But not all my work that season was welcome. In anticipation of my first rice season, I'd earlier arranged to grow rice at Cóndi Hiraande in a tiny plot generously loaned to me by Doro Thioub, although I think he secretly figured his gesture would seal my marriage to his son Oumar.

"No Pulaar husband yet?" he asked one afternoon as he led me toward my plot. "Oumar has salary," he added, in case I needed reminding.

"Nope," I responded. "Where plot?"

We reached it. It was small, but I didn't mind. I mostly wanted to see what it was like to be a member of Cóndi Hiraande. I still harbored some crazy notion that I might help replace Doro with Mamadou's younger brother, the gentle but effective Sadyo Konaté.

Yet however small my plot was, I immediately wished it would shrink in half. Within a week I was swearing at it. Breaking up that heavy clay soil with my two-dollar jalo was like turning boulders into gravel with a pick. It was backbreaking labor, and one hour so engaged with the sun burning overhead was enough to send me to bed for the rest of the day. I soon wished I could rid myself of that dastardly plot all together, as my hands were swollen from blisters, my legs were so water-chafed I could barely walk, and my back ached even when prone.

"How come a SONADER worker doesn't know rice?" Sadyo Konaté asked with a lopsided grin one day as he waded into my plot's water to help fix my canal.

I grumbled. "Look my hands, I can't hold jalo more." I displayed the large angry blisters that covered both hands.

"No, not the hands of a Fuuta resident." Sadyo flipped up his sunglasses as we stood there in the standing water. I looked enviously at my companion's thick, muscular, and deeply calloused hands. I hadn't really noticed them before.

"For people of the Fuuta, all day long, pick and shovel, pick and shovel. Sometimes it changes. But only because it is shovel and pick, shovel and pick."

His humor surprised me. I laughed and he chuckled. I looked at Sadyo and felt a glow of warmth for this gentle man. And, glad for the distraction he provided from this backbreaking work. Sadyo, I was coming to realize, was one of Civé's hidden jewels: quiet, attentive, hardworking, and with an endearing knack for appearing by my side whenever I needed him.

"Stick to your head," he said wading past me, flashing a shy smile and tapping the side of his head as he did. Then turning he pointed to my hands with a grimace. "You see what pick and shovel all day gets you."

"Maybe I try next shovel and pick?" I responded, hoping to delay his departure. We both laughed as he moved past me. I looked at the standing water around me, then watched Sadyo as he climbed up onto the diggette, rolled up his pant legs, and then rubbed his hands dry on his face. I gazed around at all the others in the distance bent over while laboring away in their gigantic plots.

Eventually, I had to concede that as much as I wanted to learn by doing, the sheer agony of growing rice was just too stiff of a price to pay for some vague hope that I would gain insight into Cóndi Hiraande's problems. Nor was this strategy especially effective, as the only knowledge I acquired was about how ill-equipped I was to farm in these conditions. Sadyo was right. Best to stick to advising, not actually doing.

Yet I did learn to become nearly as frustrated as everyone else was with my employer SONADER. First, it failed to deliver the diesel for the pumps until the rice shoots in the nursery logged thirty days. At thirty-five days, my plot finally received the water it needed to transport my seedlings. In the case of Becce, Mamadou confronted this challenge by loaning the cooperative cash to buy diesel in Matam, Senegal. But Cóndi Hiraande had no such champion, and even if it did, such a person shelled out money at his own peril. And so, with the seedlings' roots burrowing more firmly onto their temporary abode, we awaited SONADER's fuel.

Later that season, the fertilizer arrived two weeks late. Next the motor pump broke, making a chaos of irrigation schedules. With each unsolved problem, rumors flew, and tempers flared. Just being in the fields proved an unpleasant experience, making me long for Becce's order and good cheer.

This farming experience also taught me the tough economics of growing rice. At the end of the season, my tiny plot produced a burlap bag bursting with rice. But my 400-ouguiya SONADER bill (about $7) would have cut that bounty in half had I paid it in rice.

Adding in the hours of help others donated to me, and the cost of meals I provided in return, it was easy to see that growing rice was a losing proposition. No wonder the village youth aspired to city work. I would too. More than once I longed for the ease of simply plucking seed down in the dieri or joining my neighbor Harouna in the quiet solitude of fishing.

It is a risky life, farming on the margin as these villagers do. I couldn't picture ever being able to buy rice at a grocery store without thinking of aching backs, empty bellies, and an inept government agency. I found it completely understandable that so many parents wished for at least one of their kids to acquire a salaried job. Imagine! A stream of cash that arrives whether the rains or SONADER's diesel comes, whether the fences need mending, or the camels come stomping, whether the locusts arrive or even whether a mosquito bite turns into a nasty fever that takes four days to break.

Being completely exposed to all forms of misfortune left little room for planning. I realized my strong propensity to plan everything came from the privilege of living a plannable life. *If Allah wills it* is not how I have learned to understand what transpires around me.

***

On days not out suffering at Cóndi Hiraande, I happily trotted out to Becce. Right around 7 a.m., Mamadou stopped by for coffee and bread. Like me, he was a planner, and this was becoming our common bond. After discussing some upcoming event, off we set to Becce, I half-jogging along as he conducted business with others, made decisions, mulled over problems aloud, and then created new plans until it was time to scramble over Becce's gate.

Such days at Becce were long ones. I usually left after the day's third prayer, entering the village around 5 p.m. completely famished. Usually, I arrived with Mamadou. Within minutes, a young girl from the Ba compound delivered a bowl of rice and fish stashed from lunch. A few minutes later and Mamadou's young son Abou scurried up from the gully carrying a bowl containing similar contents. Often, the treasurer Kebe, Amadou Demba, Sadyo Konaté, the town crier, or some other farmer would join us. All who passed by were urged to 'come eat!' Those gathered inspected each option, then selected the best. My washing bowl was passed around and someone would issue a quick blessing. While I'd happily join my guests as we dug into one bowl followed by another, I always leaned back from the huddled men whenever a woman passed by, asking her to "come eat," though I knew she wouldn't.

During the tea that followed, the conversation would turn to the fruit tree proposal or any other project on someone's mind. By the time the river had surged and begun its retreat, the proposed orchard was mapped out, with all its details inscribed in my notebook. It was now up to me to follow through on my promise to find Civé a funder.

Chapter 23

Transitions

The daily demands of Becce and the comraderie it offered rescued me from my otherwise solitary state. Yet I found life in Civé to be stressful, with each day presenting a new reason to flee. My deeply cracked feet were sometimes so painful I could barely walk. My skin also itched so furiously it felt like something in it was alive and scratching to get out. Sometimes pent-up emotions left me depressed and listless. I'd never before realized how important talking with others was for keeping me sane. Yet my communication skills were akin to drawing with a roller brush.

Most often, though, my desperation to leave came from a total lack of privacy. It seemed my every word was captured and my every action recorded, all looped endlessly for any who took interest. And that would be everyone.

"Your stomach is running," my mom said to me one day while handing me a tin can filled with a sweet, milky beverage. "Drink."

I thanked her, returned home, and then discretely emptied the can's contents in my back yard, not imagining that a beverage made with murky river water was the ticket to stanching a sudden, nasty bout of diarrhea. This act of hers was exceptionally thoughtful, but I couldn't help wondering: How did she know? I pondered that question as guiltily I watched that precious liquid seep slowly into my sandy backyard.

A couple of things helped me blunder on when I felt I couldn't. Before leaving for Frogmore, I worked as a research assistant at the

University of Hawai'i's East West Center. A thoughtful Australian researcher took interest in my upcoming assignment and gave me two pieces of advice.

"The mosquitos may be awful. Get a floppy hat and dangle wine corks from the rim," Doug advised me. "I promise. Not a single mosquito will bother you."

Even if it worked—and I was doubtful—there was no way I would wear a hat that would make me look even more ridiculous than I already did.

Doug's second piece of advice proved more useful, though. "Keep your work and personal diaries separate. Don't mix them up."

That suggestion proved immensely helpful. When writing in my work diary, I kept to the facts: I recorded conversations, tidbits shared, vocabulary learned, and detail on the cooperatives' accounting. When I set that aside and picked up my personal diary, I could let loose my frustrations, longings, discomforts, and comments about people or situations that drove me crazy or made me desperate for the Rapide's arrival. I was, I guess they call it, 'compartmentalizing.' But Doug was right: this approach helped me both do my job and manage a turbulent emotional life.

My expanding language skills also helped my incongruous isolation within Civé's crowded fish-bowl environment. Still, eventually I had to succumb to a mounting desire to escape. Usually that meant a ninety-minute hike upriver to Matam, Senegal to collect my mail and pass the evening with other Americans at a house the Senegalese government rented for its volunteers. There I'd usually find another volunteer, and we'd happily pass time within the compound's tall concrete walls, reading, showering, sitting before a fan, drinking beer, eating peanut butter, and enjoying the ease of English. Till next morning, when I'd take a deep breath, re-tie my headscarf, and head back to Civé.

Occasionally, I ventured north to Nouakchott, but that trip was long and tough, so I only went when summoned by an overdue shot, the Christmas holiday, or some training session. Yet once there, the American community welcomed us like kids returning from college. Each night the American Club hosted a large gathering of Nouakchott's Western community; when volunteers arrived, those present at the Club would treat us to a beer, a slice of pizza, or even invite us home to watch a football game or a newly released movie. At Christmas, the American community opened their homes to us, making sure each of us was hosted by a family. Within their spacious homes, we were provided a private room, tubs to soak in, and refrigerators stocked full of French cheese, Belgian chocolate, and American bacon.

Other visits to Nouakchott required crowding into the modest concrete compound in the center of town that Peace Corps rented for us. There I'd be sure to find a boisterous reunion, loud music, animated card games, some unusual adopted pet, a visiting local boyfriend or girlfriend, and a large dose of the drama that came with our unusual and challenging lives.

Apart from the American Club, Nouakchott offered a few opportunities for tourists, although I never mustered the courage to see what the nation's zoo had on tap. But we did occasionally organize outings to some of the local attractions, like jeep rides along Mauritania's lonely beaches, the Atlantic on one side, the Sahara on the other. On one such trip amidst dust-filled salt air, we barbequed meat while watchful but puzzled seagulls loitered nearby. Then as the tide rose, we filed back into the jeep, and once again traversed the wind-swept beach, this time watching the sun lower itself over the ocean. For a brief but dazzling instant, the setting sun filled the hazy sky and rough sea with a surge of rich colors before quickly slipping below the horizon.

I was less drawn toward such group outings, however, than to those with a friend or two. The volunteer Julie and I had become best friends, and when she was in town, we'd be inseparable. We'd sit or walk the streets for hours, usually ending up at a new French bakery in town where we'd share an expensive croissant. Or we'd dream up new outfits—Julie was good at that—and search the outdoor market for fabric. Sometimes we hit the one Western boutique in town where our passports allowed us to buy Bailey's Irish Cream. If we went to the American Club at night, we sat at the bar and talked with the completely charming manager, an openly gay German by the name of Walter who surprised us with detail on Nouakchott's vibrant underground gay community.

Nouakchott was drab. But it was also a choice destination for its many immigrant residents. The thick ring of shanty towns encircling the city attested to this. Quickly assembled dwellings and tents sprawled deep into Nouakchott's surrounding desert, temporarily sputtering out until someone arrived to pitch yet another. To the city's west, the dwellings petered out several miles before the ocean, leaving a long stretch of flat empty scrub brush separating the city's western fringes from a single lonely hotel-nightclub built by a French company on sand dunes overlooking Mauritania's choppy seas. Those empty quarters between city and beach, frequented by roaming camels that delighted in its salty fare, were mostly used as a final resting spot for unusable construction material. Except, that is, when on occasion the American community congregated there for a game of softball, affectionately referring to this chosen locale as Camelstick Park.

A popular draw in Nouakchott was its large marketplace housing row after row of small, impoverished vendors selling recycled metal, bowls of charcoal, or even fifty-cent haircuts. Surrounding the stalls sat others peddling their wares—a handful of roasted peanuts wrapped in a strip of newspaper, a spoonful of tomato paste delivered on stiff brown paper, or a small plastic bag of henna tied tight with string. If I asked any vendor where to find dates, locally made cooking pots, or wooden prayer beads, he'd abandon his post to thread me through the market to the exact merchant I sought. Other than its dire poverty, very little in Nouakchott echoed Dakar's rambunctious, noisy, colorful, and aggressive street life, and the capital's hidden charms grew on me.

By the time my second year rolled around, Civé had become a more comfortable place to live. One change was that Julie had managed to move from her original post of Lexieba to the village of Koundel, a mere eight miles downriver from me. During her illness-plagued six months there, the two of us made regular visits back and forth on the Rapide. With the hint of a family she provided, and the occasional clandestine glass of Irish Cream, I was feeling more at home.

I also found that while out of Civé, the village summoned me back. I wondered if the white powder had managed to save the cabbages, if the missing six cows belonging to a Fulbe household had been found, or if the young girl in the Ba compound had recovered from malaria. Eating and drinking at the American Club left me feeling guilty and increasingly ill at ease. One evening, I wound up at the bar sitting next to a kind middle-aged embassy official, and we soon fell to discussing agriculture in Mauritania. To my great surprise, he carried on at length about Mauritania's need for better machinery and technology. He concluded that the country shouldn't expect to grow much when everything was done by hand.

"But how are they supposed to buy those machines? Where does the money come from?" I asked. As I did, I couldn't help but smile at the thought of Amadou Demba shouting merrily out of a tractor's window while driving it back and forth across Becce's soils.

"And what about all the people who would be left unemployed?" I added, realizing how preposterous this image was.

"We did it in America. That's why we're rich and they are poor," he answered, taking a swig from his German beer while rolling its cap around in his hand. Across from us, the manager Walter rolled his eyes as he wiped a beer mug dry.

This comment missed a key insight of economics I'd learned in college: When land is more plentiful than labor, as was true in our early history, investing in machinery makes sense. If not, as is true in most poor countries, machines just don't make sense. You can't make money off them.

It was commonplace to find that Nouakchott's westerners had no inkling of what it was like to live with Mauritanians. And most were none too interested to find out. Once Civé became my reference, I grew increasingly uncomfortable with the riches into which I was born, and haunted by all we consumed. For the cost of butter and jam on toast in the morning, you could buy five doses of malaria medicine. An ice cream cone would get you 10 pairs of sunglasses, the key to saving eye sights from the sun's ravages. Soaking in a hot bath, I'd find my thoughts wandering to my hard working, worn-out neene Taanooy, who had never bathed in anything other than cold river water. And opening the refrigerator in a typical American's home in Nouakchott? The food you'd find crammed in there equaled the cost of the fertilizer, seed, and tools needed to feed a large family for an entire year.

By my second year, too, many of my Peace Corps friends had begun to return home, including my neighbor Julie. I gravitated to the Civéan community living in the capital, a large group that welcomed me with open arms. Most lived in Nouakchott's 5th District. Here lived Mamadou Konaté's serious younger brother Souleyman and his family; an affable Army officer by the name of N'Diaye and his delightfully saucy wife Faba; and a handsome young Fulbe man by the name of Djigo, a distant relation to Djeinaba, and a man who having studied in Scotland, now taught English at the national university. Soon all trips to Nouakchott included long visits to their 5th District homes, where our conversations inevitably turned to the growing list of projects coming out of Civé.

***

Spending time with Civé's Nouakchott residents also meant being drawn into their problems, for Pulaars do not live discrete lives. On one trip, the Peace Corps chauffeur Demba, who I learned had married a woman from Civé, pulled me aside.

"Keyti, my wife is very sick. Do you think you could come visit her? I think she needs tubaak medicine," he confided with a worried tone.

"What her problem? What makes her body sick?" I asked.

"I don't know. It has been a year now. She gets worse each day, and now does not eat, arise or pray. We've had a Marabout visit but…" His voice trailed off.

One blustery, dust-filled afternoon I got permission for Demba to drive me to SONADER's office. Once out of sight, Demba turned right off the capital's main paved road, and soon we passed the 5th District's large sprawling marketplace. Then we left behind Nouakchott's wholesale meat market where groups of men bartered over camels, goats, and long-horned cattle. On we continued, soon leaving behind the factory that bottled all of the Coca-Cola and orange Fanta consumed by the nation's residents.

I was confused. Why was Demba taking me out here and not to his house? Soon I understood. It turned out this gracious man who worked with wealthy foreigners, lived smack amid one of Nouakchott's largest shanty communities. After negotiating a maze of tight sandy lanes, we pulled up before a jumble of corrugated metal, plywood, and plastic.

As was true of most Nouakchott homes, those in the shanty town were blessed with neither electricity nor running water. Even mid-day, Demba's home was dark for lack of windows. After we ducked below the entryway, he led me to a room in the back where his wife Maimona lay on a mat. I sat down next to her.

"How are you? How is your body? How is your tiredness? Are you sleeping in peace?" I asked, while trying to hide my horror. Maimona's bones protruded from her skin, her voice was raspy, and her eyes lay sunken in her head. Very slowly, out from beneath the worn blanket came her hand, and she placed it on mine, her thin skin as soft as a baby's.

"All is well, I am at peace, God is great," she responded in a weak voice. "How is your mother? How is your work? Are your people well?" she asked.

After a brief visit, I told Demba that the Peace Corps nurse might know something. It was awkward being cast in the expert's role on a matter I knew little about. Yet having access to people with expertise and money did, in some important sense, make me an expert. Eventually the Peace Corps nurse did visit Maimona and gave her some red pills.

"Thank you," reported Demba next time I saw him. "You are a good person. If Allah wills it, Becky will check on Maimona again in a month. Allah is great."

"May Allah will it," I responded.

After that, Demba always shook his head sadly when I asked after his wife. I wondered how he managed the jarring juxtaposition between days spent within the rich American community, and nights spent nursing a wife quietly dying in the dark.

Much later, after I had left the country, Demba wrote to inform me that his wife was no longer with us, ending his message with the philosophical reminder to us both that 'Allah is great.'

Chapter 24

The Loan

Despite that first torrential thunderstorm, the rainy season that year failed. A few sprinkles did make the baked mud as slippery as ice. But by August, stunted crops leaned in the dieri. Early September, one day of sprinkles followed another and many turned hopeful. With prayer beads in hand, off they trudged back to their dieri fields with large planting sticks propped against shoulders. Soon the soil was reseeded. Eventually some managed a meager harvest of shriveled sorghum heads and undersized melons. But the rains that year were too hard and too few for the dieri to be anything other than stingy.

October arrived, and with it the hard work of the rice harvest. By the time the sun was one palm high, men were already squatting beside dry rice stalks. With a small hand sickle, they swung hard once, twice, three times to cut through broad handfuls of stiff stalks, each hard swipe accompanied by a grunt and bead of sweat. Meanwhile, all capable of it ferried off bulging eight-foot-wide bundles of the fallen stalks, carting them off to a cleared area just past the perimeter's reach. Women then swept up thick handfuls of the long reeds and began vigorously thrashing them against overturned rusty barrels, *bang-bang-banging*, until the rice lost hold and shattered to the ground. All day long, the deep rumble of those hollow drumbeats filled the air.

"Let's sing," someone would occasionally call out, and lyrical voices would arise while the random beatings turned into coordinated drumming. If still fresh, a few young girls would even halt their work to add playfully suggestive dancing to the merriment.

During harvest, everyone worked, even the youngest. Those not yet waist-high were handed a large tin to scoop paddy rice from the ground into recycled burlap bags. During breaks, men carefully and tightly stitched each bulging sack closed with cloth strips attached to oversized needles. Then donkeys were led in and held steady while sixty-pound sacks of rice were strapped to their backs. Finally, a stick-bearing boy would silently accompany the beast back to the village. Then night came, and everyone would lay exhausted but happy, nursing hands sliced raw by the stiff dry stalks. Until daybreak, that is, when all set out with steely cheer for a repeat performance.

'Don't romanticize the farming life,' I wrote to my mom in shaky penmanship one night with a hand too swollen to close. As an afterthought, I added, 'And send gloves.'

To my relief, the harvest ushered in *Dabunde*, the cold season, which meant digging out my sweatshirt and thick sleeping bag and enjoying lunch bowls piled high with tasty vegetables.

***

One Friday morning early in Dabunde, I awoke to braying donkeys. It was quiet and cold, so I lay reading in my sleeping bag, knowing no one except my young bread deliverer, Kalidou, would dare appear in such frigid weather. But as morning lengthened, I began to wonder if something was amiss. While Friday was the holy day, usually by now I would see a handful of farmers headed to the perimeters, especially since the vegetable season was in full swing. Yet so far not a soul had travelled my lane.

At last I crawled out from the warmth of my bed. I dressed and, passing more braying donkeys, descended the banks to a river now flowing so high I had considered joining the village boys and diving off some nearby cliffs. Images of my pagne being stripped from me and flushed downstream kept me from acting on that whim, however.

On the banks that particular morning, I found only a few young girls washing the night's dishes and day's clothes. I filled my plastic tub with water, placed a rolled-up headscarf on my head, and with effort hoisted the tub up and rested it atop my scarf.

"May we pass the morning in peace," I said as I headed up the banks.

"May you live," a few called after me.

Typical, and yet not quite. Apart from the donkeys, the river was too quiet, the village too still, and too few birds lined the shores.

The cool weather, I figured as I steadied myself up the banks. It was a season that seemed to bother people (and maybe birds?) more than did the interminable heat.

Once home, I carefully lowered my tub to the floor, and then started the lengthy process of filtering and treating its cloudy contents. Then back to the river I headed to wash a crusty bundle of clothes.

This time, though, I found myself alone. It's like I've come to the shopping mall on Christmas, I thought. I quickly washed my clothes, then rinsed them in the swiftly flowing river. Back home, I dangled each article from my fence.

While so engaged, my mom Taanooy called out to me from across the lane. I waved and greeted her.

"Me, I'm coming," I called out with a wave, a greeting which usually meant, 'I'm coming later…maybe.' I had a report due to my Peace Corps supervisor Stan, and my plan for the morning was to finish it.

With my final item hung, I picked up my empty tub, then turned to enter my hut. An eerie darkness enveloped me. Stiff winds followed. What seemed like dusk rushed in with alarming and disorienting speed.

Taanooy's calls became urgent, her panicked arms waving

frantically across the darkening lane.

Looking northeast toward the rocky hills of Dow Hayre, I now saw why. A gigantic billowing sandstorm, so large and thick it was blotting out the sun, was churning our way. The edges of it were clearly discernible as it plowed towards us, its trajectory and speed unmistakable.

My heart leapt to my throat, and I was overcome with a fear like one I knew from my youth when after emerging from the ocean, lungs bursting, I would find myself confronting a towering wave about to crash and send me into uncontrolled somersaults.

We'd been warned about these winter sandstorms, when blistering winds came swooping down from the Sahara, picking up and depositing vast amounts of dust and sand along the way. Over the decades the region had lost so much groundcover that now these storms had intensified and increased in frequency. So large and powerful were they that each year they carried away something like one billion tons of dust and sand, the particles sometimes winding up halfway around the world.

And now several tons of debris were about to assault Civé.

I rushed inside to close my two back shutters. Then standing in my hut's threshold, door in hand and heart in mouth, I watched my neighbors scramble to grab pots, mats, and jalos before fleeing inside.

Frozen with both fear and fascination, I remained standing with my door ajar as the billowing orange sandstorm hit. It was darker than dusk, the sand pelting down like a violent rainstorm while unsecured items hurtled by. I couldn't make out my fence located a mere twenty feet away and was oblivious to the fact that by then my clothes had spun away to join in the mayhem.

It didn't take long for my hair to fill with sand, my eyes to sting, and my curiosity to end. I wrestled my front door shut, and with the help of a flashlight, settled in amidst swirling dirt, pelting sand, and an image of Dorothy's house spinning in the eye of a Kansas hurricane. Could these Harmattan winds uproot a mud hut?

Sitting, I tried to read but couldn't. I kept wondering if there was something else that I should be doing: Hiding under my matla? Running across to the Ba's to the safety of their concrete building? Standing in a doorway? I recalled those times during my youth when at 11 a.m. sharp on the first Tuesday of each month, alarms blasted from the local fire station. Upon hearing it, we'd take turns practicing how to respond to a tsunami, an earthquake, and (yes) a nuclear attack, depending on which disaster the alarm was signaling. What was the right response to a violent sandstorm, I wondered?

Lacking an answer, I stayed put. For thirty minutes the wind howled, the sands strafed, roofs ripped, cast iron pots cartwheeled by, unprotected animals wailed, and my heart pounded. Then finally, utter silence.

I waited another ten minutes before inching open my door, peeping out, and then slowly venturing into the gloom. There through the thick fog I found my neighbors taking stock of their losses. I retrieved my satala then crouched in my front yard to wash sand from my face. Glancing around, I belatedly realized that of course my clothes were long gone. Only then did it dawn on me that this was the message my arm-waving mother had been trying to convey to me an hour earlier.

And then emerging out of the dense haze, she appeared before me. Taanooy scolded me for losing my clothes. Looking around she declared, "This really wasn't a bad sandstorm. It does not harm." Turning to leave, she correctly predicted, "Your clothes will come home." With that she disappeared back into the thick orange fog, clucking at me as she did.

Reentering my hut, I surveyed the scene. Sand was everywhere. My books were covered with it. My drinking water was filled with it. My mats and sheets were coated with it. With eyes stinging and head pounding, I felt disoriented, unsure now if it was 10 a.m. or 4 p.m. In this stupor I picked up my two-foot-long broom, and began the long task of ridding my house, clothes, and porch of their sandy layer.

An hour into this endless task, Amadou Demba arrived. With the air still clogged with dust, he appeared before me cast in its ghostly orange glow.

"So, that was a sandstorm," he pronounced with a chuckle as he emerged from the smoky mist. "But it does not harm," he qualified.

My throat was now sore, my head still clogged, and I felt achy and irritable. Still, I welcomed the diversion of his company.

Amadou Demba removed the remains of a cigarette from his front pocket and placed it unlit between his lips. Entering my front room, he grabbed a mat and emerged to unroll it on my dinndeere. Then he sat and lit up the cigarette stump.

I told him about my clothes, which caused him to erupt in raspy laughter. Then he repeated almost verbatim what everyone else by then had told me: "You shouldn't wash clothes when sand is coming."

"I don't know sand arriving," I countered somewhat defensively, to which he gave the same instructions I'd already heard.

"Just look to the sky where the sun rises," he said between drags, turning his back to me to point toward Cóndi Hiraande and Dow Hayre. "Smell the air. It will be cold and dry. And the donkeys go crazy."

I knew that I would never be able to pick up on the subtle signals that all the villagers found so obvious; after all, the donkeys often went crazy. I thought that next time I'd pay closer attention to my neighbors' frantic arm waves. For me, *those* would be the clues that something was amiss.

Amadou Demba soon rescued my charcoal bag from its resting place in the gully behind my hut and began making us tea. Whatever plans I had had for that day were now scuttled, and I gladly joined him. That morning ordeal had left me trembling inside.

In no time Amadou Demba was fanning smoking charcoal.

Looking up, he said with a chuckle that I must wash my ears. I checked them to find they were caked with sand.

"And aspirin fixes your headache," he instructed as he flicked a disoriented dung beetle out into my sandy yard.

An hour later, the third round of tea now simmering, Amadou Demba steered our conversation toward the just-ended rice harvest. I could tell his message was important as he first jostled me awake, then checked to make sure I followed every bit of his story. I knew that like so many, Amadou Demba hadn't yet paid his SONADER bill for the just-completed rice campaign. A week earlier, Kebe and I had once again calculated each member's bill, and Amadou Demba owed a whopping 10,000 ouguiyas; nearly $200.

Usually, farmers paid their SONADER bill by selling the organization a portion of their harvest. An oversized SONADER truck carting an industrial-sized scale arrived in the fields just as the rice was being packed into burlap bags. Soon thereafter, the truck lumbered off, hauling with it a fat portion of the village's rice. From what I could tell, this was the only one of my employer's many responsibilities that it faithfully fulfilled.

"There it goes," said Mamadou one afternoon with a long look as a large SONADER truck rumbled away from Becce. 'It' was the rice.

Everyone resisted this way to pay SONADER. No one wanted to watch a huge helping of their annual food supply depart in a truck bed bound for Kaedi. Indeed, successful farmers like Mamadou Konaté paid SONADER by selling cows, goats, or sheep, or by using the proceeds from their vegetable sales, Violet de Galmi onions in the case of Mamadou. A few others relied on money sent by kids employed by the Mauritanian government, Zouerate's iron companies, or Nouadhibou's fishing industry. Like many farmers, though, Amadou Demba had none of these options. And nowhere to turn. Until now.

"And so," he concluded, his tale now told, "I will no longer be a person with problems once you loan me 7,000 ouguiyas." He then turned to steep our third cup.

This request left me stunned. People always asked me for money, usually to meet some desperate health need like transporting someone to Kaedi's hospital after a falling beam mangled their leg, or after a wife or sister had suffered through two days of labor. Usually, the request was for 100 or 200 ouguiyas. Only once had someone asked for as much as 1,000 ouguiyas. In that case, a Fulbe neighbor sheepishly asked me for that amount to herd his cows north to M'Bout, where they would fetch a fairer price. I agreed.

A week later the man, a Becce fellow by the name of Awdy Ba, came through my gate carrying a calabash full of milk.

"Fatou Wane. Wane, Wane, Wane." he said with a big smile. "Everyone from M'Bout praises your name." He handed me the bowl of warm foamy milk, reached into his pocket, and then gave me a crisp 1,000 ouguiya note.

"You must come for dinner tonight," he added. "Wane, Wane, Wane." That night he killed a chicken and boiled three eggs, insisting that I eat one of the three entirely by myself.

So, 7,000 ouguiyas was a magnificent sum.

But I was rich, and the amount only equaled half my monthly salary. A few days later I gave Amadou Demba a small stack of ouguiya notes I kept stashed in my sleeping bag's zippered pocket.

"I'm in your debt, sister. I'll pay you back, you'll see. You'll be eating my money soon. Thank you, my sister. Thank you, thank you," he repeated over and over for the next several days. I was sure he would make good on his debt, so I brushed off his need to reassure me.

Still, this transaction brought to mind Mamadou Konaté's repeated attempts to explain the dilemma those SONADER bills presented to the village. I knew Mamadou was anticipating the unhappy conflict members faced once Kebe presented each with the scrap of paper representing their SONADER bill.

This also explained why Mamadou was so effective: by helping villagers in debt, he became their backstop. There was no bank to borrow from, and certainly nothing like a credit card. The only thing that existed was something like a modern payday lender in the form of the boutique owner Samba Anne. And this source came with same downfalls; it was absurdly expensive. Many who needed money wound up asking Mamadou.

In fact, two years prior, Mamadou had loaned my landlord 10,000 ouguiyas for his SONADER bill. I discovered this was why I paid Mamadou my monthly $15 rent instead of my actual landlord. Mamadou was generous and people trusted him. But they also owed him. The respect he inspired and influence he exerted came in large part, I believe, from the way he used his money.

Indeed, the fact of the matter was that cooperative members who didn't pay their SONADER bill left everyone on the hook because the cooperative expenses—fertilizers, pesticides, motor pumps, diesel, and oil—were collective ones. Not only did the cooperative have to parcel these out among themselves, but they also had to figure out how to get members to pay. If just one person balked, the entire cooperative was on the hook. SONADER was like the landlord who doesn't distinguish which of your roommates hadn't paid her rent; even if you had paid your share, you were still responsible for the total amount.

Becce's business-like culture, with Mamadou doubling as banker, helped ensure that each member's bill got paid. And so it was that cooperatives like Becce kept SONADER happy. But it also meant their members' rice ran out months before the next harvest. As Mamadou explained it, the farmers lacked credit, as no one would lend them money since they lived hand to mouth and had no assets.

No one, that is, except me, as Amadou Demba had just happily discovered.

Chapter 25

Rice and Credit

A few mornings later, the tall figure of Mamadou Konaté filled my doorway. So cool was it that he arrived wearing a blanket draped over his boubou. I set down my coffee cup and novel to add water to the small canister on my gas stove while Mamadou entered and took a spot on the floor. He continued some conversation he'd started with himself having to do with a stream of visitors that morning. Picking up my Jane Austen novel and flipping through it, he mumbled about some matter having to do with money.

"What's this about?" he asked, changing the subject by tapping my novel.

I paused at length to consider. "It about women when men have all power and there are castes that limit what you do," I said.

"Oh. It's about the Fuuta then."

I let out a surprised laugh. "No, England. Here England." I reached up to point out the faded green country on my long-forgotten map.

Mamadou twisted around and squinted, studied the map a bit, and then looked back at the book, again flipping through its pages. "So, England and the Fuuta are alike," he said with an amused tone and nod of his head.

"Yes. But this story was long ago. Before *fergo* of Oumar Tall," I said while handing Mamadou a small pot of boiling water along with a platter with coffee makings.

"Ah." Mamadou mused at my novel's historical placement.

For those in the Fuuta, Oumar Tall is a towering historical figure, one combining Martin Luther's religious conviction with George Washington's military and political acumen—with a few miracles added in for good measure. Aside from the Prophet Mohammed and Oumar Tall's patron, the Saint Ahmed Tidjiane, Tall is probably the most revered person in the Fuuta.

Born at the tail end of the eighteenth century downstream from Civé, Tall came under the sway of this recently deceased Algerian saint Tidjiane. Tall was made a leader, or Sheikh, of this Sufi order, and was determined to extend the Tidjiani Brotherhood to West Africa.

About this time, the French were conspiring to conquer the Fuuta, and were making steady progress doing so. Moving upriver, they built forts and planted flags. Meanwhile, Tall arrived preaching religious authority, local autonomy, and Islamic statehood, messages countering France's plans, gaining him many followers—and enemies. Tall struck out to present-day Mali, home of the heathen Bambara, and his followers joined him in his famous *fergo*, or migration, to fight infidels and spread Tidjianism. Tall achieved stunning military successes, and eventually conquered several Bambara and Fulbe nations to the east. From this emerged a large and powerful Pulaar empire extending from Timbuktu to present-day Guinea.

The alarmed French, meanwhile, engaged in devious and violent efforts to first secure the Fuuta and then extend their domain east to the Niger Valley, the heart of Tall's new empire. The French considered Tall to be a dangerous religious fanatic and continued muscling their way upstream. Forming alliances with some local leaders, the French rewarded their supporters with redistributed land, and attempted to ensure that their opponents regretted their opposition. One particularly awful campaign occurred in 1857 while the French were building yet another fort in Matam, Senegal. Under the direction of the military and political leader General Louis Faidherbe, who led France's colonialization efforts in this part of Africa, troops burned 30 nearby villages to the ground. Today, Fuuta residents still recount the names of those clans who supported the French. Unfortunately, this would include some of the influential Wanes from which I hailed.

Alas Tall's empire to the east proved to be short-lived. While escaping some rebellious locals in Mali, Tall met his end when gunpowder exploded. Within a couple of decades, the French had snuffed out all remaining resistance to their rule, eventually gaining control over much of West Africa. Tall's jihad did leave an important legacy however, as it spread Tidjianism across the Sahel. Like Martin Luther, his legacy remains.

***

With a sweep of his arm, Mamadou pushed the long sleeves of his boubou over his shoulders, and carefully poured water over a spoonful of Nescafe and large lump of sugar. He placed my book aside and changed the topic.

"Becce needs some white powder. I'm going to Kaedi today to buy a sack from SONADER," he said while sipping coffee.

Amadou Demba's loan was still on my mind. "People are paying their SONADER bill?" I asked.

"Slowly. Everyone wants a loan from me. But this week two paid."

"Amadou Demba one," I commented. "He take loan from me."

Mamadou put down his coffee cup and swallowed. His arched eyebrows conveyed his utter surprise.

"So that is how!" he exclaimed. "How much?"

I paused. "7,000 ouguiyas."

This time not just his eyebrows arched, but both eye sockets as well.

"You were the giver of 7,000 ouguiyas? Really?" Not believing his ears, but seeing my confirming nod, he sat back, rearranged his turban, picked up his coffee, and then slowly sipped it.

Pursing his lips to stifle a smile, he waited a moment, seemingly mulling over a response.

"Amadou isn't a repayer. He can't," he finally stated with certitude. Then once again he picked up my novel and squinted at the two elegantly dressed beauties gracing its cover.

A feeling of incomprehension passed through me. Of course, Amadou Demba would pay me back, I was certain Mamadou was wrong about that. I held my tongue, not wanting to protest, and tugged at my bread while conflicting thoughts swirled about. Then Mamadou, who by now had lost interest in the matter at hand, began reviewing the list in his head of Becce members still owing their SONADER bills.

"Amadou Birama 14,928 ouguiyas. Oumar Deh 10,340 ouguiyas. Sadyo Mosque 12,433 ouguiyas…"

While he recited this mental list, I regained my bearings. At length, I asked Mamadou the question that still bugged me.

"The payers, where they get money for SONADER bill?" I stumbled.

Mamadou started to explain, but soon my head was swirling.

"Wait. Stop." I put my sleeping bag aside, and went to retrieve pen, paper, and my trusted Casio.

It took me an hour or two to get all the details straight. But when I thought I did, I passed my calculator over to Mamadou for his inspection.

"That's about right," he murmured after confirming the number with me. He pursed his lips and nodded. While he couldn't read or write, Mamadou knew numbers. And he knew when they were right.

According to my calculations, each year one-third of Civé's rice harvest was carted off to Kaedi. When you didn't have a tubaak to lend you money, you paid SONADER's bill in rice.

What I learned from Mamadou was that it wasn't just SONADER that hauled away villagers' rice. Residents used their harvest to repay debt owed to the local merchant, Samba Anne, a man who kept tabs on the state of everyone's rice fields. After estimating the harvest of each, his credit flowed. Or didn't. Once the rice was in, Samba Anne collected his share, which he valued at SONADER's rock-bottom harvest-time price. Men arrived at Samba Anne's closet-sized store lugging tubs of it. Mr. Anne weighed each tub, then transferred the grain into a large burlap sack. Once full, he sewed the sack shut and began another. These sacks made their way to Kaedi alongside SONADER's, where machines dehulled the paddy into ready-to-be-cooked rice, a task the village women did manually. Thump. Thump. Thump.

The problem was that once a family ran out of their remaining paddy rice, the only rice available to buy was the dehulled variety. And it was expensive. Hence the dilemma; instead of re-buying the cheap paddy rice you had sold, your only option was to buy the expensive processed version. It was like selling hamburger at discount prices when you have no money, and then having to buy prime rib at peak prices when you have no food.

According to Mamadou, Civé's families typically turned their last burlap bag of paddy upside down six months before the harvest. To stretch things out a bit, they might cut meals in half, skip one here and there, or ship their kids off elsewhere to eat. When times were especially desperate, some even handed their children over to wealthier families to serve as domestic servants, as at least then their children would eat.

With Mamadou's detailed explanation of household economics, I had just calculated the extra amount the entire village spent by selling their paddy at fire sale prices, and then buying it back six months later as expensive processed rice; roughly 600,000 ouguiyas *each year,* $13,000. It was this figure that I had just handed to Mamadou.

"You are sure?" I asked, wide-eyed, certain that such a monumental figure could not possibly be right.

He tilted his turban back, then settled in slumped against my mud wall. "Everyone knows it." Once again, he examined the cover of my novel, commenting this time on the green countryside in the background. "That's a land of rain," he remarked.

I looked out my open front door to where some farmers were just then passing by. Their torn clothes and repaired rubber slippers took on new significance. True of most, and for sure true of Amadou Demba, they were probably caught in this cycle of poverty. It took several months before I realized that Mamadou was right: As much as he might like to, Amadou Demba had no ability to repay me.

I turned back to Mamadou, who was now putting numbers into my calculator while chewing a hunk of bread. He looked up.

"Last year, Becce got a 100,000-ouguiya grant from SONADER. With it we bought eight tons of rice paddy."

I came to understand that years back, when the cooperative manually extended Becce to grow vegetables for tubaak engineers working at the dam up north, SONADER had rewarded the cooperative with a 100,000-ouguiya grant. At Mamadou's insistence, Becce used this money to buy its members' rice after the harvest. It was enough to purchase eight tons of paddy.

"Where you store it?" I asked, not sure I completely understood.

"The small storage in front of my compound," he answered while continuing to plug numbers into my calculator.

Stunned, I now finally realized what those two Haratin laborers had been building in Mamadou's lane the previous year.

Just before the last rice harvest was in, Becce members began borrowing from this stored rice, promising to replace whatever they borrowed after their harvest was in. Paddy for paddy in a one-to-one exchange. No more hamburger-for-prime rib.

"Two weeks after we transplanted rice, all eight tons were gone," Mamadou concluded. Except for the merchant Samba Anne, all were wildly enthusiastic about this newly affordable rice supply. But this pilot project was too small. The estimates we'd just calculated meant that this affordable supply met at best 10 percent of what the village needed.

Civé needed a very large loan—about $20,000 I figured—to store enough paddy rice to get villagers through the year. And they'd need a very large storage facility. According to my calculations, such a warehousing of the village's rice would save the village each year more than was required to buy several motor pumps outright and dig several wells.

"We do this," I said, with a sense of urgency. "We build this warehouse. We convince people for money."

Mamadou looked up with a startled expression. After a pause, he said, "OK, good, good. This is what we need." I promised Mamadou I'd write a proposal the next time I went to Nouakchott. I'd look for some organization to fund this rice storage project, just as I had begun doing for the new village orchard.

"Perfect," Mamadou replied with a surprised note.

By now it was late morning. Mamadou put down his coffee cup, placed the hard tail end of a bread loaf in his mouth, and slipped off his blanket.

"I have to get to Kaedi," he said as he folded his blanket and arose from the floor.

I watched Mamadou as he strode off toward the village with what appeared to be an extra bounce in his step. I crossed over to greet the Bas, and afterwards decided to go greet everyone in my neighborhood. Strolling down my lane, I took in the clear blue sky and detected a faint scent of honey in the air. Another fine winter day in the Fuuta.

Chapter 26

A Proposal

The next morning was irrigation day. Before the sun rose above Dow Hayre, I had affixed my headscarf, closed my front door, and was ready to head to the fields. Entering the lane, I spotted a familiar bobbing head and billowing boubou emerging from the gully. *I thought he went to Kaedi.* I stood by my fence awaiting Mamadou's approach.

"Where are you headed?" Mamadou called out as he strode my way.

"To Becce," I answered. "You are not a leaver to Kaedi?"

"No Kaedi today, no Becce today," he said as he brushed by to set himself up on my veranda. "I sent Kebe to Kaedi for the white powder." Looking up as I stood wordless, he added, "Today we are writers of a proposal. Make me some coffee."

Slipping off my backpack, I responded, "Of course." I opened my front door as Mamadou began setting up a working space on my porch.

To say we wrote the proposal together is a stretch. Even though he'd never written one, Mamadou arrived knowing what to say and how to say it. I sat adjacent to him on my dinndeere as he rattled off key points between swigs of coffee and chomps of bread. Soon, an outline. Then a draft. Then over and over we punched numbers into my calculator, me checking his calculations and he mine. Even after we agreed on amounts, Mamadou took another hour to check and recheck every calculation, squinting over columns of numbers he'd written in his large unpracticed penmanship, making sure all was accounted for, even the weight loss that occurs after paddy rice dries, and then again after it is dehulled.

Finally, our work met his approval. Brushing the breadcrumbs off his boubou, Mamadou gently folded sheets of calculations and tucked them carefully in his boubou's front pocket.

"That's it," he said with quiet certitude. "Now you are a traveler to Nouakchott."

I used to bristle at Mamadou's endless commands. Now I had come to depend on them.

And so, a week later I settled into the Peace Corps office and began typing. Our entire proposal took less than five pages. The last two sentences were Mamadou's: 'One of the main hindrances to self-sufficiency in the village is the structural problem of cash flow, and the necessity of using precious paddy rice to pay for agricultural debts and village necessities. This proposal is the solution arrived at by the village to solve this problem.'

I scrolled that last page out, then carefully gathered and stapled the five together. I felt sure we had a solution, not only for Amadou Demba, but for everyone in Civé. It was one that would outlast me. It might take a while, but surely someone would grasp the urgency of Civé's dilemma.

Chapter 27

CRS

One morning, shortly after returning from Nouakchott, I was on my porch having breakfast with Mamadou. I don't remember what we were discussing, but suddenly he paused, then shifted gears. He then announced that the time had come for me to work with the women. This had always been my intention. The year before when I had nearly snapped my neck lugging water up to the women's new garden, I had planned for this activity to be a steppingstone. But the women were difficult to understand and hard for me to befriend. Unlike their male counterparts, they didn't have time to hang out and drink tea with me for hours on end. I conversed with them in snippets, and aside from a few like Djeinaba, my mother, and my next-door neighbor, Sarr's wife Athia, I wasn't getting to know many of them.

"What I do?" I asked Mamadou after his pronouncement.

"Call a meeting," he said, as if that settled it. "They want to work."

Obediently, I followed Mamadou's instructions. Aided by a group of older women, I organized several lengthy meetings under the shade of my neem tree. Within two months, a plan developed: We'd get some of them trained in vocational skills, and then secure the supplies needed to put those skills to work.

Soon, nearly every one of the village women had put a 100-ouguiya down payment on this new Civé Woman's Cooperative, as we called it. The members then divided themselves into one of four income-earning activities: gardening, tie-dying, crocheting, or sewing. With over 6,000 ouguiyas in seed money and a chosen leader for each of the groups, the cooperative was in business. All that remained was the financial support to turn their plan, soon in the form of a fifteen-page proposal, into action. During my now frequent trips to Nouakchott, I spent my days searching for people to fund fruit trees, a rice warehouse, and now this new Civé Woman's Cooperative.

One week I hit the jackpot when Catholic Relief Services enthusiastically responded. Its country director, an American by the name of Steve Hilbert, was fresh from graduate school and embarking on a new career in the aid business. Steve was ambitious, smart, and most of all, in search of good projects. The Women's Cooperative intrigued him. But he was simply captivated by the rice storage project. His mind raced as he peppered me with questions.

"Your project needs someone good with numbers. Do you have anyone? How many villagers are literate? How do you weigh rice in the village, and how much can you weigh at once?" Steve took interest not just in our projects, but in the village itself. He began wondering if Civé might serve as a model for the entire region.

A short time later, Steve, whom the villagers still to this day affectionately call Estef, visited Civé. A careful shepherd of his organization's money, he wasted no time in assessing for himself this village's potential. During Steve's three-day stay, Mamadou barely strayed from his side, spelling out each opportunity he saw and listening intently to all Steve had to say.

The day before he left Civé, Steve stood before a large noisy crowd.

"To the people of Civé," he began as the crowd turned dead silent. "I have seen your work. I have heard your problems. I have listened to your solutions. I will return to Nouakchott tomorrow. My organization wants to support you. I will ask our bosses to help support you by funding both the Rice Warehouse and the Women's

Cooperative."

As soon as Kebe had translated these words, cheers rang out and dancing women pressed in on a beaming Steve. That night, the smell of roasted meat wafted throughout the village alongside the sound of festive drumming.

Three months on, Steve's pickup truck returned and out he stepped.

After warm greetings, he delivered his glad tidings. "I am happy to tell you that your news has reached New York City, and people in our headquarters there have listened. They have listened carefully and asked many questions. Now they want to support you, your hard work and your good ideas. They will fund the warehouse and the woman's center."

Kebe didn't have to translate for people to recognize good news when it is delivered: Cheers immediately went up.

Before Estef departed, the village leaders organized a celebration in a flat area above the ravine splitting Civé in two, a place where the women had decided to locate their new CRS-funded cooperative building. There, Steve placed a symbolic brick in the location where this new Center was to arise. Then the large crowd moved to a neighboring spot where Steve was handed a small neem tree to plant next to where the new rice warehouse would arise. Drums rumbled, women danced, and boys of all ages ran around kicking a new soccer ball Steve had gifted them. Then several of us donned our new white "CRS-Mauritania" T-shirts and modelled them before Steve's camera.

It took only a few months for a beautiful new yellow-painted cement building to arise on that knoll. Before packing up and leaving town, the Senegalese builders added one final touch. In crooked black lettering across the front of the building, they inscribed: 'Civé Woman's Cooperative.' On the building's river-facing side, they drew quaint colorful pictures of women engaged in the cooperative's activities of sewing, tie-dying, gardening, and crocheting.

A few months later those builders returned, and across the dusty courtyard there soon arose an imposing cement warehouse capable of housing 100 tons of rice.

CRS's generosity seemed infinite. In addition to funding these structures, it gave Becce an $18,000 loan, enough so the cooperative could purchase eighty tons of paddy, or ten times the capacity of Becce's pilot project. Once stored, this supply would later be resold to villagers at the smallest of markups.

About a year later, just before I left Civé for good, profits from this warehousing project began piling up, and Becce used them to dig the village's first well, appropriately located smack between those two spanking new structures. Here was positive proof that so much of the village's resources had previously been shipped to Kaedi.

CRS also financed a two-month Nouakchott-based training course for three women to learn crocheting, tie-dying, and machine embroidery. Afterwards, the three returned to Civé to instruct the others.

Good news kept coming. My mom's church in Hawai'i—many members of which kept tabs on me through the neatly-typed versions of my letters that mom produced and generously distributed—sent the Women's Cooperative $500. The woman used this to establish small 'boutiques' operated out of select women's bedrooms. Each boutique sold a wide range of products: the basics of tea, sugar, oil, and powdered milk, but also women's products such as henna and scented soap, the decorative tape used for dyeing hands and feet, and special oil for the tight braiding of hair.

We managed to put the merchant Samba Anne out of the loan business. Now he no longer monopolized village sales. It felt as if the sky was the limit.

Chapter 28

Women's Work

During my childhood, I often felt like anything was possible. One morning two friends and I decided to buy a horse. By afternoon we had a plan. With a couple of paint cans in tow, we began knocking on neighbors' doors, telling whoever answered that for $3 we'd paint their rusty mailboxes. Shortly our street was lined with all kinds of creatively painted mailboxes.

But then we stopped to calculate the number of boxes we'd have to paint—and then repaint—to buy and keep our pony. In short order, the bills in our coffee can lay on the window counter of Kailua Drive In. A few minutes later, and the three of us were chowing down on double hamburgers, crispy fries, and the tallest malts available.

It didn't take long for me to think that the Women's Cooperative was headed for a similar fate, one where reality smothers even the brightest of plans.

First the success. As planned, three young village women (including my friend Djeinaba) travelled to Nouakchott to attend classes at a government-run training center. There they learned to tie-dye, crochet, sew and embroider fabric. The instruction was excellent, and the women proved to be bright and creative. Two months later, they returned to Civé, and set to work teaching the skills that would soon gain the women financial independence. Well, that was my agenda. Theirs was simply to earn cash.

Then came the not-so-successful parts. I had worried about

who exactly would buy the women's new creations.

"Who will buy you cloth?" I had repeatedly asked the women.

"We buy lots of clothes each year. For Juulde Koorka, Tabaski, Mohammed's birthday, baptisms, and weddings. Let's keep that money in Civé," came the women's chorus.

But when Tabaski rolled around, relatives in Nouakchott, Zouerate, and Nouadhibou shipped clothes to the village. *Argggghhh*, I thought to myself as I watched the recipient of a new outfit cry out in joy. Like food aid that harms local farmers, the largesse from family members was undermining the women's enterprises.

Yet even without such gifts, the promise these income-generating activities held just never materialized. It was easy for me to sell the women's beautifully tie-dyed tablecloths to Nouakchott's American community. Walter, the manager of the American Club, bought a dozen to display on his tables. But outside of this small western community a day-and-a-half away, there just was not enough disposable income locally to support the women's enterprises.

Worse, though, was that their business activities were hindered by the women themselves. They complained about the selection of products, and sometimes about the maker. To my dismay, when a woman had the money to buy a new piece of clothing, she often took off for Matam.

Transforming the women into merchants also didn't go so well. While many had a keen knack for business, they lacked two essential elements for success: trust and literacy. With only a couple of exceptions, the women eyed one another suspiciously. And illiteracy made it hard to convince the women that they weren't getting the short end of a deal.

"Why does she have a new necklace?" I heard a younger woman at the river's edge scowl one day as she eyed a shopkeeper washing her clothes downstream.

One way around such distrust was to choose women with impeccable reputations for merchants, and then get me to review the books. Reluctantly I agreed, with the proviso that someone be trained to replace me. For this the women selected Mamadou's teen-aged daughter Kelly, who as a graduate of Kaedi's junior high school could read and write.

Soon Kelly and I were making weekly visits to the lady merchants' abodes. There we checked supplies, counted money, calculated profits, and handed each woman her personal earnings. With much fanfare, each week we announced how much had been deposited into the cooperative coffers. After a particularly lucrative week, the profits piled up to an astonishing $10.50, an amount so amazing that the town crier took it upon himself to bellow this out to one and all. "The women merchants made $10.50 this week. Their scarves are bulging. I'm looking forward to meat." Ballal delivered not just news, but also editorials.

This 'control,' as the women called it, was far from what I would call a business-like affair, as business could not be separated from socializing. Our five monthly controls each took a full day, leaving me at the end of each stiff and with a pounding headache. And then when I was out of town, no 'control' would take place.

It was clear to me that the women needed a leader who inspired trust, a female version of Mamadou. To keep the cooperative going, I held meeting after meeting with the women leaders. Mamadou often came to observe, while across the village, his counterparts ridiculed our efforts.

"They are all like children, and when they meet, they'll be like unmilked cows," scoffed many men.

Mamadou's support kept the women going, though, and he took to advising me behind the scenes, such as, for instance, telling me of co-wives who didn't get along or whose families complained of unequal treatment.

One morning over coffee, Mamadou was fiddling with the new pair of glasses I'd brought him from Nouakchott. After a final adjustment, he mentioned in passing, "Penda Sow and Rougui

Diop got in a fight yesterday at Cóndi Hiraande."

"Fight?" I asked, not sure exactly what he meant by that.

"Yes. They took Rougui on a cart to Matam's dispensary. She'll be OK."

That sort of fight. I knew the two women were neighbors but didn't know much more about them. I was considering what to do with this information when he added, "They made up. But make sure they are apart at the meeting today."

I thought Mamadou relied too much on me. I had neither the language skills, the cultural understanding, nor the abundance of patience needed to guide the women. Plus, I'd be leaving in less than a year. Yet maybe collectively the women could pull off what Mamadou accomplished alone?

That was a long shot, as the cooperative leaders themselves were often absent.

"She has a headache," reported a young boy sent to deliver a message from a leader while we awaited her.

"Her husband just returned from Nouadhibou," the gathered women knowingly commented.

To my great dismay, Djeinaba, who was herself a vice-president, stopped attending meetings altogether. Everyone knew why: her husband Tall was openly angry that she had become preoccupied with 'women's affairs.' Djeinaba had decided that her time was better spent keeping Tall's blood pressure down.

It was just a year earlier that Tall had announced he was taking a third wife. One result of that threat was that Tall divorced his Malian wife Fadima, which left Djeinaba as Tall's sole wife. I never understood exactly what Tall got from that arrangement, except now that I saw Djeinaba remaining at Tall's side, I figured it was somehow related.

Women had to depend too much on their husbands, straying from their partners' wishes at their own peril. If I were Djeinaba, would I choose the women over my husband? I doubted it. Power and resources, which is what Tall had, usually trumps any solidarity among those without. I hadn't fully realized how difficult it would be to wrestle away some independence for the women until the afternoon I visited Djeinaba after she missed a meeting. I found her in her compound fanning her dozing husband while a teapot simmered by her side.

"I had a headache," was about all she said while feigning fatigue.

And then there were the meetings themselves. Women were terrific at organizing the shopping, sweeping, water-carrying, washing, rice-pounding, haako gathering, clothes dying, cow milking, wood-collecting, on and on the chores went. Their work began at daybreak and continued through sickness and pregnancy, with infants strapped on backs and toddlers at their feet, until long after the sun had set. In a typical day, they lugged fifty-pound tubs of water several hundred yards, pounded the husk off a couple kilos of paddy, walked several miles while gathering wood for fuel, dug up sweet potatoes and picked bean leaves. Women worked, worked, and then worked some more.

But running a meeting? They wandered off topic or interrupted one another. Sometimes one would drag up an old dispute, or insult someone who wasn't there, only to find another shout back to defend her cousin.

On more than one occasion, I thought to myself with despair: *I've created another Cóndi Hiraande!* All we lacked was Doro Thioub's buffoonish presence.

During one especially ineffective meeting, I sat quietly under my neem tree listening to the women address a particularly thorny issue: how to share the cooperative's growing profit. The merchants' successes were building up the central bank. But the five of them began wondering aloud why the results of their efforts—the $10.50 a few weeks earlier—were shared equally with those who did nothing.

The women needed to figure out how to split the profits. For the first few hours, three or four conversations occurred simultaneously, with no group paying much attention to the other. The cooperative president, a woman named Sala, led the meeting. Sala, who by now was a good friend of mine, was a smart older woman of about fifty. She had a sharp wit and a charming toothless smile.

That day Sala stood by the trunk of my neem tree and occasionally commanded the attention of all by hollering and waving her arms, hoping for a bit of short-lived silence.

Sometime earlier, Mamadou had arrived. He now sat several yards to my left, his back against my hut's side wall. Occasionally I glanced his way to see him sitting face to the ground, his long knees folded up around his ears, his fingers wrapped around his freshly shaven head, a turban by his side. Sometimes I noticed him suddenly sit up to consider with great interest a ripe neem seed that had dropped near him. I wasn't sure what he made of this meeting. Was he daydreaming? Thinking? Perhaps like me, simply wishing he were any place else but here?

As dusk approached, Mamadou finally stirred. He drew himself off the ground and unfolded himself to his full height. He dusted off the back of his boubou, slipped on his pointy yellow shoes, and head held high, wrapped his headpiece around his head. He then slowly but decisively walked to the front.

President Sala moved aside, and the crowd immediately hushed; even the fussy babies stilled themselves. Standing aside the trunk of my tree, Mamadou began speaking. First his voice was low and quiet, sounding like he was thoughtfully mumbling something to himself. Slowly his tone rose and sharpened, and his pace quickened; then for a full twenty minutes, he chastised the rapt audience.

"You women want to advance. But you will never advance if this is how you talk to one another," he scolded. They all nodded in agreement.

"We move ahead by moving together. Raindrops are what fill the river, and our individual work is like that of a raindrop." His voice rose, fell, then paused for dramatic effect.

"All of this is Keyti's fault," he then snapped, a pronouncement that jolted me from my misery. "She should have provided you the leadership you lack. She can't start you on this road and then leave you without a cart. She can't just wake you up; she needs to show you how to get out of bed and down the road."

So goo bonii limmore aayiima, I lamented to myself, recalling Tall's pronouncement about Cóndi Hiraande.

Without leadership, you have nothing. Was I the 'goo' who was 'bonii'? I felt simply awful. I knew his criticism was strategic. But perhaps it contained a grain of truth? Were the women's failures my own? I wasn't sure, and Mamadou's comment stung.

With that final pronouncement, Mamadou was done. Up went the sleeves of his boubou, and without looking at a soul, out he walked from my sandy yard before turning left toward the village.

The small crowd watched until Mamadou's head disappeared down the gully. Then some babies started fussing. Dusk was now full upon us. The village's fósinaaji had already gathered in the alley; with tin can necklaces, the young boys sought scoops of food in exchange for evening blessings and recitations from the Koran. One-by-one the women arose, some tying infants on their backs while others took a minute to get their tired and stiff bodies off the ground.

"We're difficult, we know. But we're learning. We want to follow the road ahead. You and Mamadou will see," they promised as they took their leave.

President Sala and her daughter Aissata helped me fold up my mats and store my matlas before they too took silent leave. This was definitely one of my most demoralizing days in Civé. I had helped spearhead this cooperative without realizing how complicated it was, or how much effort it would take. Some months ago, I had finally given up on Cóndi Hiraande. Giving up on this cooperative felt like I would be giving up on everyone.

With the women gone, I did what I always did when I didn't know what else to do: I went to the river. Soon I found myself in a hard 200-yard swim to Senegal against a river intent on pushing me downstream. Once afoot, my low feelings took over as I watched a branch in the river speed quickly toward the Atlantic. I sat breathing hard on Senegal's weedy riverbank, feeling completely alone. Tears plopped into the mud. Behind me the red sun was setting while the winds were rising. A sudden chill spread over my wet body.

I looked to the dim shores across the river. I could just barely make out the animated voices of the women and kids as they packed up riverside, and could see a few older men from my neighborhood crossing the gully, heading no doubt to the mosque. From the direction of Cóndi Hiraande, I made out a young herder returning from the dieri, a large herd of long-horned Zebu cattle trailing behind. One-by-one the cattle peeled away, each obediently returning to their separate homes. A light smoke above the village signaled the early stages of dinner. To my right, I took in my barely visible home perched above the steep craggy cliffs arising from the river. Silhouetted against the darkening sky, my hut looked like something out of *National Geographic*. Yet to me it appeared not striking, but lonely—no men leaving for prayer, no cows returning from the dieri, no women pounding grain, no laughter, no dinner fire.

I lingered on Senegal's steep muddy banks, absentmindedly plucking at the long grass by my feet. But darkness was quickly settling in, I was chilled, and the river was strong. I knew that I had to cross back before somebody dispatched a rescue squad. Villagers were accustomed to me swimming and bathing at night, but they scolded me when I did, warning me of hippos, river monsters, and the mystical forces that arose after dark. I always stubbornly ignored such warnings, wandering off with a wave of the hand while leaving them to fret over my fate. After a while, everyone just decided that tubaaks were immune to the same spirits that menaced their lives, and simply clucked their tongues as I trudged down to the dark river.

Into the cool, shadowy waters I slipped, gliding until the current caught me. In my sad and chastened state, I felt I should check both sides for river monsters. Seeing none, I began stroking, stroking, stroking upstream to cross back into my Mauritanian life.

Once my toes finally felt the soft mud beneath, and now exhausted, I waded out. Turning, I looked far upstream. And there, in the final light of the evening, I could just barely make out my gently swaying neem tree. It was then that I felt my lesson keenly: Civé was like a fast-moving river, and I like someone trying to swim upstream.

Chapter 29

Madame Diaw

As demoralizing as that day was for me, the women soon experienced a huge success.

Catholic Relief Services had provided them with a monumental grant, so big it funded a small two-cylinder Lamborghini motor pump. After learning this, the women set about securing a two-hectare plot of land for this pump to irrigate. Shortly, they identified just the spot in a flat, deeply cracked waterfront parcel located between Cóndi Hiraande and Becce.

This ideal piece of land did, however, come with one minor hitch: it belonged to the Diaws, who lived in Senegal. It was common practice for people on one bank to cultivate land on the other. Before Mauritania's independence, the river was just a body of water, not a political boundary. The Pulaar saying, *maayo wonaa keerol*, literally the river is not a border, serves to remind Pulaars that ethnic bonds trump national identity.

But the river often has served as a political frontier. Many times in the past, advancing Moor tribes caused Pulaars to flee south across it. And then in 1960, the northern banks of the Fuuta became the independent country of Mauritania and the southern banks, Senegal. This change made little practical difference, as the region's farmers and herders continued to cross back and forth as they had for centuries. In fact, in the 1980s, about one-fifth of the land on the northern banks was cultivated by those, like the Diaws, with Senegalese citizenship.

But those traditional practices were now contested. Both the Mauritanian and Senegalese governments had passed laws banning traditional land tenure practices such as these so that its own citizens could gain land claimed by foreigners. With new irrigated perimeters on both sides of the river, the competition for land had stiffened and both national governments were keen to restrict ownership to its citizens.

My first brush with tension over these changing land-tenure rules occurred shortly after I arrived in Civé. One clear morning during the vegetable season, Amadou Demba scrambled down to the river to yank Becce's motor pump to life. The engine roared, and immediately water exploded from it like a broken fire hydrant, hurling Amadou Demba into the river. Climbing back onto the platform, he managed to shut the pump off; soon a huddled mass announced to those of us peering down from the banks above that the pump had no sealants. Someone had stolen them, I heard people say, rendering the pump useless. Through some ingenuity, days later the cooperative rigged up a temporary fix.

I was sure I was not understanding this episode. A piece of the motor pump, stolen?

"Who do this?" I asked Kebe one morning. "Thief motor pump?"

"I don't know," he responded, turning toward Senegal. "Someone over there." He pointed across the river.

Perplexed, I left it at that.

I forgot about this odd incident, chalking it up to some adolescent boys pulling a thoughtless prank. Until nine months later when a similar event occurred upstream. The Mauritanian village of Dolol was amid its first ever rice campaign. Deep into one moonless night, a piece of Dolol's motor pump went missing, leaving to wither in the fields an entire season of rice. In this instance, there was no doubt who the culprits were, as across the river lay the village of Odobere, whose residents had long and loudly claimed ownership over Dolol's rice perimeter.

The confiscation and redistribution of land is a constant in the Fuuta's history. In the late 18th century, the Pulaar empire that controlled the Fuuta was chased to its far eastern reaches just upstream from Civé, by leaders of the rebellious Toorodɓe caste. In the process, both sides rewarded supporters and punished opponents by redistributing land. Decades later, the French did the same as they moved upriver and tried to counter the appeal of the agitator Oumar Tall. In fact, it was the French who a century earlier had taken Dolol's land from residents of Odobere and transferred it to those in Dolol.

Closer to home, the Fulbe who settled Tokomadji in the early 1900s wanted the riverfront land Civé had assigned to its Bambara residents. These Fulbe successfully lobbied French officials in Kaedi for the right to this strip of land, an act that Civé's Bambara residents unsuccessfully contested. And then of course SONADER also took land, almost at will, and redistributed it according to its own priorities and objectives.

What occurred in Dolol was thus a rehashing of a long-standing historical conflict over who owned Dolol's waalo fields. Residents of Dolol and Odobere produced rusty WWII rifles and shouted threats across the river until some elders from afar intervened. The missing pump piece was produced, and as part of the peace agreement, a handful of Odobere residents received parcels in Dolol's perimeter. Only after I learned of this did it occur to me that Becce's stolen sealants might have traced to some similar dispute over the rights to Becce's fertile waalo fields.

At any rate, the plot the women had staked out belonged to the Diaws in Senegal. While legally they could take it, the women did not like this option.

Sala explained their reasoning to me: "The right road is to put our request to Madame Diaw. It was the road of the past, and we honor those roads. And now, her household no longer has men. We will appeal to her own honor of our roads. If she does, she will say yes to our request."

And so, a few days later, President Sala, two other cooperative leaders, Mamadou, and I gathered to cram into the arriving Rapide. Twenty minutes on and we reached the Rapide's endpoint of Matam, Mauritania. We descended the taxi, passed the ever-empty customs shack, and proceeded down the river's wide shallow banks. That day a pirogue was parked riverside, already fully loaded down with tied bundles of firewood, hobbled chickens, sacks of charcoal, large bowls of bissap leaves, and numerous passengers. With rubber slippers and presents in hand, our party waded into the river and climbed aboard.

Once on the other side, Sala led us through Matam's bustling open-air market where shiny balls of pounded indigo leaves, stacks of miniature watermelons, improbably shaped gourds, scoops of peanut butter, bags of dried baobab leaves, glistening hunks of fly-covered beef, and dangling rubber slippers were for sale. We continued through nameless dirt lanes, each anchored by a merchant's small shack.

Madame Diaw's flat finally stood before us. She appeared and graciously accepted all of the various gifts the women produced, then reciprocated in her front room with tufam and tea. An hour later, the prolonged greetings, news, and recounting of milestones over, Mamadou turned to the topic at hand.

"Allah is great, but the rains fail us, and we are poor. Our poverty does not kill, but it tires us," he said, leaning forward for emphasis as the women clicked their tongues and gently rocked their bodies in agreement.

Mamadou then wound around to the plight of women.

"Thanks to Keyti, the women have gained a tubaak pump. The future brings hope to the women. They can pull together as one."

It seemed to me a masterful presentation, appealing to both traditional Pulaar values of solidarity and progressive ideas of a better future.

"We need to take the road that leads us forward," he ended in earnest, and then sat back against the blue concrete wall as a platter with teacups was passed his way.

Mamadou's performance seemed to have its intended effect. Madame Diaw nodded throughout his speech, murmuring approval at the right moments. Then it was her turn:

"Kaaw Mamadou, you speak the truth. Koumba, my grand-daughter, is part of this future, she will pull along side of you. We must all take the path forward, if Allah wills it, otherwise we all pull apart and we remain poor. Kaaw Mamadou, you are wise and a person in good standing. Allah's blessing be upon you." While speaking, she signaled to her young granddaughter making tea on the floor beside us.

Faint afternoon calls to prayer soon drifted in through an open window which, after all had prayed, drew the meeting to a natural close. Bidding our farewells, I noted with satisfaction the respect-ful nature of that departure: repeated last names, hands touching hearts, and generous dosages of Islamic blessings.

Exiting the Diaw compound, we pulled aside to avoid a dozen musky goats accompanying a tall thin herder. After he passed and the dust settled, I uncovered my face, and in good spirits, turned to the others. Long, silent faces greeted me.

"So now you farm?" I asked with a hopeful tone as we walked down the lane.

Sala shook her head. The others remained silent as we wound our way back through the market and down to the river. Soon we were sitting on Matam's steep shady bank a few dozen feet above the river while a slow-moving pirogue plowed its way toward us. The women mumbled something to one another, but I couldn't make it out. Mamadou, meanwhile, uttered not a word. The pirogue now jutted up on shore, we rose. Sala then turned to me, downcast.

"Keyti," she said, her voice thick with disappointment.

"Madame Diaw cried for us. But an eye can cry, even when not sad." The others all murmured their agreement.

"We got an eyeful of dust," a woman named Malaaɗo added for emphasis as she shooed a pecking rooster out of her way.

And with that comment, I understood. Pulaars rarely answered any request with a direct 'no;' I never could distinguish when yes meant yes and when it really meant no.

Once back in Civé, the news of our failure spread. Soon one and all labeled Madame Diaw a *saboteur*.

"She's jealous. She doesn't want us to succeed," Djeinaba complained to me that night over haako. But it had always seemed to me a lot to expect. Why should Madame Diaw just hand over her land?

Yet to all but one present in Madame Diaw's living room that afternoon, the writing was probably on the wall; neither she nor any one of her descendants would ever seed that dusty parcel again. It wasn't until years later that I figured that part out. In the meantime, a shiny new Italian pump was on its way to Civé, and the women still had no land on which to put it.

This hard-fought battle for land had not been won. Success would require a different tactic.

Chapter 30

Messur Lamborghini

The next day Mamadou announced that the women should just take Madame Diaw's land.

At first all objected. "This isn't the right path forward," Sala unhappily confided to me as she sat on her dinndeere stitching together a cracked gourd bowl.

But the labelling of Madame Diaw as a saboteur had been quickly accepted by all, and the women's hearts hardened against her. It didn't take long for them to agree to this course of action.

But before beginning the back-breaking work of converting Madame Diaw's waalo parcel into tillable land, Sala first came to me with a request. I was sweeping my porch when she entered my gate.

"Keyti, we will take this new road and plow this land. But we first need the paperwork the master of the land in Kaedi gives. Can you get this for us?"

Sala's request surprised me, as I imagined few in the village owned this title she wanted me to obtain. But perhaps the threat of Madame Diaw's claim made the women uneasy. So, I agreed: "I will visit the master of the land this week, if Allah wills it."

And thus began repeated trips to see the top government official in Kaedi, the region's *prefet*, or governor, a Moor by the name of Monsieur Ould Louleyd.

Initially, I found the prefet 'out of town on business.' Then, after repeated appearances, out of the blue his receptionist told me I must first pay to have the land inspected before any title could be issued.

"But this land has been visited," I protested. "An official with Water and Forests came to see that no alive trees would be axed."

"There," was all he said, pointing to an old rusty typewriter sitting lopsided and neglected in the corner. "First write up your Request for a Site Visit."

In other words, someone required a bribe, I mumbled to myself.

Miffed, I approached the typewriter and considered my options. Just then, some giggling sounds emerged from the prefet's office. I peered in, wondering if maybe he'd been there all along. There I spied two spectacularly dressed young women lounging on couches. One looked up and laughed. With an air of authority, she called for me. "Tubaak. Come here."

Thinking maybe I'd find the prefet with them, I entered. Alas, they were alone.

Disenchanted, I excused myself.

"Tubaak. The prefet will be back in two days," the one on the left giggled between sips of her orange Fanta.

I left the office in a sour mood, one that became sourer yet when greeted by the long line of Toyotas and Land Rovers parked outside. These were all bought with foreign aid so that self-important government employees could be chauffeured around in them. I merged into a street filled with Kaedi's daily state of affairs: braying donkeys, aggressive cigarette venders, smelly garbage, urine-stained sand, and the pungent odor of a dead goat or cow, I wasn't sure which. That afternoon, everything was unpleasant. Why can't I just make a simple transaction by looking up a number in a phone book, picking up a working telephone, and making an appointment that someone keeps?

I went through my limited options until all that was left was the obvious: ask Nalla. Nalla, a nephew of my 'father,' was a high-ranking government official in Kaedi. I had met him on several occasions, and each time felt he reveled too much in his Big Wig status. But if anyone could help me get the women's permit, it would be this Big Wig, Nalla.

***

Around nine that night, I arrived unannounced at Nalla's large, gated compound; several government-issued Toyotas were parked outside so I knew he was home. A guard opened the iron gate leading to a courtyard, and shortly an older woman invited me inside. Nalla and his second wife had just finished dinner, and they escorted me into their living room.

A forty-watt bulb on the ceiling struggled to fill the room with its eerie light. The room was plush, surrounded by thick matlas covered with expensive cloth, and rugs decorated the concrete floor. On a shadowy wall I made out an Islamic prayer written in Arabic alongside a picture of a shrouded heavy-set Nalla during his recent *hajj* to Mecca.

Once seated on the matlas lining the room, we all complained of the heat; it's worse in Kaedi, we agreed. After a few minutes, I turned to the business at hand.

"The women farmers have a new pump, Allah is great. They have land to farm," I began.

"Allah's blessing is upon them," interjected Nalla's wife.

"Yes," I continued. "Now Allah willing, they need permit. But the prefet not in. What should I do?"

Nalla was clearly surprised by my information, but also interested. "The women have land?" he asked. "Where is this land? And who are the women?"

I began to answer him.

"I have heard of this cooperative," he interrupted. Then he fell silent.

In the dim light, I noted his jaw clench. His wife looked down at the floor, then called out to her daughter to hurry with the tea. To my complete surprise, Nalla then sat up and erupted in an angry scolding.

"Why do the women want this land?" Nalla pulled glasses out from a front pocket thickly embroidered in gold thread and put them on. Sitting up, he glared at me. Then in a commanding voice, he barked out: "This is… Cóndi Hiraande… cooperative… They lie, they… ten years ago."

His words came out too quickly and garbled for me to make sense of them, and my alarmed state did not help. Yet Nalla's conversion from host to hostile lecturer couldn't be clearer. After a long tirade, he tore off his glasses, threw them aside, and sat back against the wall. His wife handed him a pillow and a fan, and urgently called out to their daughter for tea.

"Besides, they are peasants, they know nothing," he said, giving what was obviously his final pronouncement on the topic. His wife murmured her assent.

In my bewildered state, I felt my chest tighten and the dim room sway. Bereft of words and completely confused, I simply announced my departure.

Apparently, not all Pulaars are incapable of saying 'no' to your face, I groused as a minute later the groaning iron door closed and locked behind me. Nalla wants to sabotage the women's garden. But why?

Now I had no other option than to hope that the lounging beauty in the prefet's office had been right about his return. So, two days later, I was back in his waiting room, determined to stay put until I had permit in hand.

And wait I did.

Finally, after several hours, the revving of a car engine filled the waiting room, followed by silence and car doors slamming. Then in came the prefet, a throng of others trailing behind. I quickly arose while shifting my paperwork, then summoned all five feet of my height while stationing myself between the prefet and his office.

My presence surprised the governor. I quickly explained my purpose, and after looking me over for a few seconds, Mr. Ould

Louleyd invited me in.

My heart pounded as we entered his office. The prefet sat at his desk, but in my nervous state I chose to stand aside a metal chair next to one of the couches encircling his office. Before he could ask a question, I handed him my paperwork. Mr. Louleyd took it, eyeing me as he did. He looked over the papers, noting that all seemed to be in order.

"You have gained permission to clear it," he remarked.

"Yes, not much grow on the land, the trees die long ago," I assured him. "Only one or two tree stump. It has been fallow for many years, no one grows anything since the drought."

Tapping his pen on the desk, he put the paperwork aside, then leaned back in his chair.

"Do you eat haako?" he asked after a bit, sitting farther back in his chair, and looking at me with curiosity.

Filling my lungs with air, I pulled up the chair by my side and sat down. A second later I answered. "Yes, I love it. It is very tasty. Especially with peanuts. I just learn how to make it. My friend Mairam, she's an American. She lives in N'Beika and speaks Hassaniya. Last month, I make her haako and…"

The prefet interrupted my senseless monologue by pulling out a sheet of paper, filling it in, signing it, and pressing his stamp into it.

"May we pass the afternoon in peace," he said flatly, turning toward the exit.

I thanked him profusely and then left as fast as I could. With permit #373/DCK now firmly in hand, Madame Diaw's land had legally been transferred to The Civé Women's Cooperative.

The next day I returned to Civé. That afternoon the women gathered at their new parcel. After much chanting, drum rolling and high spirits, President Sala waved the permit for all to see, then made a short speech, thanking the Americans, Estef of CRS, Mamadou, me, and most of all, Allah. As I stood proudly watching, a lump rising in my throat, the women ceremoniously swung picks into that arid clay pan that now officially was theirs.

***

A few months later, the rice storage facility had yet to be built. The rice was turning from dark green to dry golden, and the river was beginning its retreat. As the sun descended over Senegal, I entered Civé riding shotgun in a truck. Mamadou followed close behind in a second. Each one was filled to the brim with newly purchased supplies for the women's center, and construction material for the yet-to-be-built rice warehouse. Our noisy arrival brought the entire village out, and soon a cadre of men set to work unloading sack after sack of cement, rod after rod of long reinforced iron bars, a few chairs, and four sewing machines. The last item to emerge was large and heavy, carefully packaged and tied down to protect it during its bouncy trip: a handsome, diminutive, bright yellow two-cylinder pump.

As the Lamborghini appeared from the truck's recess, a chorus of instructions arose from the crowd as to how best to maneuver it to the ground. Once ashore, President Sala grabbed a horse cart from a nearby home, and without further ado, the pump was hoisted atop its bed. A dozen women promptly escorted it out to their new plot of land. There, two men tied the pump down along the riverbank, and one-by-one, each woman present climbed aboard Messur Lamborghini (as they dubbed the pump) to sit astride him, as proud as if the pump were her throne. The women were so happy you'd imagine it was each one's wedding day, this odd metal contraption their groom.

With Messur Lamborghini now securely in place, the first vegetable season could begin. After it did, every day women arrived in the fields to tend their vegetables. As those vegetables ripened, women waylaid me, eager to show off the collection of coins, even a dirty, torn bill or two kept securely tied within her headscarf.

Messur Lamborghini might be even better than a groom, I thought to myself, but aloud I cheered their success: "Allah is great!"

Chapter 31

Traditional Medicine

While I strove for progress in Civé, it was obvious others mistrusted that progress was possible. Given that setbacks were part of villagers' daily experience, their resignation to the status quo probably offered a saner approach to life.

There was, for instance, the fact that those in the Fuuta were frequently assailed by bad health. One chronic ailment affected nearly everyone, eye problems. And no wonder. With its hot dust-filled air, frequent sandstorms, and the unrelenting glare of the sun's rays bouncing off bare land and river alike, the Fuuta was just brutal on eyes. Upon reaching middle age, it was common for vision to give out, first becoming blurry, and then blotted. "Like a sandstorm," was how Amadou Demba's mother described her vision to me one day.

And in the worst cases, you would go blind altogether. Younger kids seemed to perpetually battle Apollo (conjunctivitis), with cases so severe that their eyes were glued shut for days on end. And once one kid got it, so too did all the rest, as children ate from the same bowl, drank from the same cup, and slept in the same bed.

As common as eye problems were, though, Sira Sy's bout with blindness opened mine. Sira and her husband Awdy Ba were Fulbes living on the village knoll not far from my hut, near where the new Woman's Center now stood. She was an elder among the handful of Fulbe families that had fled south from M'Bout to settle in Civé. Their compound consisted of a couple of round mud huts and some pens for their goats and cows. Sira was a member of the women's garden cooperative, and her husband a member of Becce. Both were quiet, hardworking, and simple folk who mostly stuck to their own.

Awdy and Sira had two boys. Their oldest, Moussa, was a bit older than me and lived up north in the desert town of Zouerate where he worked as a manual laborer in the town's iron mines. Whenever Moussa was home for a spell, he'd work just as hard as his parents did: plowing the fields, repairing fences, patching thatched roofs, and tending to their animals. Like his parents, Moussa was formal but friendly, reserved yet hospitable.

Sira and Awdy were always extremely kind to me, and I often stopped by for a visit. Yet sometimes I carefully circumvented their compound for fear that they would drag me in, install me on a mat with pillows, make tufam, then run around to find charcoal for tea, while having some child fan me. I never knew how to politely extricate myself from such situations and hated accepting food from people I knew might not have eaten that day. So instead, I just relied on strategic avoidance.

One day at Becce, I was inspecting the maturing rice fields for signs of locusts. Awdy saw my approach and called out.

"Fatou," he exclaimed with a wide grin. "My son Moussa is home from Zouerate. He brought a bag of rice, a block of sugar, and 5,000 ouguiyas. Please come over for dinner tonight. We're having meat."

That evening I arrived as a bright purple sky was giving way to the nighttime humming of crickets. Soon darkness and chirping enveloped us, and Moussa, who with his big-round, white eyes and broad smile peered across the dinndeere at me, took on the appearance of the Cheshire Cat. To the entertainment of all, Moussa began testing my language skills. He laughed in amazement at my butchered Pulaar, and soon all present were challenging one another to find words I would mangle, admittedly not a particularly hard task.

"Now you speak English," I challenged Moussa after this

entertainment had run its course.

"OK," Moussa said, and everyone gathered closer.

"Here word. English. You speak. Ready?"

"Ready," said Moussa, his Cheshire grin shining at me through the darkness.

I paused for effect. "Supercalifragilisticexpialidocious."

Hysterics broke out as Moussa tried repeatedly to get beyond 'supercal.' Then in good cheer everyone else tried their best to beat his effort.

After much laughter and good cheer, a few nodding heads signaled bedtime. I bid everyone a night of peace and exited the compound while quiet banter and chuckles lingered in the cool air. A light breeze with hints of honey drifted my way as I descended the knoll: the patouki trees were in bloom, their scent evoking the luscious smell of white ginger back home. I took it in as in front of me the river shone bright with a late rising moon. It was a perfect evening, which ended with me bundled under my neem tree sleeping deeply.

***

Bright and early the next morning, Moussa stood smiling at my door. In outstretched hands, he held a large gourd full of fresh cow's milk.

"Fatou, I will bring you a gourd every morning," he promised.

I thanked him as I took the gift, thinking of those who would now go without. I set the gourd down and standing up, managed to convey that the Ba compound across the way sent me lots of milk.

"Every day I get milk. My stomach never lacks it. Praise be to Allah."

I felt bad saying this and suspected that Moussa knew that it wasn't true. His head sank to his chest. But then it lifted, and his wide grin reappeared. "Then I'll bring you meat every day. The Bas don't do that."

It was difficult to say no to Awdy and Sira, and now their son Moussa. But doing so meant occasionally I *had* to say yes.

One instance occurred months later when Moussa was again in Civé on holiday. One morning I ran into him while crossing the gully.

"Fatou," he called out with enthusiasm, looking and sounding all the world like his father. We greeted each other, and I soon found myself begging off a dinner invitation for that night.

"But then you must come with me on a trip this week. I will show you real Fulbe life," he exclaimed, beaming.

After some further discussion, I figured out what he meant. And with no excuse at the ready, I agreed to accompany him to a Fulbe village some distance to the north where we would spend the night.

Several days later, I joined Moussa aboard a donkey cart headed for the small enclave of Toulde Boumbe. There lived members of Moussa's extended family, they too having descended from the M'Bout region. Soon the two of us were picking our way through the lands beyond Dow Hayre. On we plodded, with Moussa pointing out various nooks and crannies, all of which had names: Saylalla, Wendou Dieri, Bade Bodeje, Toborocki, and others. Like street names, every piece of land had been mapped out and identified, though to my eye it all pretty much looked like dry scrub brush.

A couple of hours later, the few huts of Toulde Boumbe appeared in the distance. Moussa's clansmen let out shrill cries as Moussa and I approached, the two of us now walking beside our exhausted donkey.

The next eighteen hours were delightful. The Sows killed a goat, showed off their sorghum fields, escorted me to their seasonal river channel from which they fetched their water, served countless rounds of tea, and told stories while someone strummed an elongated five-string gourd instrument. The night was magical as we slept out in the open under a stunningly clear sky, the air infused with the tang and sweat of cattle. I had never seen stars as numerous and clear as I did that night. Then came breakfast of meat, tea, and promises to return. Soon Moussa and I were back aboard the cart, calling out blessings as our donkey retraced its path home.

The Sow's extraordinary hospitality, coupled with a sleepless night left me exhausted and sluggish. I listened numbly as Moussa prodded the donkey along with a ari, ari, aaarrrriiii, orders accompanied by sharp raps from his switch. I took in the vast landscape before us: barren, yes, but also beautiful. The day was calm and quiet, the sky was clear, and except for our plodding donkey, we were completely alone. Occasionally I spotted indentations where rainwater had collected and could detect the remains of millet stalks. But otherwise, I saw no evidence of people for as far as I could see.

About halfway home, Moussa jolted from the cart, pulled out a knife, and cut a small branch from a nearby berry-bearing tree.

"Fatou Wane," he exclaimed, waving the berries at me. "Do you know what this is?"

"No," I said with a yawn, my daydreaming now broken.

He pulled out a goat's bladder full of water. "Rub these berries on the inside. The water doesn't leak out." He handed me a couple of the red berries and I rolled them over in the palm of my hand. I kept my own stock of water in a metal canteen and had never really reflected on the challenge of transporting water.

"See that hole over there?" he continued. I looked to my right and saw a very large burrow dug beneath a rock outcropping.

"Heende," he declared, forming his arms into a wide circle. I looked blank. Then he patted his back. "Wujo."

The rising sun sent my arms inside my boubou and I stretched out my scarf to cover an exposed neck. *Can we just get back to Civé?* I silently pleaded.

"Une tortue?" I tried.

"Yes. Heende. Tortue." His enthusiasm picked up just as mine waned in the growing heat. A tortoise. I had no idea they lived here.

"And see that bush over there? Boil the leaves and drink the water when your stomach runs. I'll get you some." He ran to strip off some twigs, then presented me with a scraggly bouquet. This was surely the main ingredient of the concoction my mom plied me with whenever she noticed my frequent trips to the backyard.

Moussa made our austere surroundings spring to life, every rock, tree, and bush producing something of value. I looked at Moussa and his Cheshire Cat smile, and it pained me to imagine him spending his days hauling iron ore in the desert, sweeping offices, or whatever it was he did in Zouerate. I searched for another subject.

"Moussa, how your mother?"

Some months earlier, Sira's vision began dimming until one day 'the sun did not rise,' as she put it. Nor did it again. I occasionally visited Sira to see if the sun had risen, but I always found her on her dinndeere 'sewing' or sifting through rice, trying to be useful with eyes that stared off vacantly.

"Allah is great," she'd say, and then change the subject. One day I slipped her a bill and urged her to visit a pharmacist in Matam for medical advice.

"Allah is great," Moussa responded to my inquiry as he climbed aboard the cart and slapped the donkey on. "But she can't see. She told me you gave her money. I went to Matam and got her some pills. But they didn't help. What can you do?" He shrugged, and then once again swatting our immobile donkey, added: "ari, ari, arrii, arrrriiiiii."

"She go to Matam, so the pharmacist see her," I protested. "I take her."

"Thank you Fatou. But it's no use. This is not a sickness for tubaak medicine. She needs African medicine. She needs a Marabout. When I get 3,000 ouguiyas, if Allah wills it, I'll call one here from Senegal."

I didn't like the idea of paying 3,000 ouguiyas for a Marabout. For 3,000 ouguiyas, they could send Sira to Kaedi with its real hospital and real French doctor. But Moussa barely listened to me, and finally I said no more. Anyway, I was sure the family could never come up with 3,000 ouguiyas, nearly $50. We continued in silence, and after a short spell, the first of Civé's homes spread before us.

***

A couple of weeks later, I went to say goodbye to Moussa before he returned to Zouerate. He saw me approach and ran out, his arms spread wide while exclaiming, "Fatou... Fatou... Fatou Wane... Wane, Wane, Wane."

I entered his compound, walking across a thick layer of goat pellets as I did, then held out my hand.

"Ba, Ba, Ba," I responded.

Moussa ushered me into his compound while we continued our greetings. He tried to sit me down on his dinndeere, but I protested, saying I could not stay.

"Fatou, please, please, sit down. There is something important to see." Before I could slip from his grip, he had me sitting. His hand grasped in mine, he called for his mother.

"Sira," he called out, his mom apparently inside her hut. "Sira, come see Fatou Wane. She's just arrived. Come greet her."

"Fatou," Sira exclaimed emerging, interrupting my developing plans for an escape before tea began. "Fatou Wane. Fatou. I can see you."

Startled, I sprang up and turned to face Sira. Reaching me, she grasped my hand and then began squeezing my forearms hard as if pressing her delight into me. Sira's face was only a handspan away from mine, and I gazed into eyes bright with life, tears swelling before large droplets tumbled from them.

"Praise be to Allah," said everyone watching as I stood there speechless as Sira continued to pulse her energy into me.

"My good son Moussa sold two goats," she finally explained.

"Three days ago, the Marabout came. And now I am cured," she finished with a broad smile.

Later, I learned a Senegalese Marabout had treated Sira for two full days using a combination of herbs, Koranic citations, and incantations. And around her neck now hung his final cure: a small leather amulet housing a Koranic verse selected just for her.

Stupefied, grinning, my eyes now brimming with tears, I marveled at Sira's seeing eyes, and said the only thing one can at such a moment: "Praise be to Allah."

Chapter 32

Intrigue in Nouakchott

I never figured out what type of health problems required the spiritual intervention of a Marabout. Sira's vexing eye problem for sure, but no one called a traditional healer for a bout of malaria or a nasty case of Apollo. For daily problems like these, villagers visited the local nurse, assuming he was in town. Each then implored him for *lekki*—medicine. The word lekki in Pulaar also means tree, which was the source of most medicine until the French introduced pills, liquids, gels, surgical procedures, and oddest of all, injections.

Given how costly any ailment was, I found villagers' cavalier attitude toward their health mystifying. Almost all refused to invest in preventative items like bleach, sunglasses, umbrellas, and mosquito nets, yet they would pay unaffordable amounts for expensive cures.

On this, though, the health system was partly to blame. The village nurses rarely preached prevention, maybe because their treatment provided a lucrative side business. Once, young Maimona across the lane developed a fever that alarmingly topped 104 degrees. After seeing this on my thermometer, I accompanied my neene across town to see if the nurse had malaria lekki.

"I do," he replied to our relief, then added: "But I bought it myself. That will be 800 ouguiyas." I paid it, but my mom muttered the whole way home, calling the nurse a bandit. I'm not sure that nurse ever went out of his way to explain the importance of paying eighty ouguiyas for a mosquito net.

Another contributing factor was the uncertain lives villagers led. The tangible and present cost of an 80-ouguiya mosquito net could loom larger than the hypothetical one of missed work and 800-ouguiya medicine. Who knows what Allah will bring?

Turning to traditional medicine also made sense given the awful state of the nation's health care system. Rather than inspiring confidence, it aroused dread. During my second year in Mauritania, my real mom came to visit. Unfortunately, she arrived with a severe ear infection that only got worse. Week two and the American Embassy directed us to the Nouakchott hospital. There, a line of seriously ill people, some moaning and others unconscious, spilled out for a hundred yards, with family members camped under nearby trees cooking meals, changing bandages, and providing comfort.

As we stood in horror, taking our place in that week-long line, an Embassy official suddenly appeared and shepherded us away. Within minutes we entered a dirty concrete room decorated with splashes of fresh and dried blood. Soon a French doctor entered. He apologized for the surroundings and complained about the supplies. After a quick peek in my mom's ear, he filled up a used needle, wiped it clean, and then injected her with some liquid.

Ear infections, like malaria and conjunctivitis, are pretty easy to diagnose, and the cure is both known and effective. You can't argue with success, and villagers didn't. But many of their ailments—chronic back pain, shortness of breath, dizziness, aching knees, migraines, and loss of vision—were difficult to diagnose. For these, do you turn to an impersonal, overworked, and frequently awful health system? Or do you summon a marabout who spends a couple of days bedside trying individualized concoctions while also providing comfort and sympathy, not to mention hope?

***

The village's dire need for better health services was obvious to all in Civé. Everyone wanted a decent nurse, medicine that worked, and better health-related knowledge. The women in particular spoke to me about their desire for someone with whom they could discuss 'female problems.' The women leaders developed a proposal to train a young woman to serve as a paid nurse/educator in the village. To our delight, the Red Crescent, as the Red Cross was called, funded it. Eventually, I figured out that many Nouakchott nonprofits had more funds than projects to finance.

Most importantly, though, the German organization GTZ latched onto our fruit tree project. Its director read our proposal, and as I sat across from him in his Nouakchott office, he enthusiastically asked me to return with Becce's President.

Back in the village, I told Mamadou the news. Mamadou was eager to leave, but first had a few affairs to tend to. He wanted his onions to mature beyond the stage where they often rotted at the neck, and Becce's diesel supply needed replenishing. Most importantly, his wife Fati Diallo was nine months pregnant and, Allah willing, a baptism awaited.

Mid-February, Fati Diallo gave birth. A week later, the smartly bejeweled and beaming new mother emerged from her seclusion to a crowded courtyard. Soon Thierno Ly strode in. After Fati snipped a lock of the baby's hair to present to the imam, Thierno Ly recited from the Koran, then tied a leather charm around the infant's neck. A loudly protesting chicken was produced, its blood was spilled, and then Thierno Ly announced the baby's name: Abdoulaye Mamadou Konaté.

It was a son! Straightaway two goats were slaughtered, and the festivities began.

Hours later, just before lunch was scooped from cast iron pots into large enamel bowls, Mamadou's mother, Koumba, got up to help. She handed the fragile bundle of Abdoulaye to me. Wrapped in a white blanket crocheted by the women's cooperative, the infant sported a miniature sky-blue knit hat still much too big for his tiny but chunky face. I cradled him, noting the high cheek bones that marked the Konaté clan. After a few minutes, Abdoulaye fidgeted, and Koumba wandered back to retrieve him.

"May Allah give him a long life," I said as I returned the baby to his grandmother, then joined others eagerly gathering around lunch bowls topped with mounds of goat meat and fried onions.

Shortly Mamadou and I were off to catch the Rapide. A farmer sitting shotgun gave up his seat to Mamadou, and I joined this man in the truck's bed. The two of us crowded in with a half-dozen people squatting amidst bags of cabbages, sacks of charcoal, bowls of hot peppers, and a single goat, its four feet bound together.

Two flat tires and five hours later, we arrived in Kaedi.

Next morning, Mamadou and I caught a packed early morning taxi from Kaedi to Nouakchott. While on the road, the taxi stopped between the towns of Aleg and Boutilimit where two men in a forlorn hut served us greasy rice and gamey meat that left me with a stomachache. As we pulled out, the sand dunes beyond rose up, all of them trimmed by euphorbia bushes, or 'living fences.' This was part of the international community's efforts at holding back the desert. *Hopefully these transplants are proving more effective than my mud stoves*, I thought as I watched them disappear behind us.

Having by now made several trips to Nouakchott with Mamadou, I had begun staying with him at his younger brother Souleyman's home in the 5th District. Logistically, it was easier than remaining in the Peace Corps house. Plus, that often-deserted lodging was lonely, and when volunteers were in town, they were usually from a new year's crop of recruits; ones who, unlike my own cohort, I had not tightly bonded with during four months crammed together. The choice was easier, too, because I really liked Souleyman, as he was a spirited and good-natured young man. Lucky enough to have a salaried job, he and his family lived a comfortable life in their relatively spacious concrete home.

The following day we headed to Peace Corps for my check-in. After a swift thirty-minute walk, we approached my organization's two-story Spanish-style tiled house and chanced upon the chauffeur Demba hanging out in the sandy parking lot. He and Mamadou stationed themselves beneath a flowering leucaena tree, while I trotted up the few stairs leading to the front door. I checked my mailbox before heading upstairs to see Stan, as I had something important to discuss with him.

Tucked beneath a thick envelope containing Crystal Light, in my mailbox that morning I found an unstamped letter with the return address 'Peace Corps Mauritania.' Perplexed, I opened it. The contents of that letter floored me. Like most volunteers, I did my best to steer around the obstacles Peace Corps created for its volunteers. Like suspicious parents, the staff often invented reasons why we couldn't do whatever it was we were doing. But here in my box was a strongly worded letter reprimanding me for some vaguely phrased charge of poor conduct. Signed by Stan, the letter threatened to send me home. With a mixture of disbelief and vulnerability, I hurried up to Stan's office. Upon entering, I sat down and placed the letter in front of him. His new beard and switch from western wear to a colorful kaftan fueled my growing sense of bewilderment.

"What is this?" I asked, pointing to the letter, as my mind raced in too many directions at once. This had to be a mistake. Or perhaps I *had* done something terrible?

Stan glanced at the paper in front of him, then his eyes started darting around the room. "Oh, yes. That… That letter." He cleared his voice and fiddled with a stuck drawer.

"Well." After a brief hesitation, he continued. "You haven't been keeping us up to date. We're here to support you, but we can't do that if you don't tell us what you're doing. You can't just go around doing whatever you want. You must work with us. You must be a team player. There are rules. We work hard on your behalf, and you need to respect the chain of command."

Chain of command?

Stan continued, each word strengthening his conviction that I was guilty of some yet-to-be-specified crime. His chest seemed to puff out as the color in his face darkened.

"What did I do? What are you referring to?" I finally blurted out while leaning forward.

"We know what our volunteers are up to. We find out. But not the right way. You need to respect that. You need our permission before you do anything." The stuck drawer suddenly burst open and papers, pills and pens spilled to the floor.

This arbitrary hierarchy I had supposedly not adhered to, and the need for *permission*, struck a raw nerve I hadn't realized existed until that moment; I was irritated by Peace Corps' lack of support. Other than providing vaccines and occasional transportation, what did anyone in this richly appointed building do, anyway?

"Stan, what are you referring to?"

"We know you went to the Catholic Reserve Service for projects. Steve Hillford told us everything," Stan crowed while hastily gathering his things from the floor.

"Hilbert." I corrected him. He could get the name of the organization wrong, but not Steve's name.

He wetted his lips while wedging the drawer back in. "This is not how things are done in the Peace Corps.

"Jim...I mean the director, he heard from Steve Hillgard last week at a reception. A director can't be caught off guard, knowing less than others. The director should know more than everyone. He shouldn't have to pretend. He is, after all, the one who must approve your projects. Not Steve." His eyes avoided mine. With a note of finality, he concluded: "You work for Peace Corps, not some Catholic organization."

On Stan's cluttered desk I spotted a large overflowing plastic inbox filled with mail.

"Probably if you look there, you'll find letters about my activities," I said, my anxiousness having now turned into exasperation.

Small beads of sweat were forming on my boss's forehead and upper lip. He glanced at a watch-less wrist. "I have an appointment with the Agricultural Ministry. I'll have to look later," he said as he stood up.

But it was too late. I had already found a host of unopened letters from volunteers, and three from me now lay in front of him.

His eyes twitched; a strained chuckle arose from his throat. Stan grabbed a folder full of papers on a chair, then disappeared under his desk to retrieve his sandals. Emerging, he suggested we have lunch together as, he said, "It's hard to communicate over such a long distance. You know how it is here. It's not easy," he added. He cocked his head to peer beyond me into the hallway. Then, awkwardly he fled past, leaving his intricately embroidered Moorish wallet behind as he did.

I stood in his office not knowing what to do. This was not what I had expected, working with locals while my own countrymen left me abandoned. It wasn't easy straddling the gap between my prior life and this new one, and Peace Corps made it even harder.

I realized at that moment that Steve from CRS had become my model. I admired his ability to work productively with both sides of the equation—the villagers and his organization—and to insist that the projects he funded actually worked. Thinking of Steve's example, I placed an envelope with a handwritten report of my activities atop Stan's wallet. With a red pen, I wrote in large letters, 'Please read this!'

A minute later, tense and distracted I emerged into the bright haze of that Nouakchott day. Mamadou and Demba were huddled in conversation; despite being preoccupied, I detected something serious in their demeanor. Both men took a small step back from the other as I approached, and their conversation stopped. I switched directions, announcing I was going across the street. Crossing the goat-filled lane, I made my way toward a nearby wooden stall, its Moor owner sitting on a mat in front, fingering prayer beads. I stood under the meager shade of the shack's corrugated metal shutter, propped open for business. The merchant finished praying, and while still mulling over that distasteful encounter with Steve, I bought some chap stick. *Could he really send me home?*

I re-crossed the lane while adding moisture to my cracked lips. Mamadou approached, rearranging his turban as he did. I waved my goodbyes to Demba in the distance, and the two of us headed east toward the main road out to GTZ, me still buried in thought.

But my stomach also rumbled. Our meeting with GTZ was still three hours away, and it was too late to return to Souleyman's for lunch. I suggested we eat at a nearby Lebanese restaurant, one favored by volunteers; Mamadou nodded his assent. Maybe, I hoped, I could find someone there to help me digest this disturbing exchange with Stan.

***

La Sahara catered to an unusual assortment of Peace Corps volunteers, foreigners, government officials, and Mauritanians with either foreign connections or money. The restaurant that day was about half full of locals and what appeared to be visiting Arabs, but unfortunately for me, no volunteers. A friendly Pulaar I'd come to know by the name of Diallo greeted us, and in a couple of minutes had taken our orders.

After our meal of roast chicken and fries, Mamadou asked about tea. Diallo smiled politely and said there was some being made out back, and he'd include us. So, we settled in for another hour. Mamadou used this time to look over the paperwork we'd brought for the GTZ director; though he couldn't read, he wanted to identify each separate document during our upcoming meeting.

"This is map of Becce, and here is where the fruit trees will go," he practiced while pointing out places on the crude drawing laying before him. Pulling out another paper, he placed it carefully on the table, squinted, then continued: "Here are all our expenses.

260 • Growing Mangos in the Desert

This 5,000 ouguiyas…" He stopped and looked up and I nodded my agreement. "This 5,000 ouguiyas is the cost of an expert from the research station coming to graft our mango trees." He continued on, explaining the amount and purpose of each expense before reaching into the sack for yet another document to discuss.

Our first round of tea came and went. Now alone in the restaurant, Mamadou continued reviewing documents, numbers, and facts. I meanwhile, mulled over my options. If Stan were to send me home, maybe I could seek refuge in the hills behind Civé, just as followers of Oumar Tall had done when French soldiers plowed the river in search of adversaries. So engaged, I failed to notice that Mamadou had fallen silent. He finished his water, turned to me, and then paused.

"Do you know Fara Ba? The professor?" His question seemed to come out of the blue.

I surfaced from my ruminations. "Yes, of course," I answered. "Why?"

Fara Ba was a tall, smart, and personable Pulaar who taught literature classes at the University of Nouakchott, coordinated Peace Corps' language trainings, and during my own training had one night donned an orange wig to impersonate me. Fara was immensely popular among us volunteers, as he always spoke to each of us in whichever of the four local languages we were learning, forever complimenting us on our progress. I looked at Mamadou, suddenly sensing there was reason for alarm.

He glanced around. "He is in jail. Arrested two nights ago along with some others." He picked up his empty water glass and drained it of its last few drops. Then he continued quietly, while inspecting the cloth napkin in front of him: "They say he's trying to… organize Pulaars to overthrow the government."

"Wow." My eyes widened as I leaned forward. I too glanced around. Diallo came out from behind the beaded curtains that separated the kitchen from the diners, carrying a tray with a teapot and two empty teacups. I watched him pour out *saani*, possibly detecting a knowing glint in his eye as he did. I wondered whether he belonged to this Pulaar movement I'd heard rumors about.

I watched Mamadou pick at his remaining fries, then pushed my own plate with the few left towards him. Suddenly it dawned on me that *this* was what he and Demba had been discussing an hour earlier. I sipped my tea, watched Diallo depart, and then told Mamadou how much everyone liked Fara Ba.

"Maybe the American Embassy help him out." I leaned forward a tad more. "Everyone knows the government is… against blacks." I couldn't think of a better way to word it. But rumors among volunteers had spread that the Mauritanian government was cracking down on the non-Moor, black Mauritanian population because of some underground movement.

"Yes. Things are tense." The restaurant's screen door banged as two middle-aged Bidhan men entered. Mamadou gathered up the papers around him. "It's probably nothing," he murmured, bringing an end to the conversation as he pushed his chair back. He placed all our papers back in a thin plastic sack and looked toward the motionless beaded curtain until *fartak*, the final cup of tea, made its way through.

Chapter 33

The Moor Shopkeeper

An odd mixture of emotions coursed through me as we got up from our table at La Sahara. The encounter with Stan left me demoralized, even though I was now pretty sure nothing would come of it. The fate of Fara Ba was on my mind, and I felt something ominous brewing. Yet I was also thrilled with the long-awaited meeting with GTZ to which we were headed. The restaurant's door banging shut behind us, Mamadou checked his watch, rewrapped his headdress around his face, and then in the smoky air, raised his arm for a taxi.

Our meeting with the GTZ director could not have gone better. Mamadou not only remembered which documents were which, but he amazed us both when in response to a question, he sketched out exactly where the pidgeon pea bushes and prosipis trees, serving as windblocks, would go. As Mamadou detailed how each and every cent in our proposal would be spent, the director grew visibly excited. Soon we were meeting other GTZ officials, drinking orange Fanta, and then parting with promises, handshakes, and most importantly, a stamped letter assuring us of all the funds we had requested.

Before we could return to Civé with the good news, however, Mamadou and I had one final important business transaction to attend to.

While the capital's proximity to the ocean left Nouakchott with a relatively cool climate, the following day was not. It was over 100 degrees and humid. Midday we lingered after lunch, hoping a slight drop in temperature and a welcome afternoon breeze would make our upcoming negotiation less steamy. Between leisurely rounds of tea in Souleyman's living room, I lay next to a woman by the name of Faba. She and her husband were both raised in Civé and now lived in Nouakchott. Faba and her family lived a block from Souleyman, and nearly always came for meals. That afternoon, Souleyman was snaking a very long cable from his car's battery through an open window and across the room to a black and white TV set; his house lacked electricity and a big soccer match was starting.

Amidst this activity, I mentioned to Faba that my dad had just remarried. Faba discussed her cousin's recent divorce, and I pulled a small photo of dad out from my wallet. Soon this picture was circulating about the room, and when it came full circle, Faba tucked it into her headscarf, letting me know with a smile and cocked eyebrow that this photo was now hers.

Around 5 p.m., Mamadou and the other men returned from the nearby mosque. A flickering game of soccer had begun, and males from the neighborhood were cramming into Souleyman's living room.

"Let's go," announced Mamadou.

So off we headed for our final errand: for a third time, we were headed to the shop of a Bidhan merchant to attempt a complicated arrangement. We wanted this man to sign papers saying he had sold us sewing machines for $150 when, in fact, he hadn't. His receipt would get us the cash needed for the bribes and other expenses we could not account for. To be reimbursed, CRS required careful documentation. So, we were being careful.

Well, I guess you could say we were cooking the books. Whatever it was, it wasn't easy. Especially since CRS's strict reimbursement requirements left unavailable to us the usual routes by which money could be secured.

The Moor store to which we were headed was one of the very few places in town selling sewing machines. Its merchant, a Monsieur Ahmed Ould Vall, had been interested in the deal

Mamadou proposed, but was understandably perplexed by the odd couple we presented. He was wary. So off we went on our third and final attempt to convince Mr. Ould Vall to sell us a false receipt.

Life in the city center that afternoon was beginning to stir as our taxi deposited us near a landmark Peace Corps volunteers affectionately referred to as 'the dead tubaak pile.' There stood a gigantic eight-foot-tall mound of used western clothes with individual items on sale. Whenever I passed it, I couldn't help but wonder if some personal item of mine might be buried within, especially after a volunteer digging through it amazingly produced a ragged Boy Scout shirt with his troop's number still visible on its sleeve.

Moving along, we crossed the sandy street, then turned down a narrow alley, where the merchant's store lay beyond a corner business selling recycled metal. Before entering our shopkeeper's establishment, Mamadou hesitated, then turned to me: "I know what to do," he asserted with confidence.

Mamadou pushed through a rickety screen door while I followed behind. We found ourselves alone amidst dusty rows of shelves containing pipes, shovels, barbed wire, screws, paint, a camel's saddle, a dusty shortwave radio, chewing gum, and a few catalogs. Above us, a malfunctioning ceiling fan noisily tried to spin.

Monsieur Ould Vall appeared from a backroom, uneasily eyeing the two of us. Mamadou greeted him, and the shopkeeper immediately retreated behind a row of half-empty listing shelves. Shroooppp, Shrooooppp, Shrooooppppp, wobbled the fan above.

Mamadou coaxed Monsieur Ould Vall out by speaking in Hassaniya, a language he spoke more poorly than his faulty French. Ould Vall stepped forward, craning his neck to look beyond us and past the door. He was a small man, standing five feet tall, bald, and had the translucent skin of someone who never toiled in the sun. That afternoon, he wore a beautiful clean white boubou made of thick damask with intricate embroidery along the neck and sleeves. We exchanged some formalities, and in a low, demure voice

Mamadou reminded him of our purpose.

Just then, a skinny, dark Haratin Moor in a thin boubou, wearing fake plastic eyeglasses, and smelling of both perspiration and cologne, entered the store carrying a plate with a teapot and three small glasses. Mamadou continued his steady, respectful patter in Hassaniya. My thoughts wandered as I surveyed the shelves. I glanced at the fan above, then inspected a faded, torn poster on the wall advertising a tropical beach getaway in the Canary Islands. I sighed and wondered what options would be left once Monsieur Ould Vall gave us his definitive "no."

Meanwhile the young man standing patiently aside us poured out three small cups of tea and presented the platter to us. Monsieur Ould Vall sat down behind a wood desk, and Mamadou courteously beckoned me to pull up a dusty metal chair and sit directly across from the merchant. After fidgeting with my boubou to make sure my legs were covered, I picked up the tea glass on offer. As I did, Mamadou switched from Hassaniya to broken French.

"You know, Keyti here is America. She tell me she think you like one father. She don't no father. She miss father. It lonely no father. You know? Yes. You know?" Wide-eyed I turned to look at Mamadou, not sure I had understood him.

Mamadou turned away from me to give his glass back to the awaiting servant now fiddling with his outsized glasses. I turned back, but not daring to meet the merchant's gaze, I looked down at my feet, feeling incredibly awkward. I listened as Ould Vall shuffled through some papers on his desk and then swore at a bothersome fly, the seconds ticking away, the noisy fan above still struggling to spin. Mamadou was silent. Ould Vall was silent. Our tea bearer was silent.

I looked up. "Yes. Yes, it true. And you looks even like my father." I managed a weak smile, assuming the role cast for me.

With those words, the merchant's indecision disappeared. He opened the bottom drawer of his desk, took out a receipt, wrote everything out exactly as we wanted, got out his rubber stamp, and placed it with emphasis on that receipt. Eyeing me, he handed Mamadou his business card. In return, Mamadou slipped him 2,000 ouguiyas, and bowed as he praised him, while I, head spinning, quickly stumbled toward the door. Ould Vall called out to say goodbye, and I managed a feeble, "See you soon," before dashing outside.

Once around the corner, Mamadou tucked that coveted receipt in his boubou's large front pocket. Then, all smiles, he looked down at me and promptly handed over Monsieur Ould Vall's business card. "This is yours," he said, while patting the receipt now safely tucked away. "That *was* easy, wasn't it?

"Now time to buy something for Abdoulaye," he continued, as he swept up his boubou. And off we headed toward the now bustling marketplace to search for something to bring baby Abdoulaye.

***

That evening, back home in the 5th District, we once again lingered on matlas after dinner while my friend Faba made tea. I lay next to her while across the room Mamadou slept. To the best of my ability, I recounted to those still awake most of what had occurred in the Moor shop that afternoon. The others, understanding most but not all the story, laughed heartily.

"He gave you a card?" queried Faba as the laughter died down, raising her eyebrows and giving me a naughty look. "Give it to me!"

I dug the card out from my wallet and handed it to her as laughter in the room exploded once again. "Look, she kept it! Monsieur Ahmed Ould Vall, Importer/Exporter," she read. Everyone roared again as Faba waved the evidence for all to see.

Inspecting the card again, Faba cried anew, "Look. Isn't this a phone number? Who has a phone? Let's find one and call him right now. He's waiting for you!"

By now all were in stitches, folded over, and holding their

sides while Ould Vall's card circulated around the animated room. Mamadou stirred, then slowly moved upright. The others pelted him with questions, and soon, embellishing each detail in hysterical fashion, Faba proposing additional ones while passing around the photo of my dad, Mamadou retold the story of how he procured that false receipt from Mr. Ould Vall.

With that and the retellings that followed, residents in Nouakchott's 5th District had found their evening's entertainment.

Eventually, midnight arrived and Souleyman's wife Aissata distributed sheets and pillows to the remaining guests. Soon the sound of deep breathing filled the living room. I lay smiling in the dark, feeling some pity for Mr. Ould Valla. But I also imagined my dad's reaction upon hearing this day's tale. In the dark room, I could almost hear his hearty laugh.

Chapter 34

A Pit Stop In the Sahara

The fruit tree project was in business, and Mamadou moved into high gear. On our trip back to Civé, he decided we would stop at the research station to order our 1,500 tree seedlings.

I dreaded that taxi ride from Nouakchott to Kaedi. Drivers crammed as many people as they could into their small sedans, always more people than there were seats. And once on the road, passengers faced the unpleasant choice of either rolling down the window to let the hot air circulate or leaving it up to avoid being pelted by driving sand. Assuming, that is, that the window even worked.

And it wasn't just the windows that barely functioned. One time between Kaedi and Nouakchott, a thunderstorm hit. As lightning streaked the sky, thunder cracked and rain fell in buckets, I discovered our taxi lacked windshield wipers. No matter, though. The driver took out a rag, scooted up his seat, and manually cleared the window shield as he drove. After a few minutes, he gave that up and instead stuck his head out the window, completely soaking those of us silently smashed in the car's backseats.

Taxi drivers also thought nothing of deserting you, as the only schedule they followed was the one leaving them with more coins in their pocket. If they had one passenger too few, they just stayed put. Once a driver abandoned several of us at some desert outpost to wait out the night under the stars saying that Allah willing, he would leave the next day. Come night, I borrowed a sleeping pad and sheet from Mauritania's equivalent of a Starbucks, a small dark, windowless shack made from corrugated metal with a single bench for its patrons. The main drink, Nescafe, consisted of a spoonful of instant coffee, hot water, and a quarter cup of sweetened condensed milk. Healthy, no, but so delicious I often indulged in two.

That night I slept on my pad alongside other marooned voyagers. Around 2 a.m., a young man in a similar predicament joined us, lying down perhaps ten feet from me. He must have turned my way just as a thin moonbeam cast its pale light over my sleeping body. Soon shrieks of terror pierced the air as the poor soul streaked barefoot across the otherwise silent dirt lot, yelling, "Ghost. Ghost. My Allah it's a ghost!"

The next morning, with a mixture of embarrassment and laughter, the traveler bought me my twenty-cent cup of Nescafe and hunk of bread before we both went our separate ways, sending our greetings to those at the end of each's journey.

All to say that I feared long taxi rides, especially the one between Nouakchott and Kaedi. It was with great relief, then, that for this trip the chauffeur Demba offered us a ride. Demba was driving another volunteer along with his fencing material to Kaedi, and to our good fortune he had room for two more.

Except that halfway to Kaedi, the volunteer David fell ill. Demba reluctantly decided it best to return to the capital, and so he deposited Mamadou and me at the nearest road stop that promised alternative transport south. On the fringe of the Sahara Desert, this dusty intersection just outside the town of Aleg was a reasonable place to hope a passing truck would stop for us.

We waved goodbye to Demba and David as they U-turned on the highway. Mamadou and I then took turns scanning the dim horizon, one of us taking refuge under a shade structure fifty yards from the paved road, the other sitting roadside under the spare protection of a stunted gawdi tree.

After several hours, Mamadou wandered away from our station, and soon returned with some boxed orange drinks and wafers tasting like animal crackers. He acquired from a small customs booth to the east.

"Why there is customs out in middle of desert?" I inquired.

"To make money," Mamadou replied as he examined his crackers before cautiously eating them.

"Oh. Makes sense," I responded while reaching into the bag for my own handful.

Naps followed, then the hour of prayer. Mamadou began to wash himself with the sand that substitutes for water when there is none. He took out prayer beads stored in his boubou's front pocket and turned to the east.

I was used to seeing people prostrate themselves so close to me, rocking and endlessly reciting the Tidjiani litany specific for each prayer time. Yet I always felt like a voyeur, even though no one seemed bothered by my presence. After praying, the devotee just picked up where he or she had left off, whether finishing a joke, braiding a child's hair, arguing with a neighbor, transplanting rice, or in Mamadou's case this day, returning to a nap.

Several hours on and it was my turn to watch from the road's shoulder. The intense sun was beastly hot, so I walked slowly up to the short thorny tree under which Mamadou lay asleep. "Hey, the time touches me," I said loud enough to rouse him.

He rubbed his eyes then looked west toward Nouakchott, the road shimmering with the heat. No vehicle had passed for a couple of hours. "No one comes while the sun touches our head," he said as he raised himself from the ground, brushing off his boubou. "We will both wait in the shade."

As we slowly returned, I figured it was time to tell Mamadou my news.

"The fruit tree project is funded." A spare click of his tongue indicated Mamadou was listening. "The rice bank and woman's garden now starting," I continued. Two clicks. "It not good time for me leaving Civé. I think I stay many moons longer. So, I can see the trees growing."

We'd often discussed the timing of my departure, now a few months in the future. We were both pressed with the many milestones still to accomplish. "That would be great, great, that would be great," Mamadou said with a surprised look.

"This week, I ask Peace Corps for permission," I added, referring to the envelope I'd left with Stan.

"And your family? Your family agrees?"

"You mean my dad?" I chuckled, and he pursed his lips to stifle his. "Yes, I write. They agree."

"OK, OK. We hope you get it. That would be great. There is much work to do, too much work. You must continue your work with the women." He fell silent, brushed aside some pebbles on the ground, and then covered his face to shield himself from the large lazy flies bumbling about. He stretched out on the hard ground, converting his turban into a pillow as he did, and soon was lightly snoring.

I took in this desolate flat rocky locale with its intense sun and cloudless sky. Down the road I could just make out the Mauritanian flag flapping alongside the custom's booth, and far beyond that the first of Aleg's shadowless buildings that blurred into the dusty surroundings and sandy desert sky. For some reason this seemed a perfect spot, quiet, peaceful, completely unpretentious. I put aside my book and marveled at my luck of being able to enjoy the serenity of this spot on the edge of the Sahara.

***

Too soon, that moment of contentment vanished. I quickly became tired and stiff, bored, hot, thirsty, and very hungry. To cope, I began rocking back and forth, rolling my shoulders, ankles, and wrists to loosen some of the strain. Meanwhile, Mamadou was now awake and mulling various problems over, taking a calculator out when a new thought occurred to him. I tried listening, but my mind was too foggy and tired to focus.

Are there tarantulas out here? was about all I could concentrate on.

Late afternoon, a dozen or so full taxis and a handful of large lorries passed by, but none heeded our waving arms. The sky turned orangish-red, the flies disappeared, the winds picked up, and the temperature dropped. The sky near pitch dark and the air now cold, finally a Mercedes truck loaded down with thirty tons of flour slowed then stopped. For a small fee, the driver had us clamber atop his load before he took off at a top speed of ten m.p.h.

It must have been around 4 a.m. when just short of Kaedi, the Mercedes stopped, and the driver shut off its loud engine. He called up that we'd sleep until daybreak. In that clear, dark, still desert air, the stars were as bright as you're ever likely to see them, a broad Milky Way painted in a bright band across the black moonless sky. If I had had my sleeping bag, I would have marveled at one more peaceful, delightfully chilly, and stunningly beautiful Fuuta night. But I had no sleeping bag, and therefore did not feel the urge to stargaze.

To fend off the cold, Mamadou and I opened our bags and pulled on all the clothes in our possession. We tossed and turned on those rock-hard flour sacks until finally at daybreak, the blessed deep rumble of the diesel engine awoke us. An hour later, up we pulled into Kaedi's truck garage.

After grabbing some Nescafe and bread, Mamadou and I hitched a ride on a horse cart to the research station beyond Kaedi's edge. There, our news spread, and soon a crowd of employees gathered as Mamadou presented the station director with the stamped GTZ letter guaranteeing our funding.

This trip had been an especially emotional one for me. But at that moment, my frustrations with Peace Corps, lingering doubt over whether to extend my stay, and concern over Mauritania's political tensions dimmed. I wandered in awe among the station's huge grove of symmetrically planted and carefully tended fruit trees.

"So. This is how Civé look like soon," I remarked.

To which Mamadou added, "If Allah wills it."

Chapter 35

Abdoulaye

It was late February 1986 when we placed that tree order. The clear air of Dabunde was quickly giving way to Ceeɗu's thick sandy and oppressive haze. I'd already noticed the uptick in sore throats, conjunctivitis, and headaches in the village, and my own staph infections were once again erupting.

Ceeɗu was not the time to plant fruit trees. Beneath a mango tree at the research station that morning, Mamadou and the director agreed on a plan. In three months, Koorka, the month of fasting, would come to an end. Civé would then send several cooperative members to the station for training. After that, the fruit trees would be delivered, timed so that the orchard would be planted before the busy rainy season.

The logistics seemed daunting to me, especially since there was no quick way for anyone in Civé to communicate with anyone in Kaedi, let alone Nouakchott. There would definitely be problems ahead. But that morning, none were mentioned. In the best of moods, Mamadou bought bags full of mangos and limes to accompany our good news to Civé.

"The future," he said with a smile, pulling a large shiny mango from his sack to admire it.

"Let Allah will it," I added.

At around 2 p.m. that afternoon, our week-long trip came to an end. We were back in Civé. After descending the Rapide, Mamadou handed me a mango for my neene, and I gave him a small bag of kola nuts for his. We went our separate ways. Exhausted and famished, I headed straight to Tall and Djeinaba's home. My stomach grumbled as I spotted their ten-year-old servant taking a pot off the fire. Perfect timing! I eagerly veered left through the small opening in their fence, and awaited Djeinaba's cheerful "Eeey-ohhhh, Eeeeyyyy-ohhhhhhhh, Keyti Baird," greeting.

But it didn't come. From a prone position on his matla, Tall saw me enter. To my surprise, he arose grim-faced and approached me without uttering a word.

"Does Mamadou know?" was how he greeted me.

"About what?" I was alarmed.

Tall dropped his voice and looked down. "His baby son died three days ago."

A few days earlier, Abdoulaye had become ill. They'd rushed him to Matam, but he died on the way home.

The mango dropped from my hand and my mouth fell open. I noticed Tall's Adam's apple moving and was aware that Djeinaba now stood beside me and had taken my bag from me. I imagined the sorrow now taking place in Mamadou's compound and grew lightheaded as my chest tightened. Abdoulaye's high cheek bones and tiny head encased in an oversized sky-blue cap appeared before me. I looked up at Djeinaba who with choked words was talking to me.

"You should go," I heard her say.

I turned around and weak-kneed, walked slowly to Mamadou's. There I found him sitting silently on his dinndeere, his shoulders stooped, a large sack of mangos and limes and a small bag of kolas by his side. He noted me enter, then leaned over to pick up his small duffle bag and put it beside him. I hesitated a moment, my eyes glued to that bag: inside, I knew, were two carefully selected baby outfits.

I made the final few steps to Mamadou's side. "May Allah bless and forgive him," I said.

"Amin," he murmured looking up a bit vacantly, then began wiggling the zipper on his bag.

Don't open it! Don't look at those outfits! For some reason, that was about the only thought that came to my mind.

I left Mamadou's side, then circulated around to repeat my condolences to others, noticing that Abdoulaye's mother Fati was not to be seen. With heavy heart and eyes on the ground, I left the compound.

***

I was stunned by the quickness with which others accepted Abdoulaye's death. True, I had missed the wailing that followed; perhaps the deep collective drama of that sorrowful day served to confine its duration. Yet soon, no mention was made of the infant Abdoulaye, and all signs of his brief presence were gone. Stoicism, I surmised, was another adaptation to so much soul-wrenching tragedy.

Indeed, the day after our return, Mamadou began the task at hand; figuring out who among the cooperative members wanted trees, and then re-dividing Becce so that three hectares of it could be converted from rice to fruit. For that, Mamadou's long strides which served as Becce's consistent measuring rod were put to work reconfiguring the cooperative's plots, all parcels reshaped and reassigned for another reason to hope: fruit trees were coming.

Chapter 36

The Training

Then, once more, those suffocating days of Ceeɗu arrived. Midway through, Koorka came to multiply the suffering. At long last the tiniest sliver of a new moon ushered in the welcome festivities of Juulde Koorka. Barely a day later, Mamadou, Kebe, and I caught the Rapide for Kaedi to begin a week of instruction on growing fruit trees.

By now Mamadou had roped me into nearly every one of his activities. In some weird way, it seemed, I had come to play the role of leather pouches worn around necks and muscular forearms with Islamic prayers sewed tight inside. But in truth, my main value was not as an amulet. Rather, my presence and poised notebook played the role that courts and the media do in our country: they seemed to keep others in check.

"Where is your notepad?" Mamadou always asked if ever he found me without.

Unfortunately, our training sessions at Kaedi's research station did not get off to the best start. Morning one, the director heartily greeted us, then insisted that we all tour his orchards. Just as our outing ended, he flipped up his sunglasses and turned to shout authoritatively to the workers lagging behind. "All right! Down to the river," he called.

I had no idea what he meant but watched as the workers dutifully grabbed picks and headed over the bank. The three of us lagged behind, watching the workers disappear down to the river. Peering over the banks, there below us trickled a distant stream winding half-heartedly through stagnant pools of water; the remains of the mighty Senegal River at the tail end of Ceeɗu.

We realized now that the station's motor pumps lay 200 yards from any remnant of the river. That day, the workers' task was to dig a channel through the river's thick soggy bottom to drain stagnant pools over to the motor pumps' intake pipe.

Realizing this, Mamadou went over to the director.

"Your workers are working hard, and we are glad. But our training?" he asked.

"Patience. Patience. Slowing down doesn't mean you won't arrive," the director responded while lighting up a cigarette. "First we must get water to the trees."

"Of course," said Mamadou, but he was none too happy.

He stood on the banks, and in consultation with Kebe, the two began estimating how long this task would take. "Too long," Mamadou concluded. "Let's go."

And so, the three of us joined the other workers in that long, laborious project of digging a trench to coax the motionless river over to the pump. By the second day's end, our back-breaking task was complete.

With pumps finally rumbling and thick, muddy water flowing, day three held promise. But mid-day, the pumps stopped, and work halted. Soon rice, meat, milk, and endless rounds of tea appeared. It turned out the director's second son had been born seven days earlier, and today was Samba's baptism, certainly not a day for work.

Once again Mamadou went to the director. All I heard was 'patience, patience,' followed by Mamadou's polite attempts to persuade him otherwise. By day four, it was evident the director had not the slightest interest in us. He paraded around in his heavily starched and conspicuously expensive boubous, drank tea, napped, and smoked coveted Marlboros, nonchalantly handing over the last centimeters of each to some grateful worker.

Mid-morning day four, Mamadou had had enough. He approached a pair of orchard workers fertilizing mango trees, and the two stopped their work and began answering Mamadou's questions. Then, for two straight days, those men taught us everything they knew about growing mangos, limes, guava, and bananas. Meanwhile, I served as the cooperative's scribe, diligently recording everything we learned: the schedule for the pesticides Lindane, Futinel, and HCH; the timing and amount of urea; the length of time to leave banana roots bathing in a chemical solution to ward off roundworms; and the height of mounds on which to plant our Chinese bananas.

At nights Kebe and I stayed up late to translate my notes written in a strange fusion of three languages only I could decipher. Soon the two of us were showing off a rich set of illustrated "How To" documents.

Each afternoon during those long days at the station, a rice bowl arrived for the three of us. While awaiting the tea that followed, out came Mamadou's small transistor radio, straightaway tuned to the only station it received. At 2:30, the deep melodious voice of a Pulaar man familiar to every resident in the Fuuta began transmitting messages from Nouakchott. Beginning with the Fuuta's far western reaches, the soothing voice slowly wound its way eastward. Around 2:50 he'd arrive at Tokomadji, signaling that Civé, squeezed between Tokomadji and Garly, was next. In silence, ears bent toward the radio, Mamadou and Kebe listened, hoping to receive word from Mamadou's brother Souleyman in Nouakchott that GTZ's money was on its way. For some reason, it was late.

Each day, the calm voice bore no such message. On the last day, even the workers joined in to listen. At 2:50 p.m., the announcer reached Civé. "Civé," he began slowly. "Demba Diop's wife must come to Nouakchott. Bring haako, bissap, and couscous. Alasanne Maladel died Tuesday night; may Allah have pity on his soul. Garly…"

Once again, no message.

Without money to buy trees, our carefully planned timeline was falling apart. The rice in Civé's nursery beds was already being transplanted. Upcoming rains could wash away roads, and any vehicle attempting to get there, especially one loaded down with trees, could be blocked for days.

Having learned all we could from those two workers, Kebe and Mamadou decided to catch the next day's Rapide back to Civé. I, meanwhile, was tasked with finding out what had happened to GTZ's money. So early next morning, I paid full fare for half a seat, and headed north.

*

Chapter 37

A Rough Road to Kaedi

In no time, the GTZ director was ready to hand over Civé's money. But first he wanted an assistant to escort me to Civé for an on-site inspection. After agreeing where to meet the following day, I walked to Peace Corps to find my mailbox stuffed with thick application packets to graduate schools. I had begun discussing with Steve of CRS my post-Mauritania career, and he had suggested several graduate programs. I tucked the packets in my backpack and headed out.

Next day, the assistant and I climbed aboard an oversized Land Rover; then one-by-one the family members of GTZ employees crowded into the back two rows of seats. Then came their various purchases: Chinese bowls, bolts of cloth, straw mats, an umbrella, hard blocks of sugar, bags of biscuits, sunglasses, and gallons of cooking oil, all carefully bundled in plastic woven bags once containing U.S. food aid. Once no other item could be wedged in, off we sped.

By midday, the Senegal River now before us, we turned east into the wide open, roadless Sahel, and one-by-one the occupants descended as villages appeared in the distance. With each stop, cheering children sprinted forth from distant homes, and then just as eagerly bolted back bearing large bundles on their head while sucking a piece of candy.

We reached Civé in record time, and the GTZ official quickly affirmed that the fruit tree project was as described. Late afternoon, a large share of the village gathered in Mamadou's courtyard.

Surrounded by wide-eyed Becce members, the assistant ceremoniously opened a briefcase, then slowly counted out 350,000 ouguiyas. With equal ceremony, Mamadou had Kebe recount the stacks before the silenced crowd, and then astonished murmurs arose as Mamadou signed the receipt.

Mid-way through this recount, someone touched my shoulder. "Keyti, your work is beautiful." I turned and my shining eyes locked with those of Sarr's wife, my next-door neighbor Athia. We squeezed hands then locked our arms together.

By now, the bone-dry air was increasingly humid, and a rising river confirmed that rains to the east had arrived. Early next morning, Mamadou climbed aboard the GTZ Land Rover, and raced off to the research station. There he handed over a small duffle-bag full of bills and set about transporting the treelings.

As evening approached, Mamadou re-entered the village, hanging onto the back of a large, loaded wagon full of saplings hooked to a small lawn-mower sized tractor. He directed the driver across the gully to park in front of my hut. By the time it arrived, a loud and festive crowd had gathered. Mamadou descended, righted a few toppled trees, and then told those gathered the plan: the remaining trees at the station would take two more trips. In the morning, the driver would deliver this first load to Becce. Then the two would return to Kaedi for a second, and then the following day a final third trip.

At that, loud shrills indicated that it was time for festivities. But Mamadou put an immediate damper on the celebratory air.

"Our work is not finished," he admonished everyone.

The sun now below the horizon, the sky radiated deep gold, red, and purple hues. I approached Kebe who seemed to be taking in this stunning sight.

"Rain," he murmured, giving me a sober glance before turning back to the crowd.

***

A couple hours later, abundant bowls of food from all over the village arrived at my place. A dozen cooperative members gathered mats and matlas from neighboring compounds. Despite Mamadou's cautions, my porch and yard became one festive party.

Around 10 p.m., with music blaring and a partial moon in the sky, Mamadou's young son Abou came running up to the lounging crowd. I was across the lane scooping up charcoal embers from the Ba's cooking pit. When I returned, Mamadou was gone.

"Someone important has arrived," Amadou Demba told me while taking the embers. "Too bad he missed tea," he added, as the coals' glow briefly lit up his bright smile and stubbly beard.

Sometime after midnight, the last of the party-goers departed, and the driver stretched out on my veranda. After a final dip in the river, I lay down beneath my neem tree amidst scattered moon-beams and the high-pitched whine of mosquitos. I was so charged with caffeine that sleep came late.

Early next morning found me stacking the night's food bowls, sweeping up spilled couscous, and heating coffee water. Looking up, I noticed Mamadou striding my way, his paces a bit more urgent than normal. Waving away my offer of coffee, he went to rouse the driver, and then ordered him out to Becce.

"The men of Becce are on their way," he instructed, "they will meet you there." Mamadou's rushed nature surprised me. What had I missed?

But I wasn't alone. Mamadou's snappy orders annoyed the driver.

"*Kaaw*, my breakfast is not eaten," he protested.

But Mamadou was already delivering orders to his yawning son Abou, who now stood in my yard. Grumbling, the driver arose, prepared his tractor, and soon was following Abou toward Becce. With the motor dimming in the distance, Mamadou turned to the growing group of Becce men now gathering in my lane. Then he delivered his news.

"We must hurry. Those at the station are not helpful. Yesterday, I loaded the trees by myself without help." He looked down the road. "Not even that driver helped. It will take a lot to get the trees here." He paused, then delivered his bombshell.

"And the president is coming. Sunday he will meet leaders in Matam. He will pass through Civé."

"The president?" Kebe asked. I silently thanked Kebe for this question. I was more than confused by this sudden swirl of information.

"Mauritanian President," Mamadou answered. "I was in Koundel planning Matam's reception until the sun rose." Mamadou, we learned, had just returned from an all-night meeting.

Alarm passed through the gathered men. Compounding the impending rains and the demanding rice season now underway was an uncooperative research station and an unprecedented presidential tour bringing Mauritania's president to Civé.

I knew that tensions between Moors and Pulaars were heightening, and even with my limited connections, that rumors of a coup abounded. The drought had taken a toll on the Moors' camel-herding livelihood, sending them farther and farther south. Even I could detect a trend over the last two years. Maybe the president's trip was to ensure that the Fuuta made room for Moors?

While he must have been exhausted, that morning Mamadou burst with orders. Whatever it took, he was going to get those remaining trees to Civé. Once the tractor driver returned, Mamadou gave his final orders.

"Kebe, prepare the fields for the remaining trees. Water their nursery bed. Sadyo, get Becce to prepare for the upcoming presidential visit. Buy a goat."

Then he climbed aboard the wagon headed to Kaedi. To my surprise, he turned to look down at me.

"Come on! Aren't you coming?"

"Oh," I responded, still slowly processing all the changes whizzing about. I retreated inside, and then threw some items in my backpack. Reaching to close my shutter, I caught sight of the stack of graduate school applications I had planned to begin that evening. I froze. Then hearing the deep rumble of the tractor starting up, I latched my shutter, and was soon climbing aboard the wagon while waving goodbye to my mother who stood by.

"My tubaak is a tractor rider," she called out to all in amusement. "Go in peace."

Then, at 10 m.p.h., off we chugged.

***

That ride to Kaedi was miserable. The large wagon was full to the brim with tools and remnants from the saplings. Mamadou and I awkwardly balanced on opposite back wheel coverings, steadying ourselves by holding on to the wagon's wooden slats. Meanwhile, the hot mid-day sun beat down, while the tail end of the wagon where we squatted exaggerated to the full extent possible each and every bump in the road. Six exhausting hours later, we reached Kaedi. I felt as if I had spent a full day atop a jack hammer. Descending, I wobbled, swooned, and my two legs refused all commands to coordinate with one another.

To top it all off, Kaedi greeted us with astonishing news: the following day was a just-announced national holiday, Army Day. To our deep dismay, this meant the research station would close. There was no chance anyone would work that day, least of all our exhausted tractor driver. The day after that, Friday, was our last shot, but that was the Islamic sabbath. If we missed that day, Mamadou would have to return to represent Civé at Sunday's presidential reception in Matam. Any delivery delay now would consume a week or more, putting it smack in the middle of the rice season. And if the rains arrived? No telling whether a tractor could even negotiate the muddy roads, inland lakes, and filled channels they brought.

So, after hastily regaining my balance, I spent the next six hours trailing Mamadou as with great determination he crisscrossed Kaedi to engage in negotiations I only partially understood. But after each was complete, he reached into his front pocket and unfolded a small leather pouch. From it he produced a bill or two, and then a handshake. After leaving, he had me produce our unofficial accounting book, and gave me a name and precise amount to record. Amadou Hamidy Diallo, 500 ouguiyas. Diaw Bocar Tokosel, 300 ouguiyas. Sidy Adama Diang, 1,000 ouguiyas…

***

At 10 p.m., Mamadou mercifully called it a day. We entered a dimly lit restaurant serving thick strips of tasty grilled beef and greasy potatoes, alongside a large hunk of soft French bread. Alone in the restaurant, I plopped down on a plastic chair and let Mamadou order, too tired to even think. Knowing Mamadou had not slept the night before, to no avail I tried to summon some reserve energy.

Mamadou soon brought over two plates of food. It wasn't often I saw Mamadou tired, but even in the dim light his sagging eyes and drooping shoulders were hard to miss. He sat, and except for the sound of scrapping noises and quiet Pulaar lyrics drifting over from the grill, we ate in silence. Suddenly, the nearby open corrugated metal door rattled, and wind swirled about. The shadows in the diffuse light shifted eerily. Face down, I kept eating, my mind empty. Suddenly, though, my plate lit up. A loud crack of thunder followed, rattling the tin roof, metal door, and the restaurant's half-dozen plastic chairs. And then came the rains, a deluge that poured down so hard it ran off the roof in sheets.

Trapped, the cook, Mamadou, and I peered out as water cascaded off the roof and into the pitch-black street. Finally, an hour later, the rains relented. Slowly the two of us began wading through the dark, deserted, and flooded streets, surrounded all the while by the sweet earthy smell of mud. Around midnight we plodded up to our host's dark house. Presented with a matla, and while still muddy and smelly, I collapsed. There I remained, unaware of anything until roosters, braying donkeys, calls to prayer, a throbbing body, and senseless dreams of graduate school awoke me at dawn.

Chapter 38

Exiting Kaedi

Next morning, decked-out soldiers slogged through Kaedi's inundated streets. Behind them rambled trucks full of soldiers blaring incomprehensible messages through malfunctioning bullhorns, their muddy water splashing everywhere.

Two years earlier, the military had replaced President Mohamed Ould Haidalla with the current President Maaouya Ould Taya. The now ex-president Ould Haidalla, whom I had met at our swearing-in reception in the palace before his ousting, had himself thrown out another, even more short-lived Moor president, Mohamed Ould Louly. In turn, Colonel Ould Louly had deposed his boss, Mustafa Ould Salek. Not surprisingly, Ould Salek had rid the country of his predecessor and former friend, the long-serving Moktar Ould Daddah. Ould Daddah did *not* depose his predecessor, but only because he had none.

In 1960, the French installed Ould Daddah as Mauritania's first president. President Daddah was Mauritania's first college-educated citizen and had been singled out by the French for his diplomatic skills—crucial, they figured, in a country riven by deep social and cultural conflicts. In the small fishing town of Nouakchott, Ould Daddah took up the helm. And there he ruled for eighteen years until his buddy, Commander Ould Salek, led a bloodless coup that ushered Ould Daddah into early retirement.

These seemingly endless *coups d'etats* reflected an enduring feature of weak states like Mauritania: the surest path to financial success is to capture the state and plunder it. Beginning with independence, competing leaders of Moor clans did just this, fighting over the reins of power, sowing mistrust among themselves in the process. Whoever occupied the Presidential Palace had to watch out for others, figuratively speaking, waiting at the gates. Since the literal palace gates were forever policed by a dozen rifle-bearing soldiers, which rumor had it were a nervous lot, no one dared approach within a hundred yards of them.

President Ould Taya's arrival in Kaedi was now just two days away, and the military had sealed the town, allowing traffic neither in nor out. Even with Mamadou's untold payoffs, the chances of securing those trees, then escaping the city with a wagon full of them, seemed as likely to me as a snowstorm hitting.

Thankfully, Mamadou allowed us a leisurely morning, which for me included a bucket bath. Late afternoon, the sun's hot rays piercing the heavy air, Mamadou took us to Kaedi's taxi garage, inexplicably situated in an extensive pit now thick with mud. It was also surrounded from above by large pungent piles of garbage, not exactly the location where people would like to wait. But wait they did, as dozens upon dozens of stranded voyagers lingered on overturned metal drums beneath acacia trees, awaiting word that the military and road conditions would permit them to leave.

Our purpose here was to rent a pick-up truck for the next day. By draining the balance remaining from the merchant Ould Vall's false receipt, we managed to do so. Mamadou doubted that the station's tractor would survive the muddy roads ahead of us, and this pickup was our insurance policy.

***

Thankfully, Friday's skies contained not a hint of clouds. Early morning, Mamadou and I skirted muddy lanes to return to the taxi garage. But the driver and his rented truck were nowhere to be seen. Soon we learned that he had been lured away by a higher-paying client; someone from the president's party, no doubt. A Pulaar woman with a baby strapped to her back called out to us from a dark dwelling, then emerged to return Mamadou's down payment. Mamadou then turned to me with a frown as he tucked the money away. He perused the taxi garage, considering his options.

"We have no choice, we must go with the single wagon," he finally decided. "Let's go."

We mounted a horse cart and headed off to the research station. Once beyond Kaedi's tight confines, Mamadou turned to inspect the lands before us.

"Hmmm, the land is wet, the road soggy," he mused aloud.

I, on the other hand, noticed just one thing: the lush green fields of the dieri spreading before us. Overnight, long dormant grass seeds had taken root and burst open at the first feel of moisture. What once had been a brown, bleak, scraggy landscape now appeared before me like a well-manicured, scenic Arizona golf course, complete with its sun-drenched red rocky backdrop.

"Wow," I exclaimed at the sight of such beauty and abundance.

Mamadou pursed his lips and glanced up at the clear sky. "Too much rain," he mumbled.

I belatedly recalled my lesson from the previous year: the amount of rain mattered less than did its distribution, as the hard clay soils simply shook off those first downpours.

Shortly after we arrived at the station, the tractor driver chugged up. But for some reason he arrived pulling a small wagon rather than the larger one used for his first trip.

"A lot of rain," he stated. "The big wagon can't make those roads. Even this small one can't." Then, scrubbing his teeth with a twig he added, "But I will try."

"*Kaaw*," entreated Mamadou, after looking over the small wagon with dismay. "The bigger one can make it. We'll take the upper sandy road, through the dieri. Our path is not through the muddy waalo."

But the driver was dead set against any plan not his own. Time was short and growing still shorter, and we still had soldiers guarding the roads to contend with. Reluctantly, Mamadou pushed no further.

"We will get as much as possible in this wagon," Mamadou finally instructed with a flat voice.

And so, the two of us began ferrying trees from the research station's nursery bed to the dusty lot where our wagon sat parked, and then jogged back for a repeat trip. First came 500 Chinese banana saplings, each wrapped in black plastic, and each we carefully arranged on the wagon's bottom. With every trip, my rubber slippers flicked streaks of mud up my legs and over my boubou, and each armload of trees left more clay pressed into my front.

Sometime during this frenzy, the director of the research station—the man who a week earlier had celebrated his son Samba's baptism—pulled up with his chauffeur. He meandered over to watch us pile banana on top of banana, standing at a distance to keep his starched white boubou unblemished while urging us to be gentle with his saplings.

With pride he then informed us that President Ould Taya would visit the station the following morning. As the director wandered away, Mamadou paused his activity, then brushed off his hands to follow him toward a low cement building surrounded by oleander bushes. I glanced at my watch—that last trip had taken fifty-five seconds—and then committed myself to ferrying another twenty armfuls before taking a swig from my dwindling water supply. Short goals, I decided, would get me through this day's unending task.

Ten rounds later, Mamadou returned, and straight away joined me in those short dashes carrying two saplings each while dodging the growing swell of recently arrived workers. With various tools, these workers prepared for the next day's guest by sweeping, trimming bushes, scrubbing walkways, and weeding.

I had previously written off the station director as yet another self-centered bureaucrat. But that day proved me wrong. Shortly he returned from his office to track down our driver. When the driver appeared, the director insisted that he secure the large wagon for our upcoming trip to Civé, not the small one he had arrived with.

"You can take the upper dieri road. Your path is not through the muddy waalo," he told him. "Mamadou will lead the way."

I stopped. Mamadou looked over at me and acknowledged my surprised look with the slightest of nods. The driver, on the other hand, was miffed. But he obediently unhooked the small wagon now loaded with bananas and took off on his single-seat tractor to dawdle the one mile to a storage shed. Meanwhile, Mamadou and I returned to ferrying trees from station to parking lot, station to parking lot, slowly chipping away at the large roped-off plot of treelings with the handwritten 'Civé Cooperative' sign staked into its middle.

An hour later, our driver steered into the parking area, the large wagon now in tow. After parking it next to the small one, he disappeared. Without exchanging a word, Mamadou and I first switched the banana plants from the small wagon to the large, and then began adding lime, guava, and mango saplings on top. That accomplished, Mamadou announced we'd try for everything. That meant now adding in the 500 prosopis seedlings that would serve as the orchard's wind block.

Two hours later, we had implausibly crammed in every single one of those seedlings. The result showcased African transport ingenuity: it would take more than a slight breeze to topple this masterpiece over. Or so at least I hoped.

"*Gussi*," proclaimed Mamadou, as he tucked in the last prosopis tree. Finished. Completely spent, I too felt *gussi*.

But alas Mamadou was not. With the sun descending in the light blue sky, he donned his long boubou over his muddy tunic, wound his turban to its full height, and switched on some reserve supply of energy I wished I had.

"Let's go," he said to the driver.

Once again Mamadou and I climbed onto the wheel covers to slowly chug the five miles to Kaedi, first winding our way through happy green fields now dotted with happier cattle. We then made our way out to a government warehouse on the edge of town to pick up our pesticide and fertilizer supplies.

"I must eat or I fall off wagon," I told Mamadou while leaning against our overloaded vehicle as the last bag of fertilizer emerged from the warehouse. I desperately wanted to lie down, but knew I dare not ask.

With that, Mamadou disappeared, then returned with a soft loaf of French bread wrapped in torn brown paper. He helped me eat that loaf, insisting that the driver remain seated while we did. As soon as the last morsel of bread passed into my mouth, Mamadou instructed the driver on.

But the driver just scowled. "*Kaaw*. Let's do what is possible and leave tomorrow. Patience is not a sign of weakness," he tried.

But Mamadou would have none of it.

"*Kaaw*," he retorted, and battling one pithy proverb with another pressed on. "If we do what is possible, we leave now. Patience is virtuous, but too much patience invites laziness. When you lead cows to the dieri, your job is undone until they are home. These trees don't live on patience. They live on soil. We must plant them."

I turned my back and stepped into the road to distance myself from this dispute, honestly not sure which side I hoped prevailed. Half-listening, I inspected the sorry state of my mud-splattered clothes. I heard Mamadou at his best, appealing to the better instincts of his people. "Allah judges us not by our actions when the cows are fat, but those we make when their udders run dry."

Yep, I sure felt like my udders were about as dry as they could get.

And then, as the sun approached the horizon, as the rains neared and Mauritania's president approached Kaedi, our driver relented.

The tractor engine came to life, and once again I climbed aboard.

At Mamadou's direction, we took a back road north of Kaedi's extensive rice fields, all kelly green with their recent transplants. A few barefoot farmers, empty lunch bowls balanced on their heads and jalos hanging from their shoulders, were heading home along our narrow, elevated trail. They stepped aside to let us pass, scratching their heads as we did.

I can only imagine what a sight we presented, puttering our way beyond Kaedi while towing 1,500 trees and a half ton of fertilizer and pesticides. A six-foot, middle-aged Pulaar hanging onto one wheel, a youthful five-foot female tubaak hanging onto the other, and a disgruntled Pulaar driver sitting atop a large bag of fertilizer while stretching out to reach the gas pedal.

But for some inexplicable reason, that evening we attracted the attention of not one single soldier guarding Kaedi's roads.

Beyond Kaedi's limits, we trundled along the sandy road while heading into the darkening sky. Above us, the clouds gathered as the sun behind us set. I was glad for the bread in my stomach, and released a deep, heavy sigh.

"Good work," Mamadou mouthed, smiling broadly as he stuck his head out from behind the wagon's rear. The jarring noise of the bouncing trailer and the loud sputtering of the tractor's diesel engine made any verbal communication impossible.

I smiled back. For a brief second, I felt the thrill of adventure course though me as I took stock of what we had accomplished, those treelings all piled high beside me. Then a foot slipped. Tightening my grip and adjusting my footing, I steeled myself for the six-hour journey ahead.

***

I lost track of how many times we stepped down from our perches to push the wagon out of the mud or scout out the road ahead. We took circuitous trips upland and into the dieri to avoid mud, gullies, and lakes. Sometime around midnight, a few hours from Civé, my aching body gave up.

"We take a break here," Mamadou instructed, seeing me slumped by the road. My head was pounding, my shoulders ached, and my calves kept cramping. "Come." Mamadou led the three of us up a small hill covered with the stumps of long-dead trees. Cresting it, I could just make out a small cluster of huts. We were in the enclave of Nema.

Approaching the nearest hut, I saw the silhouette of a woman sitting up under a mosquito net, her dim flashlight switched on. Once within earshot, Mamadou called out to her, and soon the two were warmly greeting one another.

And so, I met Ramata Konté, who it turned out was some relation to Mamadou's first wife Fati, and seemed to share some connection with the driver, though what that was I couldn't say. Ramata set to preparing us couscous and milk while I lay and caressed my trembling calves.

With that welcome meal and the more welcome matla, I fell sound asleep while the three drank tea. After no more than an hour, we were once again back on the road, a late-rising moon now offering the dimmest sliver of light.

The driver continued to follow Mamadou's navigations. At one point, our load became stuck in sand and nearly tipped over. We managed to right the wagon and locate the spilled treelings, but after that Mamadou had us walk, our pace just matching the tractor's as it sputtered and plowed through deep sand. At last, just beyond Tokomadji, we turned toward the river for the final trek into Civé.

Sometime after 3 a.m., we were coaxing our merchandise through the steep muddy gully of Caangól Lougousaloumawol, the final steep incline to Civé, when the wagon wheels held fast and refused to spin, not yielding an inch to our exhausted shoves. With Civé so close, Mamadou decided to just abandon our load.

For forty-five minutes we plodded onward, mindlessly marching through deep mud and standing water. Finally, the village emerged before us, outlined by the slice of a moon glittering above us in the hazy sky.

I have no idea what the driver thought about Mamadou roping him into this ordeal. I kept thinking about his plea nine hours earlier to spend the night in Kaedi. It was a reasonable request. Yet during that night's endless ordeal, (unlike me) he never complained. Perhaps, I figured, he simply responded to his fellow Pulaar, some cultural connection silently binding them in ways beyond my perception.

***

A few hours later dawn broke, and the good news of the trees' arrival spread. Early morning, Becce's men, wives, and children began parading out to the crippled wagon, everyone in high spirits. There, villagers gingerly hand-carried the treelings, several barrels of insecticide, and countless bags of fertilizer the 200 yards down to the river's edge. There, all treelings and supplies were loaded into pirogues, and teenaged boys began paddling the cargo six miles upstream.

Once this transfer was successfully underway, I accompanied Kebe and Amadou Demba to Becce to supervise the opposite end of the operation. With the announced arrival of each pirogue upstream, Becce's men lined up parallel to the irrigation pipeline to pass the trees and supplies up and over the steep river embankment. Youth then cradled the trees over to the well-prepared nursery bed Kebe had constructed, while the pirogues turned around to secure yet another load. Back and forth those pirogues taxied all day, the final boatful of trees arriving as the sun set. By this time, I had abandoned my supervisory job and was instead photographing the merriment of this event.

At day's end, all the trees were safely tucked into that nursery bed. Once the president had passed through Civé, the cooperative would transplant the trees into Becce's soils. Miracle of all miracles, only two mangos and one guava had not survived that grueling journey.

A year earlier, workers at the station had told me that if Civé planted an orchard, it would be Mauritania's first. This had surprised me. Why wouldn't villages want to plant fruit trees? It wasn't as if they were too expensive, and they certainly could bring extra cash.

That night, with the pitch-black sky above, I felt utterly exhausted. Every muscle in my body ached. I strung my mosquito net up under the starry skyline, and then limped inside, pulling a sheet up over me as I collapsed. The fatigue from three sleepless nights and two jarring days on that wretched tractor quickly swept over me. In the very brief moments before losing consciousness, I finally understood why no one had yet accomplished what Mamadou had just pulled off.

Chapter 39

A Presidential Visit

The next morning, my body ached. The only time I could remember feeling so worn out was my senior year of high school. Thanksgiving Day I bet a friend I could complete the Honolulu Marathon; that afternoon I began a semi-strict training regimen. Three weeks later, I miraculously crossed the finish line, then once helped to the sidelines, promptly vomited up all the green Gatorade I'd drunk along the way. For the next several days, the school stairs proved beyond my ability to climb.

Today, though, was not a time to dwell on my throbbing body; the president of Mauritania was coming! I sorted through the pile of clothes in my back room, all of which were filthy. I picked out a stiff boubou and limped to the river to wash it.

An hour later, my darkish green print boubou was dry. I slid it on, then camera in hand, hobbled across the gully. I followed the rumble of drums, smell of roasting goat, and growing parade of people leading toward Civé's western edge. Djeinaba, now visibly pregnant with her third child, grabbed me as I approached. She was dressed in a brand new, stunning three-piece outfit with a stylish headscarf, deep red lipstick, and thick gold earrings.

"Wow," I said, realizing that not only was my boubou not all that clean, but I had forgotten to add earrings. With a skip in her step, Djeinaba led me by hand to the health center, now temporarily converted into a storage room. There in the 'examination room' atop the 'examination table' lay a wide assortment of food and drink beautifully displayed in fine plastic bowls from China.

Soon some other women leaders joined us. They all led me out-side to where several short display tables were lined up along the road into Civé. These tables—actually the desks from the nearby school—faced the health center on the far side of the dirt lane, cre-ating a gauntlet of sorts through which the president's car would pass. Every one of the tables was covered with a beautiful piece of heavily waxed damask cloth that sparkled in the now-hot sun. On each the women displayed samples from their new cooperative: cro-cheted baby sweaters and hats on one, beautifully embroidered bou-bous on another, multi-colored tie-dyed cloth on a third, and on a fourth, a somewhat random assortment of onions, hoes, and irri-gation pipes. Behind each separate presentation stood two women erect and dressed in her finest, peering out from behind conserva-tive white gauze headdresses. As we approached, each broke into a wide smile.

"Look at our work, Messur President. This is from the Women's Cooperative of Civé!"

"Praise be to Allah." I returned their playful salutes.

Just then a handful of teenage boys with bongo drums passed by, followed behind by two dozen clapping and singing teenaged girls. Somehow, all these girls had acquired matching white T-shirts. They broke off from the drummer to practice some choreographed chanting and dancing, every one of them in the highest of spirits as they reveled in the rare pleasure of time in the spotlight.

Meanwhile, the women had somehow created a large, tie-dyed banner which they had stamped with 'Civé Woman Center' and tied to a wooden pole. A spirited young woman by the name of Wourri—the niece of my mom Taanooy—took great delight in twirling the banner this way and that among the crowd, like a rebel-lious drum majorette. I, meanwhile, stood in awe amidst this cele-bratory atmosphere, stunned by such a display of money, creativity, and organizational effort.

Then I recalled who was behind it. Mamadou had left his brother, Sadyo, in charge of these arrangements. I smiled, then looked around to see if I could find him. But the crowd was too thick.

Meanwhile, Djeinaba nudged me along. We continued our stroll down Presidential Lane. Beyond the Women's Cooperative tables stood a few others. One held a gigantic cast-iron pot to represent the gruel women made when high protein cereal arrived for the village's malnourished kids. On another unmanned table lay a stethoscope, an empty box of malaria medicine, and a pad and pen.

At the far end of this short corridor arose a large shade structure covered with rugs and topped by a Mauritanian flag. Expansive plastic mats mats were spread beneath, topped by a ring of matlas decorated with fine cloth and leather pillows. On those matlas sat a row of dignified male elders. An empty space among them signified the president's honored spot. Raising clasped hands, I gave a collective greeting to this ceremonial gathering.

"Wise one," responded Doro Thioub, sitting in the middle.

"My niece," Djeinaba's uncle Kalidou called out at me, waving.

"Next time the president comes, Keyti, we'll have mangos," added my neighbor, the fisherman Harouna.

"If Allah wills it," I responded with a wave and bow.

Checking behind me for any sign of the president, I noticed that a few of the village's younger men had converted themselves into 'security' officers. They wielded whistles and sticks, ostensibly to ensure that all but them remained behind ropes separating villagers from the soon-to-arrive president.

And thus passed a couple of increasingly sultry hours, until finally several young scouts came sprinting down the road. "He comes, he comes," they yelled. Civé's new security forces whipped into action, frantically blowing whistles and menacingly swiping the air, committed to turning this animated and chaotic mass into an orderly and compliant one.

Within minutes, up drove a slew of white Land Rovers with fluttering flags. Everyone, including me, pressed forward against the ropes as the entourage came to a halt. Out of the front vehicle emerged a man who hoisted a large video camera on his shoulder. After a moment, four light-skinned Moors emerged from a middle vehicle. Except for the thump of car doors shutting and somewhere a cow mooing, the air was silent, the crowd still. I realized my heart was pounding, and strangely found myself hoping the president would single me out.

Then out of the middle vehicle stepped a man. Slow to emerge, he was quickly surrounded by his four companions. He lifted his hand in greetings as the cameraman maneuvered to capture the scene.

President Ould Taya was around forty-five years old, surprisingly small, and semi-bald with a thick moustache. I caught my breath and blinked, as he looked a lot like the Portuguese father of a high school friend, one known for his raucous humor. I stifled a surprised laugh.

Ould Taya began his parade. He strolled along the gauntlet, his men remaining an arm's length away. For an awkward few seconds, it seemed neither the villagers nor the visitors knew what to do. Several elders approached from the right. Greetings and information were exchanged through a translator. Meanwhile, the bowing elders pointed to the display tables across the ropes. Ould Taya nodded, walked a few paces to his right, greeted the women, and hands clasped, walked on. About ten yards from me, he called out greetings to the men under the shade structure. *Yes, an uncanny resemblance to Mr. Medeiros.* I prepared to greet him.

But instead of continuing, the president turned and signaled. I saw Kebe approach, only to be intercepted by a guard who took the ceramic cup of tufam he held and handed it to the president. Ould Taya took a sip, returned it, then held a hand up. Bidding farewell, he climbed into his Land Rover, and disappeared behind the tinted windows. Off the entourage sped to Matam, leaving a lingering cloud of sand and dirt in its wake.

Thus came to an end President Ould Taya's two-minute visit to Civé.

The sun now directly overhead, the overdressed crowd immediately sought shade. I joined a group at the gully's edge watching the dust cloud that engulfed the convoy until it disappeared down the road. Then nothing remained of the president's visit except a dispute over whether he had arrived with five or six Land Rovers in tow. Since I had taken pictures, I promised to settle the quarrel once my film was developed.

Standing at the gully's edge looking beyond my hut toward Matam, a wave of distaste for the president swept over me. Minutes earlier I had been excited, overwhelmed by the work villagers had put into his visit. Now? He came and went without really saying hello, not the behavior I was accustomed to in politicians. I wished he'd at least greeted Sala, the Women's Cooperative president, and sat for a minute with the male elders. He seemed ill at ease. This visit was not meant to impress. What was its purpose?

Back at the gauntlet, the festivities were now winding down. A large bowl of tufam emerged from the health center and was offered to the male elders. Then out came plates of goat meat, bowls of roasted peanuts, and hunks of bread. The girls in their matching T-shirts pulled down the ropes and entered the dirt road to dance, clap, and sing. They looked like they could have remained there all day had they not quickly been called into service.

***

Despite the heat and humidity of mid-day, as soon as the president was gone, all Becce headed to the fields, everyone eager to plant their trees. After a quick dip in the river and a large dose of aspirin, I headed there too.

The afternoon before, Mamadou had assigned each of us our

role for this day. Amadou Demba would dole out the trees while Kebe would record what everyone got. I would measure out fertilizers and fungicides, and the cooperative's secretary Bayal would supervise their application.

The day was jubilant. Youth who studied in far flung cities had recently returned for the summer, and their presence infused the fields with cheer and never-ending banter. Many practiced their English on me with catchy phrases such as "How do you do Missus?" and "Baby, be mine." Two of the returning teenagers, one of them Mamadou's oldest son Mari, bore the fantastic news that they had passed the nation's baccalaureate exam, one that three-quarters of Pulaars failed. It was touching to see families reunited. But the reunions also reminded me of the two-year separation from my own. With my application to extend recently approved, I knew my own reunion would have to wait. My joy was mixed with loneliness.

Yet, I kept busy. As did everyone else. There were holes to be dug, trees to be ferried back and forth, and advice to be sought from Kebe and me. With the sun descending, kids and women arrived with large bowls of rice, fish, and hot peppers, along with tea leaves, charcoal, and sugar. The festivity in the fields now moved to the shade beneath Becce's elder, the grand old Baaba Njiia. I joined Kebe and his young son, and we ate oily rice topped with fried fish, squash, and tangy bissap leaves.

The good cheer of lunch gradually dimmed as tea was started. One-by-one, the farmers stretched out on the hard soil, a protruding tree's root or a pocked termite mound serving as pillow. Soon all were fast asleep. The youth, meanwhile, headed to the irrigation pump to splash around in the stilling basin where brown yet utterly refreshing river water swirled. To their delight, I joined them.

"Baby be mine," I called out as I jumped in the small basin, for the first time unable to resist water thirty degrees cooler than the air. I knew my time in Civé was ending, and while jumping into a stilling basin wasn't really appropriate for a female, that afternoon

I didn't care. Plus, I had always been permitted to break the strict prescriptions for women, as no one seemed to know which norms I should adhere to. I was always some vague 'other,' a status that allowed me room to establish my own category within Pulaar's fixed social order.

An hour later work resumed, and by the end of it, nearly every tree was planted in Becce's soil. The hazy sun slipped below the horizon, erasing the last of the long shadows stretching across the green rice fields. Only then did everyone slowly collect their belongings into large scarfs and oversized metallic bowls, sling their jalos over their shoulders, and head with tired bodies toward the fields' western entrance that pointed toward home.

While over the next few months a few of those trees died—despite my best efforts, a couple were burned with over-enthusiastic doses of fertilizer, reminiscent of my own zealous treatment of strawberries decades earlier—most of them flourished. Their trunks quickly stretched upward and thickened outward. The prosopis trees and pigeon pea bushes around the orchard grew rapidly, each day showing more promise that they'd dutifully protect those trees from the powerful gales that sought to strip away their progeny.

And each week, Amadou Demba started the far motor pump that delivered water to the growing fruit trees. Every week, I stood beside him and watched the water climb the bank, spill into the basin, and spread out to the hopeful cooperative members as they watched, prayed over, and even sang to their trees.

"It's not like rice," Djeinaba's uncle Kalidou Deh told me one day as we stood together watching water enter his plot.

"No, but rice not like sorghum, either," I remarked, mindful of the changes he had witnessed over his lifetime. As my time to leave approached, I was increasingly aware of how life in Civé was ever-changing, not timeless nor static as first I took it to be.

"Ha," he responded, slapping a spare irrigation pipe next to him. "You speak the truth."

Chapter 40

The Union

Seven months passed and my third Ceeɗu arrived. Each day Senegal shimmered more, new hobbled donkeys wandered the village, and more people complained of unspecified pains. Each night, howling winds littered the village with more clumps of thatched roof while the stars above dimmed. The time to leave Civé had arrived. During one of my final days, the motor pumps at Becce delivered the thriving fruit trees their weekly dose of water. Amadou Demba found me resting under a row of now large pigeon pea bushes. He laughed and promised that when next I returned to Civé, Becce would be a cool shady oasis.

"You won't have to squat under a bush to find shade," he assured me.

Sometime earlier, the orchard's banana trees had thrown out their mammoth purple blossoms, and small buds had appeared on their stalks, gradually turning into the clusters of bananas now present in every cooperative member's plot. With great pride, Amadou showed off his own clusters, counting out all ten for me before insisting that I too, count them to be sure.

He then urged me to eat one of his young bananas. It was more than a tad green, so I balked. But grinning he plucked one from a bunch and handed it over. Looking at it skeptically, I snapped it in half, and insisted we share it.

"If this what bananas in the Fuuta taste like, I must go home to Hawai'i. There, bananas are the best in world. I send you one. You will see."

Amadou chuckled at this and then repeated the same comment he'd made every day for three months. "Ah, no my sister. I am not leaving you. I am coming with you, packed in your suitcase."

We laughed, and then tossed the starchy remains of our half-eaten banana in the bushes. Surrounded by all those small but flourishing guava, mango, and lime trees, with or without Amadou Demba, it was time for me to head home.

Meanwhile, as the bananas were blossoming, the rice warehouse was flourishing. The harvest had occurred some months earlier, and the warehouse had opened for business. Farmers flocked to sell their paddy at prices above what SONADER and the local merchant Samba Anne paid. And it wasn't just those from Becce and Cóndi Hiraande who came knocking, their carts piled high with rice. So too did farmers from Garly and Tokomadji. They even came from the small village of Wali a couple hours upstream. Word had spread.

"See," was about all Mamadou had to say one day after an active afternoon of rice buying. Everyone stared in awe at the stacks of rice now piled to the ceiling. Some Becce men closed the warehouse's two iron doors, securing them with three large padlocks, three different Becce men each pocketing his separate key. This extra security measure was Mamadou's idea, a way to assure everyone that no one could pilfer the wealth within. *Trust*. It was what Cóndi Hiraande, and to some degree the women's cooperative, lacked.

Very soon, every cent of CRS's $18,000 loan was converted into paddy rice. Then, before I left, an about-face in traffic began; empty carts and donkeys lumbered up during the warehouse's posted hours, then departed with bags of paddy sold for pennies over its buying price.

So successful was the warehouse that Becce quickly made good on all its loan repayments to CRS. CRS had promised to dedicate all such repayments to other village projects. With the first repayment, CRS bought the cooperative a rice dehulling machine. With the second, Civé dug its first well, two Haratin laborers striking water the week I left.

Steve Hilbert and Mamadou hit on this financial arrangement after a daylong conversation that started over breakfast and ended over a third cup of sweet mint tea drunk under the watchful gaze of Queen Cassiopeia on her throne in the sky. Mamadou and Steve both envisioned Civé becoming a training center for neighboring villagers where they could come to learn about running their own warehouse. Steve imagined CRS assuming an active role in the region, with Civé as its headquarters. This, he explained, fit with CRS's new emphasis on community development instead of its old one of disaster relief.

Mamadou had long dreamed of building on Becce's success by collaborating with surrounding villages. He paid keen attention to price differentials, and figured out that with reasonable transportation costs, one could make a killing by selling vegetables in Nouakchott. The problem with local markets was that they were always flooded with identical products, leaving farmers forever on the short end of bargaining. Reliable and reasonably priced transportation out of the region would open up higher-priced markets.

During that one day stranded ten hours roadside outside of the town of Aleg, Mamadou had ruminated at length about the problems of difficult, unreliable, and expensive transportation. He hovered over a newly purchased calculator to figure out exactly how much money could be saved if the cooperative had a truck. After several hours, on the spot he developed the idea of banding together with the region's other cooperatives to buy one.

By the sixth or seventh hour of that roadside interlude, as my mind was getting muddled from heat, hunger, and visions of tarantulas, Mamadou's was kicking into high gear. He talked of creating a Union of Cooperatives to spur regional development. This union could buy a truck to improve commercial opportunities, it could purchase a tractor to plow fields, add land, and re-divide plots, work for which SONADER was both notoriously unreliable and prohibitively expensive.

Together the region's farmers could also learn to dry vegetables and meat. They could begin an agro-pastoral project to grow fodder during the hot season so that cows could be milked year-round, and so many goat carcasses wouldn't be thrown down the deep crevices leading to the river. Villages could buy mills so that dehulling rice and sorghum was done mechanically, saving women the back-breaking job of doing so by hand—which was, in fact, the first item Becce bought with its inaugural loan repayment to CRS.

"Soon the Fuuta will look like America," I joked to Mamadou during a final day together as we stood observing women streaming up the gully carrying paddy rice to dehull for that day's lunch. "When I come back, I think I am in my country."

Every chance he got, Mamadou sold this vision to leaders in nearby villages. A few were quick to agree. Others, however, were openly skeptical, maybe not of Mamadou's ideas so much as his motivation.

Two mornings before I left Civé, Mamadou got his wish. Beginning at 9 a.m., leaders from six surrounding villages began arriving by donkey carts. By 10:30 a.m., all were present. The meeting began under a handsome and expansive shade structure newly built next to the rice warehouse and adjacent to the village's just-completed well. A dozen men were present, all dressed in their finest and prepared for a long day of discussion. Preoccupied with my pending departure, I sat in the back that day, feeling acutely my outsider status.

Mamadou opened the gathering by underscoring the dire straits of their villages and pitching the need for them to unite. Together they could awaken others in the Fuuta.

"This Union will be like lanterns, we will provide light so others can follow," he said. I thought of the women who desperately wanted to follow Mamadou's light but were pulled in too many directions.

"If some dig and others bury, we'll never get anywhere." I thought of the sabotaged motor pumps upstream, and the now-landless Madame Diaw in Senegal.

The atmosphere was somber and respectful as late morning turned to midafternoon. Women arrived with water, bowls, and soap for hand washing. Next came savory lunch bowls of rice and large fish from the Atlantic. I joined four older men around one bowl but found conversation hard. Then came tea and naps, and I retreated to my notebook. Mamadou lay some distance away, and I wondered why after his opening speech, he had remained so silent. I guessed he just seemed content to observe the birth of this Union he'd dreamt about.

With the heat promising to stay above 100 degrees and distracted by the swirling emotions of my upcoming trip, I took leave before the meeting restarted. After a quick dip in the river, I made my way into the village to greet friends; many, I knew, for the last time. My stomach curled and eyes burned. Wearing a strained smile and bearing a heavy heart, I entered the village.

Eventually I wound my way over the Kebe's house, who lived adjacent to Samba Anne's boutique. There I sat with his wife when something caught her attention. She turned to announce, "Meeting over." I then saw that Koundel's elder, a man by the name of Moussa Diaw, was passing by on his cart. He waved and called out greetings. I went out to say goodbye.

"Everything go well?" I asked.

"OK," he responded as he adjusted his straw cone-shaped hat. Hesitating a second, he looked down and added sadly: "We elected Doro Thioub to be the new union president."

"DORO Thioub? The president of Cóndi Hiraande?" I asked startled. Doro was the last person I would have picked.

"Yep," he responded with a nod, turning sideways toward the river.

Moussa remained silent. Then with a sigh, he turned my way.

"We send our greetings to Julie. And we greet all your kin. May you travel in peace with Allah's blessings." He stroked his beard thoughtfully and gave me a sad smile.

"Amin. I send greetings to everyone in Koundel," I responded, not wanting to say goodbye.

Then "ari, ari, arrriii…," Moussa signaled his donkey on. Off he headed along the sandy road leading out of town toward Tokomadji, then beyond to Koundel. I sadly watched his departure as news of the leadership choice that had brought the long day's meeting to a close, sunk in.

***

"People are suspicious of Mamadou," Tall explained to me that night after I joined him and Djeinaba for dinner. "There's no way they would elect him. Mamadou knew that. They think he'll become too powerful. So, they elected Doro instead." Then he added sourly: "In the Fuuta, it isn't about who is effective."

Djeinaba chimed in, "Caste is still important. People don't want a slave as leader. But no one will say that."

I realized then that I had misjudged, even misunderstood, the lingering importance of caste. So much still escaped me, a message which in two years' time would be forcefully delivered once again.

Chapter 41

Farewell

That final month in Civé was difficult, I think more so than my first. On the one hand, I had much to look forward to. Steve Hilbert had recommended several masters programs combining my interests in Africa and economics. I recently learned that my top pick, Michigan State, had accepted me. It was April 1987, and I would start in September.

Then there was my dad, who soon after I arrived in Mauritania had lost his second wife to cancer. Now he had a new one I had yet to meet. My sister lived with a new beau, a college friend had an infant daughter, and my best friend from high school lived across town from my mom, where I'd be spending the summer. It was time to get caught up with those back home and move on with my own life. Yet I knew I wouldn't be writing to those I was leaving. Nor calling. And certainly not making quick weekend visits while passing through.

During my final week, I sorted through my belongings to decide what would stay and what would go. I flipped through my stack of notebooks, rereading about events from different times, like the morning two months into my stay when Koumba Binta called me a person without Allah's blessing. Our friendship had recovered from her insults, and I now knew that I should have ignored her bout of nastiness or met it with an insult of my own followed by an invitation to tea.

I looked over my rice manuals with the many hand-written

notes in the margins. Then in the back of my single-drawer desk, I found a long-forgotten list of possible projects, and immediately regretted what I had left undone. Like helping a small Fulbe enclave some miles north find money for a well. I forgot. I thought of their long miserable trek to the river during the hot season. A moment of indecision passed before I crumpled that paper up and quickly tossed it away.

There too in my drawer was Casio, my calculator, a simple device that proved its worth many times over. I spread out an old pagne, and carefully tied up the hundreds of letters I'd kept from friends, family, international organizations, and potential funders. I took down my map that now flapped in the breeze, and gently rolled it up while watching the red dot of Civé disappear.

Those days I felt disoriented and tired, and for the first time, slept in.

"Peace be upon you. Are you sick?" Mamadou stood in my doorway mid-morning about a week before I left, finding me asleep inside.

I sat up quickly, a bit confused. Dirty dishes and clothes were piled up in my blue tub by the doorway, still awaiting their morning trip to the river.

"No, no. I mean… no. I tired. I not sleep last night." I rubbed my eyes.

"There's a lot of work at Becce today."

I knew that. The fruit trees were newly grafted, and Ceeɗu was full upon us.

"Me, I'm coming. I get water first."

"See you there." With a sweep of his boubou, Mamadou turned to leave. Then he stopped. Slowly he turned back, then said: "Civéans will speak your name after you."

"And I yours," I responded. His words caught me by surprise, as I was unaccustomed to his tone and sentiment. To 'speak some-one's name' means that your memory will persist after you are no longer present, as people will ensure your good deeds and honorable character are remembered. In Pulaar's oral tradition, those who hear these stories must themselves pass them on, so that the past is never forgotten, the dead always alive.

After he left, I picked up my blue tub and shed tears all the way down to the river.

***

One of those final days found me visiting several women who had thoughtfully declared that as a souvenir, they would record parting words for me on a cassette. "Your relatives can listen, and hear the words of Pulaar speakers," the head of the crocheting group announced. "And you can translate our greetings."

I arrived late afternoon at the appointed home. With me was my cassette player, a tape, and several extra batteries. The women, some with babies strapped on their back, started to gather. They made tea and fried dough as everyone took turns talking into the microphone. Each started with fifteen minutes of greetings to everyone under the sun in America, after which each immediately wanted to hear what she sounded like. They talked, laughed, and sang into the tiny microphone until all the batteries, including the spares, had died. Next came various gifts. First, a leather pillowcase. Then some silver earrings. A bracelet. A potato into which someone had carved 'Civé Women's Cooperative.' We laughed, drank more tea, and ate more fried dough.

After the third and final round of tea was drunk, five women from the tie-dying group entered the compound with an armload of gifts. For five minutes they handed me piece after piece of beautifully tie-dyed cloth, describing each one as they showed it off. Finally, only one remained. After a pause, the head of their group, Deiko, presented it to me. Everyone stepped in a little closer as I held the cloth. It was sharply pressed, still warm from the iron.

"This one is for your mother," Deiko pronounced, "A

tablecloth." Even though they'd probably never eaten on a table in their life, the women loved making tablecloths, associating them with tubaaks and hence big profits.

I picked up the blue and white fabric, admired its feel, and said my mom would love it. "It's for the church," Deiko continued, referring to my mom's church which had sent the woman's cooperative $500. All the women grinned. I thanked them again and said the church would love it.

"Open it up," Deiko instructed. Before I moved an inch, four women grabbed the cloth destined for St. Christopher's and spread it out for me to admire. It was truly beautiful. But I wasn't sure what they wanted me to see.

"You did fine work," I assured them, "they will love it. They will eat off it and remember Civé and the women. They will always remember you; they will speak your names." At times like this, any Pulaar in my position would launch into an elegant speech, a skill I didn't naturally possess, and definitely not one I had mastered here. Still, I feebly made the best attempt I could.

"Look," Deiko said, pointing to the middle of the cloth. "Look what we did." I looked. There were some symmetrical white designs in the blue cloth, but I didn't see anything else.

By now, a curious crowd was growing around us, and kids were roaming in to check for unclaimed leftovers. Djeinaba, who often made a point of bailing me out in situations like this, realized I wasn't doing my bit here. She clapped her hands and cried out, "*Celi*. They put *celis* on the cloth."

I didn't recognize the word. I looked dumbfounded at her, hoping she'd make another stab at helping me out. I looked at the cloth again, and then it hit me. The white symmetrical patterns in the cloth were crosses. They explained: the husband of one of the women was home visiting from Zouerate and told his wife that the cross was to Christianity what the crescent and star was to Islam. The women decided to put crosses on that tablecloth destined for my mom's church, one that to this day still appears on special occasions.

"This gift is one from the heart." I choked on those words, then fell silent, too moved to say more. Someone handed me a large plastic cup, and I took the rare act of gulping down unfiltered river water.

As I did, my dear friend President Sala waved her hands to silence everyone. "No, no." She leaned over laughing, then straightened up. "It from our ability," she exclaimed, skillfully imitating my ungrammatical and thickly accented Pulaar. Everyone laughed heartily, and I put down the cup and joined them.

***

Mamadou and I left Civé on the afternoon Rapide. I started the day with a dip in the dwindling river. Then as quietly as possible, I parceled out my remaining belongings, first to the Ba's, then my neighbors Harouna and Maimona (giving their son, Sarr, Kmart's 'The American Sack'), and then to Sala who lived nearby on the village edge. For Amadou Demba, I left my large blue tub with matching blue teapot. My torn map went to Mamadou, who proudly displayed it on the wall of the cooperative's new concrete office located next to the rice warehouse. My jalo went to that dear man Sadyo Konaté who wondered about the moon, and who commented that life in the Fuuta entailed pick and shovel, but not much more.

Before heading into the village one final time, I visited the knoll above the ravine where now was located both the women's cooperative and the rice warehouse. I said goodbye to the woman who had nearly gone blind, Sira, and her husband Awdy. I crossed over to the nearby compound of Kalidou Deh, Djeinaba's uncle who had become my own. I repeated the same words dozens of times, took benedictions, shook hands, refused tea, and tried to find things to laugh at. I passed through Kebe's compound and found him repairing a fishing net with twine made from patouki roots. I sat down and went over my itinerary with him, then pulled out a gift I had tucked into my pagne: a brand-new bright blue knit hat. He laughed, put it on, and said he'd wear it as soon as Ceeɗu was over.

"But I have no gift for you."

"Send me picture of you in new hat," I requested, and while he laughed, I took off my necklace and gave it to Kebe's wife, while she promptly removed hers and gave it to me. I fingered the colorful beads for a moment, then with hands trembling, put it on.

Mid-day arrived and I continued to Djeinaba and Tall's, where I found Amadou Demba waiting for me. Djeinaba had an early lunch ready for us. It was my favorite dish, peanut maafi. A group of Djeinaba's family members came to say goodbye, as did a host of others. After one cup of tea, it was time to retrieve my luggage and so I bid my goodbyes. Djeinaba, holding her newborn son, grabbed my hand and, with both of us too choked to talk, walked with me to their gate where we embraced under her murotoki tree. With tears slipping out, I shook Tall's hand and promised to write.

Amadou Demba accompanied me back to my house where I picked up my large green duffle bag and backpack, then waited at the east side of the village for the Rapide. For the first time, I hugged Amadou Demba's bony, muscular body, and told him to quit smoking. I bid goodbye to Harouna and Maimona, Sarr, and all the Bas who had gathered. Then I climbed into the back of the pickup, waving goodbye as the sand kicked up.

The truck retraced the path through which I had first entered the village, then pulled up at the west side where a large crowd had gathered. Mamadou exchanged words with the driver, and the two passengers in front got out so I could take the middle seat between the driver and Mamadou. The villagers pressed, the driver honked, I waved, and off we went, plowing through deep sand. The heavy weight I had been carrying for days began to lift, but before I could wipe the tears from my cheeks, a loud *thud* signaled that our tire had gone flat.

***

Mamadou was a great help in Nouakchott, accompanying me to final visits with CRS, GTZ, Peace Corps, and a few other places where we'd had dealings. A couple of nights later, he, his brother Souleyman, and Faba's husband N'Diaye accompanied me to the airport, walking with me out onto the tarmac, where workers were loading our plane. Having gone as far as they could, they stood in a line, and I shook each of their hands, promising to write, and promising to send their benedictions to all my relatives. Before picking up my backpack, I looked once more at Mamadou, and said lamely, "Thank you."

"It is Allah we should thank." He smiled. I smiled and nodded, picked up my bag, waved at them all, and was the last to board.

At the top of the stairs, I turned to give one final wave but found the men now gone. I realized I could see much of Nouakchott from this vantage, the two tall thin spires of the Saudi Mosque just barely discernable in the dwindling light. The three men, I knew, were headed for their evening prayer. I sent them, and all those in Civé, a silent benediction before ducking aboard.

part three
FARTAK

Chapter 42

The Event

Shortly after I left, the political tension in Mauritania exploded. I knew it had been mounting, as a covert group of citizens had been agitating against black Mauritanians' second-class treatment. Most in the Western community were sympathetic as it was obvious to all that the high-status members of the Moor population monopolized government jobs, military positions, promotions, and business and educational opportunities. I recall a few times when Mamadou and I would find ourselves in meetings with them, and he'd turn quiet.

"You explain," he said one afternoon under his breath while we sat across from a couple of officials from the Ministry of Water and Forests. Throughout that meeting, he kept his role to nodding and verifying my claims about how long trees had been dead.

I often could sense growing social tensions, but I was also not particularly tuned in to events outside of Civé. Yet even there I had glimpses. For instance, one time two Bidhan Moors from Nouakchott drove trucks to Civé loaded down with material (including Messur Lamborghini) for the village. Sitting shotgun, my driver quizzed me on all aspects of life among Pulaars: where and what I ate, where I bathed, how I travelled, and how many locks I kept on my door. The closer we got to the Fuuta, the more agitated he became.

Once in Boghe, we turned left to take the unpaved road to Kaedi. It was then he became openly fearful, wondering what he had gotten himself into. He was attentive at each bend in the road, imagining, I guessed, that villagers were sticking pins in Bidhan voodoo dolls. I compensated with jovial banter, thinking only of our bounty in the back that I feared might soon be in a U-turn for Nouakchott. At dusk we arrived in Civé. After unloading all our supplies in record time, the two drivers disappeared into a cloud of dust. It was a notable occurrence when a Mauritanian refused an offer of tea.

We volunteers discussed the ominous shifts in the political landscape, one perceptible to me the day President Ould Taya all-too-briefly stepped out in Civé. And there were odd occurrences, for instance, the one I witnessed a few months before I left. Without explanation, a couple of Moor soldiers appeared in the village. I watched from my backyard as they walked along the river's edge with guns on their shoulders, asking all they chanced upon for their identity card. If the villager didn't have it—which hardly anyone did—they were fined 2,000 ouguiyas. All day long the soldiers patrolled the village, randomly stopping people and searching homes.

"They were looking for Pulaars planning a coup," Mamadou flatly explained to me later.

We volunteers picked up what we could from the diplomatic community. But our main source was whispered conversations with Mauritanian friends, such as the one I had with Mamadou over tea in La Sahara café. Before I left, it was common knowledge that an underground organization of black intellectuals called FLAM, the French acronym for African Liberation Forces of Mauritania, had published a manifesto detailing the numerous injustices black Mauritanians suffered. That document was covertly distributed but not hard to find, and more or less called all black Mauritanians to arms.

When I left Mauritania, tensions were continuing to escalate. A few months prior, nearly all black government officials had been recalled to Nouakchott so that their possible association with this shadowy FLAM movement could be examined. Upon arriving one night at my host's house in Kaedi, his wife informed me in a worried voice that her husband had just been summoned to the capital. As residents with sharp and not-very-distant memories of the political control they once held over the Fuuta, Pulaars were the main target of suspicion, especially its elite Fulbe clan.

The government arrested and tortured over 100 people, almost all of them Pulaars. In April 1987, the same month I left, word on the street was that a couple dozen Pulaars had been convicted of treason. Without any kind of press, it was hard to distinguish truth from rumor. After I left, information was scarce, and the few letters I received were filled with warm greetings but empty of news.

Soon ensconced in a new life, I forgot about Mauritania's political woes and instead only wondered if the mango trees had blossomed, if the woman's cooperative was functioning, whether Doro Thioub was providing the Union with leadership, and if Messur Lamborghini was still delivering on his promise of wealth to the gardening women.

I was thus unaware that Mauritania's political climate had deteriorated to the point of no return. And then it exploded. Almost two years to the day after my departure, the peak of the hot season arrived. Some Fulbe herders in the Fuuta's far eastern edges had crossed over into Senegal with their gaunt Zebu cows in search of fodder. Tension between these Fulbe herders and the Soninke farmers on the southern banks had been rising, as the two groups disputed who had rights to the land. This time, as the Fulbe and their cows approached the farmers' drying sorghum fields, the Soninke farmers confronted them. Eventually, they chased the shepherds and cattle back across the dry riverbed.

Back in Mauritania, those Fulbe herders located some sympathetic Moor officials who supported their claim to that land. Several Mauritanian soldiers accompanied them back across the riverbed. A tense encounter ensued, and the soldiers wound up shooting dead two Soninke farmers, then hauling a dozen others off to a

Mauritanian prison. Sometime during the day's violence, a Soninke farmer was tied to a camel and dragged behind, a practice evoking times past when Bidhans punished their runaway Haratin this way.

Two growing and festering land conflicts were thus inflamed by this incident: one over the rules governing land rights, and the other between settled farmers and roving herders. That these conflicts were being expressed through historical patterns of ethnic oppression did not bode well for their easy resolution.

Indeed, the spark lit that day did not dwindle. It spread.

About a week later an identical incident occurred downriver in Matam, Senegal. There, the river had been reduced to a stagnant pool, with animals from the north regularly streaming across. One morning, some residents of Matam, Senegal seized goats found rummaging through their gardens, knowing these intruders belonged to Moors across the river. The Moor goat owners were furious and stood in the river channel shouting for the return of their goats, while above them Senegalese residents threw rocks their way, yelling back that their animals should remain on the river's northern banks.

Fortunately, no one was killed. But several Senegalese farmers were arrested by Mauritanian officials, then carted off to a Kaedi jail cell. Protests, shootings, and a couple of deaths followed, and soon retaliatory attacks spread hundreds of miles away to Dakar, Senegal. There, thousands of the capital's ubiquitous closet-sized Moor shops that dominated the commercial scene were pillaged, burned, and destroyed, and a handful of their Moor owners killed by vigilantes. Tens of thousands of Moors fled back north to their homeland.

Meanwhile, several hundred thousand black Africans made the reverse trip, some expelled from Mauritania because they lacked proper documents, often because officials had just confiscated them. Riots erupted in Nouakchott, and quickly became deadly. Moor gangs controlled the streets and murdered hundreds of black Africans in the open or after breaking into barricaded homes.

As this violent period began, I was nearing the end of my master's program at Michigan State and considering post-graduation employment options. One morning, I went to my favorite coffee shop. Settling into a window seat, I opened the *New York Times* to find a story splashed across its front page detailing the mayhem and killings taking place in Dakar and Nouakchott. In a bewildered state, I screeched back my chair and spilled coffee on the floor. A feeling of shock and helplessness swept over me, and I looked around, wondering if there may be some mistake in the story.

All day I kept this news to myself and avoided conversations with others. My memories of Civé had always evoked daily life: long walks to the fields, dust storms, the daily calls to prayer, women scrubbing their feet at the river, Mamadou scolding some Becce member for being tardy, my 'mother' poking fun at me, or the knowing look of Djeinaba. These images were now crowded out by ones of battered heads, deadly chases, and lifeless babies. This political development was one I had completely, naively, overlooked. And now all I could do was read about it in the alarming but impersonal language of journalists who included no news of Civé. I felt guilt and dread.

I tried to find out more, but reliable news was hard to come by, and much of what I learned came from reports written long after the fact. Once I managed a return to Civé, I was able to fill in the detail.

After the violence and mayhem in Nouakchott ran its course, the Mauritanian government announced it had thwarted a coup, and then followed up by purging the military of nearly every one of its black officers. Several thousand were imprisoned and tortured, including three army officials from Civé. One of these, Kalidou Konaté, was Mamadou's distant cousin and now husband to Mamadou's beautiful and talented daughter Kelly. Another officer, N'Diaye, was Mamadou's cousin and the husband of my friend Faba, who had teased me for keeping that Moor merchant's business card. N'Diaye had been one of the three men to bid me adieu on the tarmac that hot night two years earlier. All three Civéans were tortured but then thankfully let go. However, their release, along with thousands of others, was accompanied by legislation absolving the military of guilt for the death of 500 captive officers, all of whom were tortured to death.

"The country needs to look forward, not backwards," came the official reasoning for this amnesty. So embittered was the officer Kalidou Konaté by the horrors he saw and treatment he experienced, that he left his three wives and countless kids and fled the country penniless. Eventually, he gained refugee status in France where he remains today with his very large immigrant family.

This crackdown soon concentrated on the Fuuta and its residents, and in 1990 the military marched in to occupy it. Many Fuuta residents were labeled as Senegalese and sent packing. In some cases, the military chased every last resident of a village into Senegal. Then on their heels, Moors descended to claim the newly abandoned lands, animals, and fertile soils.

The main target for expulsion were those residing in the hundreds of small Fulbe enclaves sprinkled in dieri lands north of the river. According to Human Rights Watch, in short order the military emptied two-thirds of such villages. All told, half of the Pulaar population on the Mauritanian side of the river was expelled, most landing in refugee camps in neighboring Mali and Senegal.

This occupation was particularly intense in the region around Civé because of the region's history. This eastern stretch of the Fuuta had always been its most productive and densely populated area. In times past, it was here that Fulbe kingdoms had held court. In more modern times, it became known for its fierce opposition to the French, in part because of its location so far upstream that a dry riverbed provided rebels a seasonal refuge from the river-bound French. The last pocket of resistance to the French died in 1891 when its leader, Abdoul Bocar Kane, was assassinated just north of

Civé.

Dozens of small Fulbe enclaves near Civé, such as the one that hosted me and the blind woman's son Moussa, were emptied and refilled by Haratins. One night fifteen miles to the west of Civé, all members of the Fulbe hamlet of Nema were chased across the river. It was in Nema at a peaceful spot atop a small knoll, that Mamadou, the tractor driver, and I stopped one moonless night to revive ourselves with couscous and milk. Shortly, Nema was repopulated with dark-skinned Moors and renamed with the Arabic name, Dar-es-Salaam.

After chasing out its residents, the military turned to occupying the region. The dead town of Matam, Mauritania was transformed into a military headquarter. Soldiers came to reside in Civé, and soon accused twelve of its families of being Senegalese. Each had a day to head south. They did. The village baker Alasanne fled with his family. So too did my next-door neighbors the fisherman Harouna and his wife Maimona. The merchant Samba Anne fled back to his village across the river from Kaedi.

The village's imam, Thierno Ly, also originally hailed from Senegal, and was also given a day to leave. In a poignant display of resolve, the dying Samba Ba arose from his hammock once he learned this. With the aid of family members, he crossed Caangól Laddéegi and then climbed Civé Dow. He entered the imam's compound to await the returning soldiers. When they arrived, he informed them he would go to Senegal in place of the imam. After some indecision, the men threw up their hands and left. Just months before he passed on, Samba Ba, Civé's one-time Jom Wuro, had managed to pull off one final remarkably magnanimous act.

The news was rarely so good though. In some villages, residents were forced to swim across the river at gunpoint, some drowning in the middle. A few Civé residents, such as Koumba Binta, the woman who during my first months had given me a jealous scolding, simply fled in terror, heading south like so many of her ancestors had done in the past. The Pulaar proverb, *Maa rewo ronkaa nde worgo hodaa,* captures this feature of life in the Fuuta: "When the north is bad, the south is occupied." In bad times you may have to abandon your homeland.

Meanwhile, unemployed Moor shopkeepers, those no longer living in Senegal, descended on the Fuuta to open shops. Westerners and western organizations in Nouakchott fled the nation's violence and unstable political situation. As it shuttered its doors in the capital for good, CRS left all of its plans for Civé behind.

The timing of CRS's departure could not have been worse. Only two weeks prior to the violent outbreak, CRS had organized a region-wide workshop in Civé, one attended by leaders from a dozen nearby villages, a step in turning Civé into its regional headquarters. Somehow the decision was made in Civé to pay the event costs upfront with money stashed away by the women merchants. CRS would reimburse them later. Given the distance between Civé and Nouakchott, I imagine this arrangement made sense. But before any reimbursement occurred, CRS had fled the country, bringing an abrupt end to the women's now-bankrupt entrepreneurial activities.

When I first heard these tales five years afterwards while visiting Civé, my body went numb and I failed to hear the rest of Djeinaba's tale, except some reference to 'Allah is great.'

I wanted to cry out:

"No. This is not an instance when Allah is great, or Allah wills it." But I didn't. I just bit my lip, then went to the river to swim across.

***

According to the Mauritanian government, the military's presence in the Fuuta and its expulsion of black Africans were necessary measures to protect true Mauritanians from their enemies across the river. For two years, Mauritanian and Senegalese soldiers stared at one another across the water, guns at the ready. But the government's real agenda was to resettle the region and reclaim its resources. For six months, Civéans lived under the watchful eyes of soldiers who banned residents from trips to the river except during two designated midday hours. During those hours, gun-bearing soldiers accompanied villagers as they performed chores and gathered water. Other than that, people remained in their compounds, especially after villages witnessed uniformed officers shooting at fisherman a few miles upstream, heard of shootings and rapes elsewhere, and learned that eight miles downstream in Koundel, a troublesome villager's head had been cut off and displayed on a pole.

There were many other instances of violence and humiliation. Mamadou Konaté became a regular visitor at Matam's now well-staffed military post where he skillfully built friendly relations and bought favor. He arranged for the Becce cooperative to take turns preparing meals for the occupying soldiers, treating them as honored guests. Providing food to anyone was especially difficult as few dared to venture out to their fields. A severe food shortage led Becce to one day take out the three keys to the three locks, then open the iron doors of its warehouse. In short order, all seventy tons of the rice within was gone.

For two years this brutalization continued, a period now euphemistically referred by all as 'The Event.' One might be tempted to describe it as 'ethnic tension,' or more ominously 'ethnic hatred.' But the terror was not directly linked to ethnic hatred. For decades, domestic resources had been shrinking while competition for them grew. This challenge came mixed with the region's long history of contested land rights, now heightened by the goldmine international funders had created through their investments in motor pumps, bulldozers, fertilizers—and now I realized, Peace Corps volunteers like me. Unbeknownst to me, my efforts had been directed at stoking these tensions. Allah had help.

Chapter 43

The Aftermath

Shortly after that shocking article in the *New York Times* appeared, I finished my master's degree. I then landed a job evaluating agricultural projects in Africa. Our clients included the World Bank, the U.S. Agency for International Development, and the U.N.'s Food and Agriculture Organization. I often found myself touring Africa's rural areas in large, air-conditioned Land Rovers. Whenever we stepped out into the hot humid air to meet with farmers, the first thing I did was scan the crowd, wondering which farmer was deeply in debt, who was the true leader, and which one was, well, a buffoon who shouldn't be taken seriously. But soon our entire team would be dashing back into a cool vehicle to head for the capital.

Then there was my husband and family, developments that didn't square with frequent jaunts to Africa. So, I set my eye on becoming a college professor, and entered a PhD program in economics. I tried to maintain contact with friends in Civé, but communication was spotty. Even after The Event abated, little news came my way.

Shortly after the birth of my first son and about halfway through my PhD program and nine years after I left Mauritania, I finally arranged a trip to Civé. Late one morning and with no advance notice, I stumbled exhausted out of the back of a pickup truck headed from Matam to Kaedi. I was on the edge of the village.

Unbeknownst to me, Tall and Djeinaba had recently constructed a large concrete building here on the edge of the village just where I descended. Mamadou was coming from their place and stood a dozen yards from me when I hit the ground.

"Good morning," I said, straightening up after picking up my bag, then covering my face as the pickup's spinning wheels began showering me with dust.

Mamadou just stood staring at me, mouth wide open.

"What?? Just like this! You come?" he said in a familiar scolding tone. He rushed over, grabbed my bag, brushed it off, then ushered me into Tall and Djeinaba compound, talking more to himself than to me as he hurriedly led the way.

Tall and Djeinaba were both home and upon seeing me immediately let out cries of astonishment.

"My eyes are lying today!" Djeinaba exclaimed in disbelief as we hugged. "How did you get here?"

"Huh!! Don't you know how to write?" Tall said in a high-pitched voice, a grin spread across his face.

Mamadou, meanwhile, stood speechless, pushing his turban back and scratching the top of his head. He then announced he had business to attend to in Kaedi but would be back this evening.

Back and forth to Kaedi in one day? I thought. My *ears* must be lying. How does that happen?

Shortly, I was installed on a mat in Djeinaba and Tall's courtyard, and endless rounds of tea began. Word spread, and many visitors began stopping by. Sometime mid-morning I fell fast asleep, and remained so over the next twelve-hours ("Is she dead?" I vaguely recall hearing my mom Taanooy ask). Mamadou returned that night as I stirred to life.

"All day long, to and from Kaedi, I kept asking myself: did I really see her?" He was still astonished by my appearance.

The next day, I began learning who was and wasn't alive, who had fled the country, and who had been tortured or violated by the military. Once alive enough to walk around, I began encountering Civé's numerous Moor residents and several strategically placed soldiers.

During lunch on my second day, Djeinaba and I lay enjoying tea made by her oldest son, a fourteen-year-old boy who was two when I first met him. Tall was off with Mamadou on yet another trip to Kaedi.

"Why didn't you bring Mamadou?" Djeinaba asked, using the Pulaar name for my newborn son Benjamin.

"Oh. Too young. He just too small baby. Not even two," I replied.

"Not two? In the Fuuta, we say he should be with his mother," Djeinaba replied, surprised by my logic. It was the same comment everyone said to me, making it awkward to explain how vulnerable I would feel bringing a baby to their village.

I fell silent. Then I told Djeinaba my news.

"Mamadou born had bad heart. They cut him to fix," I tried, making a mark across my chest as I did.

"What?" I had Djeinaba's full attention, as well as her son's as he turned down the music and leaned our way.

"Do you mean surgery?" she inquired, her eyes big.

"Yes. Allah is great, now he fine. But nearly dies," I explained, my voice cracking.

"What happened?" she asked.

This subject was a difficult one for me, both emotionally and language-wise. But I had opened it, so I trudged onward. I began by drawing diagrams in the dirt beside us.

"Here is heart. Heart has blood. Blood comes here and leaves here to go to all of body. But lines cross, so heart is bad, not work," I tried. "Mamadou stay small, too small, cannot grow."

"So, what did they do?" she asked.

I gave my best attempt at a technical answer. "They cut open and fix. They move this here, and this here so heart is good," I drew as I talked. "Then they needle up his chest." I was sure my explanation made absolutely no sense.

"It's like fixing the irrigation canal," piped in Djeinaba's son Mamoudou.

"Yes. Yes. Like that. The irrigation pipes missed heart. So, they fix so heart gets blood," I said, reaching out and touching Mamoudou's leg in a show of appreciation.

Djeinaba let out a long low whistle-like noise. "Oh my Gooooddddddd. So scary." After a second, she continued: "Tubaak medicine. Wow. What it does. Here our babies just die."

"Yes. We are very lucky. Our medicine do miracle," I replied. "Ben's hospital, people come all over world. Next room was young girl from Morocco."

Another long low whistle, followed by a prayer for my son.

"Amin," I replied, wiping the heat from my forehead, and taking a gulp of water. To me, Ben's case had been a miracle.

We fell silent. Her son Mamoudou poured us saani, our second cup. After a minute, I asked the question I had been waiting to ask.

"The Event. What happened?"

Over the next thirty minutes, Djeinaba told me many stories. She explained how villagers survived the famine conditions by eating their seed corn, making haako out of the weed ulo, eating the tender shoots of the murotoki tree, and scavenging paggiri and water lily bulbs. When all else failed, kola nuts and the gum from patouki trees helped dull the pang of empty stomachs.

As Mamoudou poured us fartak, the third cup of tea, Djeinaba asked if I had heard about some incident in a gully.

"Gully? Here, Civé? What happen?" I asked. "No, I no hear. Tell me?"

She told me that during their extended stay in Civé, the occupying soldiers had taken and eaten animals at will. Djeinaba's uncle Kalidou had become a prime source because he owned one of the village's largest stocks. But the constant poaching of his dwindling herd made Kalidou angry. During a hot windy day in 1991, he complained to a higher-ranking officer, who at the time was visiting

Civé.

"He pleaded with him," explained Djeinaba. "His herds were disappearing and would soon be gone. He asked him that they eat them more slowly. The Moors are herders, they know this. The official agreed."

"So what happened?" I asked. "They stop goat killing?"

Djeinaba shook her head and looked away.

"Next day, it was awful. The soldiers came and called the men to Caangól Laddéegi. Then.." Djeinaba stopped and drank some water.

She continued: "Then they said they were calling a meeting. Outside the village."

"Like Matam?" I wasn't sure I was following her tale.

"No. They led everyone toward Tokomadji. They all had big rifles. All the men followed, and the women we wailed! So much wailing they heard our voices in Senegal. Our hearts were cut in two."

I was alarmed but confused. "What in Tokomadji?" I asked.

"Not Tokomadji. They led them to a gully." Then she added with a meaningful nod, naming the precise gully: "They led them to Caangól Pingu-Nai!"

This gully name translates to "Cow Shot Gully." It's an especially narrow gulch used in the past to herd cows for the orderly dispensing of vaccines.

"The men were trapped in there. The soldiers stood above with their big rifles! Oh the wailing! We didn't know what happened to them. I thought everyone was dead."

"What they want? What they do??"

Djeinaba wet her lips then continued. "They wanted to know who said they were eating the village's goats. Mamadou and Tall spoke up. They said the village goats were theirs to eat. Everyone said, yes yes! We are safer with you, eat our goats!"

Before I could ask, she continued: "Allah is great, Kaaw Kalidou had told his son to take a horse to Matam to get the big bosses here. They came and we ran after their truck. Everyone was angry. Everyone was scared. Then the men came home."

And, I imagined not a single one showed his face until a new day dawned.

***

Eventually, tension in the Fuuta eased, and the region returned to a new normal, one Pulaars now shared with Moor residents and soldiers. In Civé, a police box was erected across the lane from my now weather-beaten, roofless hut, just in front of the compound of my mother Taanooy and her now deceased husband Samba Ba. Meanwhile, several Moor merchants set up shop after chasing the hefty Samba Anne and his family back to Senegal. While villagers had always given Samba Anne mixed reviews, at least he was never taken for a spy.

During that visit, one woman after another came to thank me for registering their land. Apparently Permit #373/DCK had made a difference, giving them proof of their legal claim to the two-hectare plot Messur Lamborghini watered. I had initially been perplexed by their insistence on this permit; apparently, they sensed the precariousness of their claim.

But that claim proved contentious, as The Event reopened historical divisions within the village. Nalla, the high-ranking government official in Kaedi from Civé —the man who refused to help me acquire that permit—was one of the few black Mauritanians during The Event to side with the Moor government. As a well-positioned Fulbe, he attempted to cash in on this loyalty by seeking official sanction for his claim to both Cóndi Hiraande and the women's land. According to him, these lands belonged to his Ba clan and should be returned, just as land throughout the Fuuta was being 'returned' to Moor claimants. Navigating their own way through these treacherous times, some Civéans sided with Nalla. Eventually the conflict divided the village into two camps—those who supported Nalla and his claims, and those who fought them.

To counter Nalla's power, Mamadou Konaté and Djeinaba's husband Tall took the surprising step of joining the discredited government, becoming its 'elected' representatives in the village. This move was designed to offset Nalla's power. Amazingly enough, it worked: both the men's and women's cooperative managed to retain their land.

But word spread that Mamadou and Tall, now in cahoots with the government, were traitors. One night, some Fulbe on horseback took revenge. They crossed the river then pillaged the village that harbored those collaborators, carrying off their bounty into the night. Such retaliation occurred not only in Civé, but up and down the Fuuta. It harkened back to times of old, when the threat of fearless Fulbe raiders on horseback, capable of swift revenge, had for centuries helped maintain the Fulbe aristocracy's control of the region.

Not long after this, my "father" Samba Ba died, and due to his lineage, Nalla was selected to be the village's next Jom Wuro. Unlike the throning of prior Jom Wuros, though, most in the village boycotted this one.

Fortunately, Civé's fruit trees weathered that period. One of the first things I did during my trip back was visit Becce. Early one morning, I walked there with Amadou Demba. A half mile away, I caught sight of the trees looming green against the dusty grey sky.

"See! I told you," exclaimed Amadou Demba gleefully. "My mouth tells the truth!"

There before me loomed three hectares of magnificent 100-foot tall, fully mature mango trees. Unfortunately, though, there were no mangos to eat, although Amadou Demba assured me they were delicious. He pointed out his most productive tree, slapping her thick trunk as he looked up into her sprawling branches.

"I've made a lot of money off of her," he said looking back at me as he lit up the remains of a cigarette. He took a drag, and then flashed me his trademark wide grin that, except for a couple missing teeth, looked so familiar.

"I call her Keyti," he said with a deep hoarse laugh after taking a final drag.

The bananas had all died out after a half-dozen years, and the farmers hadn't had the money to replace them. A few remaining limes and scrawny guavas were still alive, but had proven fickle, requiring too precise dosages of fertilizers and too specific timing of insecticides. In a few short years, they'd be gone.

One day as promised, I visited Mamadou. It was one of few days he spent entirely in Civé, as he seemed constantly on the move. That much, at least, had not changed.

I entered his compound, my mind cycling through the many things I wanted to ask him. Then I saw him, surprisingly sitting tall at a sewing machine next to his dinndeere, his turban piled high. I had completely forgotten that as a young man, Mamadou had lived in a town up north earning a living as a tailor. Before that day, though, I'd never seen him actually sew. As he worked on his task, I greeted everyone, then sat with Mamadou's mother Koumba.

"Koumba, it is me, the tubaak Keyti. I happy see you," I said while holding her hand. In fact, I had seen her several times, but was pretty sure my visits didn't register. She was blind and seemed without memory.

"Yes, yes, how are you?" she asked, then changed the subject. "It is hot today."

After a few minutes chatting, and still sure she had no idea who I was, I saw Mamadou get up. I had a young girl take my picture with Koumba, then I got up to leave.

"May we pass the day in peace," I said to Koumba as I arose.

I straightened my boubou and before I retrieved my camera, Koumba reached out for my hand.

"Where are my kola nuts?" she asked.

Instinctively both hands shot up to cover my mouth. My chest fluttered and my throat tightened. I was speechless. Those within earshot were too, until one burst out in laughter.

"Tomorrow," I promised as I joined in the growing laughter while dabbing away tears. Koumba nodded her approval.

I then crossed the compound to where Mamadou awaited. He held out a small pile of carefully folded clothes he had just finished sewing: a miniature tunic; a gorgeous miniature midnight blue boubou with matching pants; and a lighter boubou made of colorful cloth.

"These are for my namesake," he said, referring to my son.

"They are beautiful, thank you. I send you picture of Mamadou in them," I promised.

Soon we ate and had tea while a steady stream of visitors came calling: Amadou Demba, Sadyo Konaté, Sira Sy, Ballal, Sala, even Thierno Ly.

I was glad for these distractions as Mamadou was pre-occupied with a dozen different problems associated with a dozen different people who came to see him. Without much understanding of who each person was and what they were referring to, most of these conversations went over me. When there was a break in the action, I turned to Mamadou.

"Still Jom Haaju," I remarked with a smile, referring to him by the name my mom Taanooy often used for him: Master of Problems.

"Yes, Jom Haaju. I have too many haajus, always," he replied with a thoughtful chuckle.

From Mamadou I learned that the Becce cooperative was functioning well, and Mamadou spoke to me of his many projects. He was, as I already knew, an elected government official. He also remained Becce's president.

"And President Cóndi Hiraande?" I asked.

"Doro," he replied. "Nothing has changed there."

The Union, however, had fallen apart during The Event. But

after he had inadvertently been launched into a political career, Mamadou was able to get the European Union to refund the Union and rice storage project.

"Now I am president," Mamadou reported.

"Thanks be to Allah," I replied.

After tea, the two of us walked over to where the rice warehouse was recently re-established; for the first time, I had no trouble keeping up with Mamadou's pace, as I noticed him picking his way rather than charging across the terrain.

The storage facility was open and filled with rice, just as it had been when I left nine years earlier. Mamadou directed us over to the new office he worked in, one shared with a French tubaak paid for by the European Union. On the way, we passed by the Women's Cooperative building. That structure was shuttered, and the yellow paint had faded to off-white. The building appeared as if no one had used it in years, which in fact they hadn't. I looked at the faint drawings on the side facing the river and could recognize cartoonish characterizations of each of the original four leaders, each engaged in a separate activity, one sewing, another dying cloth blue, a third displaying a crocheted blanket, and a fourth gently tending her sprouting onions. I took some solace in realizing the building had not succumbed to rain and neglect, as had my hut, but was sad that so much of what I thought we had accomplished had not outlasted me.

I had been naïve, I reflected. I had not paid enough attention to wider political considerations. But then again, maybe if I had, would I have packed it up and gone home much sooner, and accomplished much less?

We entered Mamadou's office. He sat down at his desk, put on glasses, then took off his turban. For the first time, I saw his head uncovered, and was surprised that his greyish whiskers were matched by a short crop of completely grey hair. At sixty years old, he looked surprisingly old and tired.

I turned to look at a poster on the wall of Mecca, wondering what had happened to my map of the world. On the other side of the room an air conditioner jutted out from the window.

"An air conditioner?" I asked with great surprise, glad for something to comment on. "Really?"

"The tubaak turns it on when he comes. We have a generator outside." He opened a shutter and pointed it out.

"Well. Nice during Koorka."

He smiled and paused. "Yes. It gets crowded when people are fasting."

He shifted through some papers and pulled out a letter from me written four months earlier.

"That's the letter," I exclaimed. "That when I tell you I come here. To visit."

"Yes, but saying you are coming, and coming. They aren't the same. Usually, they aren't the same. Anyway, we didn't know when you would come."

We turned to discuss his son Samba, who had been lobbying his father for permission to come to the U.S.

"I bought ten hectares of land by Matam, and a motor pump. Samba wants to go to America. I want him to farm. But things here are still not settled." His voice trailed off. He wanted his son to stay, but he also wanted a future for him. Would the Fuuta offer Samba one?

I imagine we both had that unspoken question.

A newly installed loudspeaker carried Thierno Ly's call to prayer all the way out to us. Mamadou rose and excused himself. We said our goodbyes as he locked the door to his office.

I continued across the gully to visit my mother and offer condolences for the loss of her husband, the old man Samba. On my way there, I reflected that Mamadou's activities continued to expand, even while age was slowing him down. He still ran Becce and its activities, was president of this new Union, was now active in politics, and constantly found himself summoned to Kaedi or Matam for this reason or that. In addition, he now had a ten-hectare plot of land along with a motor pump to irrigate it. It was too much. He wanted Samba to take his place, I knew. But I also knew that no one could *really* take his place.

On the day of my departure, Mamadou arranged for a Union truck to drive me to Matam where I would cross the river and catch a taxi to Dakar. Before I mounted the truck that morning, Mamadou made me promise:

"Next time do not just drop out of the sky. Let us plan for your visit."

"I be back soon, I not stay ten years," I promised. "And I tell you."

I quickly got in to avoid long choked goodbyes as a crowd gathered.

But that promise was not one I kept. That morning turned out to be the last time I saw Mamadou. As the truck drove off, we waved goodbye, and I turned to watch as he headed to the village to begin yet another long day of work.

Chapter 44

News

None of my friends in Civé made it to America to see the good hand we've been dealt; where rains fall, the government works, markets for just about everything exist, machinery does the grunt work, and courts substitute for political violence.

But the next generation did. Mamadou managed to send his feisty son, Samba, to America. Fourteen years earlier, while I was newly arrived in Civé, Samba and a host of other teenagers frequently took unwelcome refuge in my home. Some months later, he spent a day playing cards under a hanger during Aissata and Elimane's wedding, while nearby I cooked. And six months before I left, he spent a festive day planting trees at Becce, then splashing around with me in the irrigation basin.

Samba flew into New York's JFK airport one cold February night in 1998. I met him there armed with the thickest coat I could find. For the next several months, he lived with me and my family in our New Haven apartment where I did what his father had helped me do: integrate. A couple of Yale law students took up his cause, and through its Immigration Legal Services, gave him the legal counsel necessary to gain him asylum. Each day Samba's tall, good looks and deep commanding, at times bossy, voice reminded me of his father.

Two years later, Samba's sweet younger brother Abou followed, the young son who so often came to Mamadou's side to deliver messages, bring meals, or call his father to business elsewhere. As an adult, Abou has the quiet thoughtful demeanor of his uncle Sadyo mixed with the intelligence of his Nouakchott uncle Souleyman.

Both Abou and Samba are now American citizens, and both live and work in Columbus, Ohio. Samba lives with most of his grown children, often shuttling back and forth between Columbus and Mauritania. Abou, on the other hand, brought his wife to Columbus, and they now live in a house with all their many kids.

It was an early spring day in 2012 when Abou called. Hearing the phone ring, I gladly tossed aside the papers I was grading to answer it, gladder still when I saw it was Abou. His calls always brought news, laughter, and good-natured banter.

But not this time.

"I have good and bad news," he said, his voice flat.

His tone told me it was about someone close, not someone for whom I would have to dust off musty memories.

"He's alive, but my dad died yesterday," he continued. Initially confused, I realized Abou was telling me that his father had passed, living now in another world.

"Mama…?" I halted, my mind now racing through scenarios in which Abou had gotten it wrong. After all, how could he be sure what had transpired 5,000 miles away?

"Yesterday. In Nouakchott. He had a heart attack and died in the hospital. We thought he was getting better."

Abou added the bare details of Mamadou's final illness and unexpected heart attack. An image I've long carried of my own grandfather came to mind. One morning, when I was still very young, I learned that Grandpa had keeled over into the snow while retrieving something from his car. And that was that.

"May Allah have pity on him and forgive him," I murmured.

"Amin," Abou replied.

With nothing left to say, we bid goodbye and promised to talk soon.

The line now dead, I stared past the ungraded pile of papers before me as the spirit of Mamadou filled the room. There he was, wrapped in a sheer white sheath, Thierno Ly quietly chanting Koranic verses over him. The men from Becce somberly lowered his body into a freshly dug grave in Civé's shady cemetery. Then came those twenty-five-year-old memories where I saw myself jogging alongside his long urgent strides, listening to his constant harangues, and trying to keep up with his visionary explanations. Then conjured-up images of his last minutes crowded in, a bowl of rice and fish tumbling from Mamadou's lap and onto the hospital's concrete floor as his younger brother Souleyman and oldest son Mari unsuccessfully tried their best to revive him. *Where was the doctor? Was there a doctor?*

Unable to return to my task at hand, I called to my dog Lani and we headed outside. That afternoon, the two of us walked aimlessly up and down neat tree-lined streets beneath which the young shoots of tulips were springing to life. As the warm March air swirled, I paid silent homage to this man who had helped me carve out a role for myself in his tiny, beloved village of Civé.

It was now sixteen years since I last visited Civé. I often contemplated a return, but a career, two kids, a dog, and a husband always presented ready reasons why 'this year won't work.' But shortly after Abou's call, somehow, I convinced my seventeen-year-old son Ben, known to the villagers as Mamadou, to join me in the long trek to Civé.

Three months later, summer began, and the two of us joined hundreds and maybe thousands of others from across Mauritania, Senegal, Mali, and France on a pilgrimage to pay homage to this one-of-a-kind man of the Fuuta.

Chapter 45

The Trip Back

That trip to Civé was grueling. The first part, the trip to Dakar, went without hitch—until we reached the airport. Then we entered a taxi, me in front, Ben in back, our gear in the trunk. It was just after midnight.

Once zipping along the unlit, empty highway leading to the capital, our driver claimed not to know after all where Hotel Faidherbe was.

"I don't know this hotel," he claimed. "Plus, you pay too little for ride." He swore at me. He pulled over to the side of the pitch-black highway and without a word, got out and slammed the door shut.

"What's going on?" Ben asked, not clued into our conversation.

I had no idea what in fact was 'going on.' Heart fluttering, I put my hand on the cloth belt beneath my blouse that held money, passport, and credit cards, and recalled with a sick feeling how during my last trip through Dakar, a young rogue like this one had robbed me of nearly all my money.

I wanted Ben to stay calm, but I was deeply alarmed. I craned my neck to see where the driver was and became even more distressed once I saw how empty our highway was. In the glow of the one working taillight, I could make out the driver huddled in conversation with several young men. *Where did those guys come from? Do they have anything in their hands?*

"Mom, what's going on?" Ben repeated, this time leaning

forward.

"I don't know, but make sure you can exit quickly if we need to," I instructed.

"The luggage in the back?" he asked.

"Leave it," I said quickly as our driver headed our way.

"Got it, don't worry mom," Ben said as he moved his backpack from the seat to his lap. His tone gave me courage. He was a strong young man, and I was glad for his company.

The driver returned, slammed his door shut and then started the engine. Without any idea what to do, I inexplicably began berating him.

"We pay you good money. Take us to the hotel. You drive to Place de l'Independence and I get out there," I commanded, straining as I did to control the pitch in my voice, which was much too high. Before he could respond, I escalated by switching to the little Pulaar I could summon. "You are not good driver, you understand? We go to hotel now," I demanded in Pulaar, adding the one thing I knew how to say in his language of Wolof: "*Degg na Pulaar?*"

"No, I don't speak Pulaar. Your words make no sense," he said as he accelerated back onto the highway. *Good.* So, on I continued in Pulaar, hoping a verbal but senseless command of the car would convey my authority.

"It is sad, you there, me here, we go Fuuta, you hear? Listen? Straight ahead, turn left, no light. My mother's name is Taanooy, my father is a grand Marabout from Rosso. I go to the river to wash my clothes." I actually don't recall what exactly I said, and for sure my non-stop babble was much less coherent than this.

Still, I continued with nonsensical patter, eyes glued to the road, until thankfully I saw him take the exit for Dakar. Finally, he deposited us at a corner with a neon sign *Ho el Fa dhe be* looming above. I grabbed our bags from the trunk and gave him a stoic look to let him know his ruse did not work. Then, with Ben in front, I rushed inside the deserted hotel, shaking.

I'm too old for this, I thought, and while waiting for a clerk, began to feel simply horrible for having subjected my son to this episode, a feeling that only grew over the rest of this African Adventure of ours. *I should have paid more and arrived during the day,* I silently rebuked myself as Ben plopped down in a lobby armchair.

My wits slowly returning, I once again rang the clerk's bell, then looked up to see HOTEL FAIDHERBE boldly written above the rows of mailboxes before me.

Oh Lord, I thought in my misery, as the hotel's name suddenly registered. Why did I book a hotel named after the French general who was the mastermind behind the French conquest of the Fuuta, a man with a penchant for torching unsupportive Pulaar villages? A bad choice, one I was surely now paying for.

Fortunately or unfortunately, that trip to our hotel proved less traumatic for Ben, I think, than did the six hours spent next day at the Dakar taxi gare. The gare looked better than I remembered, but it was hot, dusty, and the negotiations nerve wracking. All day we were surrounded by aggressive vendors, people speaking incomprehensible languages, rude staring, the smell of urine, and broken promises. Drivers collected our fare, said we'd leave, and then abandoned us for an hour or two.

Ben sat in the sun fanning himself, and once seeing the food on display around us—large sides of raw beef swarming with flies, a stew with a fish head pointing up—decided he would eat nothing that day. The last straw came when he returned from the gare's 'bathroom' looking nauseous. Yep, those can be pretty awful.

"How long before we leave?" he asked with an empty expression.

"I don't know, I hope within a couple of hours. It seems no one will leave in the heat of the day," I responded trying to be hopeful.

"No, I mean leave, leave. Like leave Mauritania," he said.

"Oh," I said looking around for something of interest to show him yet finding absolutely nothing. I had tried to entice him into drinking one of those delicious coffees with condensed milk, but he didn't bite. How do you make eighteen days sound like no time at all to a seventeen-year-old?

With each hour, Ben became more irritable, and my stress level rose. As I tried to figure out how and when to leave, I felt increasingly overwhelmed. I needed help and did not see anyone around who could provide it. I never liked Dakar, and this trip did nothing to change that judgment.

"Can we just go back to the hotel?" Ben asked.

I recalled my own first night in Dakar decades earlier, and how that evening I'd been drawn back to the safety of my hotel and its welcome air conditioning.

"Keep an eye on our luggage," I replied, as our bags were now secured with a large net to the top of a nearby van whose driver three hours earlier had promised to leave 'soon.'

I scolded myself as once again I began scouring the parking lot. *Why did I think this was a good idea?* He is only seventeen. I had been twenty-four and had a month's preparation before stepping into Dakar's streets.

As luck would have it, I soon chanced upon a man going directly to Matam. He was a merchant and was willing to sell me the extra seats in his large van. While I looked him over trying to decide, he handed me his business card. It identified him as a merchant, but also a Marabout. Trusting in his religious credentials, I agreed and handed him some cash.

"We will go direct to Matam, but I must stop in Thies for a short stop. A relative died and I must stop to pray," he informed me.

"This is fine," I replied. "We are going on a *duuwaawu* ourselves, to the village of Civé."

He looked surprised. "Mauritania?"

"Yes," I replied. "I worked there three decades ago. Mamadou Konaté died in March."

"And you come back for *duuwaade*?" he said stepping back to look me over again.

"Yes. He and I work together."

The Marabout took this information in, then after a moment's reflection, reached into his pocket and returned my money.

"Allah has willed it. I will not charge you and your son," he replied. Then he excused himself to buy the last of his supplies. My help had arrived.

***

Two hours later, we were speeding north in the merchant's van. As we did, Ben worried aloud about how much hotter it could possibly get.

"It's night. Doesn't it cool off?" he asked as he rolled down the window.

I recognized his panic. It was the same I'd felt my first hot season, as if one is trapped in an oven wondering if you've yet reached the preset temperature. I again wondered why I thought a crash course in cultural and physical adaptation was the ticket for this seventeen-year-old young man, especially one wanting independence from his mom. Not a well thought out plan. I knew I was dragging him along because this trip was not one that I wanted to make alone. I appreciated his company and felt safer for it. But I knew my request that he join me ("you'll learn a lot; it will be interesting") had been a selfish one.

After an endless overnight taxi ride, early morning we loaded into a motorized pirogue parked alongside Matam, Senegal's steep banks. After paying our twenty-five-cent fare and squatting low in the hull, a warm thunderstorm hit mid-river and soaked us. As we continued across, a familiar, earthy smell of muddy water arose, stirring my body awake. I looked downriver, feeling we were close.

After waiting out the storm in Matam, I arranged for a kind one-armed Pulaar with a horse cart to bring our luggage over the now-muddy road to Civé.

Some years earlier, Mamadou's family had relocated to a large new compound on the eastern side of town, out beyond my hut, and just behind where Djeinaba and Tall's new-ish mansion stood. As the three of us reached this new village edge, there, perched outside his compound's concrete walls was Mamadou's son Samba, who had been visiting from America when his father died. He remained there still. Samba was keeping half an eye out for us, having kept our arrival secret in case we couldn't make it.

Seeing us approach in the distance, Samba let out a loud cry, jumped up, and came jogging out to meet us, his arms open and his smile wide. Soon he was ushering us into his family's compound, a quarter the size of a football field and encircled by three gigantic new concrete buildings. A large neem tree spread open smack in the middle of this grand home.

Luggage in hand we entered, and delayed cries of joy went up. I wasn't sure I recognized anyone, although all the faces looked vaguely familiar. Soon I was hugging females and holding out my hand to males. Ben, stunned into silence, sat down on a wooden dinndeere under the neem tree. The others crowded around him in a way I knew he would find annoying, particularly after the previous long, stressful, and sleepless day.

"That Mamadou," I announced. "My son, my older. Samba, younger, not come but he and Daouda send greetings." Samba was my second born, named James. I gave him the Pulaar name Samba after our current host, Mamadou's son, moved in with us just after James' birth. Daouda was my husband, Dave.

"Mamadou not carry heat. He not used to Fuuta. He drink?" I just managed, my tongue and brain not working well together.

Someone handed my son a pot of water. Samba assured us it was safe to drink, and Ben drank deeply, laid back, and then fell sound asleep. There he remained pretty much all day while a stream of visitors curiously inspected and occasionally gathered around his oddly splayed body.

In fact, Ben did not carry the heat at all. He hardly budged from that spot over our two-week stay. At first, I was alarmed, and watched him closely, once again finding myself mentally calculating the time and logistics involved in getting medical care, especially when one afternoon he arose, wobbled, then collapsed to the ground.

After that fall, a youngster was charged with sitting near him, and I was relieved to know there were always many eyes on him. Then Ben discovered he could play games on his Kindle and wound up spending hours in the shade teaching all the youth—and a few elders—to play Angry Birds. Shortly everyone was engaged in good-natured fighting over whose turn it was to play next, and Ben's spirits picked up a tad.

***

During those first moments in Civé, I greeted the compound residents, and with several sweeps of the eye, took in this palatial new home. Then I belatedly glanced around. Where were Mamadou's two widows? Samba had been busy giving orders, including one to slaughter a nearby goat tethered to a stake. But when I asked where his mothers were, he stopped to indicate an open doorway above which dark blankets covered decorative concrete bricks. Those blankets signified that the widows within were in mourning and would remain secluded for four months.

I walked over to the threshold leading to their enclosed patio, then murmured blessings into the darkness. On my left through the dim light, I saw Samba's mother Fati Diallo, Mamadou's first wife, the one who several decades earlier had lost her infant Abdoulaye. Fati was sitting on a mat on the floor. Very softly she was calling out.

"Wane, Wane, Wane."

I could barely make out her shrouded figure, but hearing her voice awoke something deep within me.

"Diallo, Diallo," I responded as I approached, the dark room smelling strongly of incense. I got on my knees, and we hugged, her body feeling alarmingly frail. A few beams of light fell gracefully across Fati's somber face, and I saw tears gliding down her cheeks. Mine slipped out as well

Quietly, we exchanged benedictions over her husband's soul. I squeezed a thin hand and sat silent.

"I return," I said, then crossed to the opposite side of the patio where sat another woman, her back against the entryway. Light from the doorway highlighted her features; her face appeared sad, puffy, and considerably older than the woman stored in my memory. It was Mamadou's second wife Kadiatou Demba.

If Mamadou's first wife Fati had been like a mom to me, Kadiatou was like a sister, one who liberally employed her wicked sense of humor to tease me. I sat next to her, and we embraced. First joy, then sadness, then a rush of long-forgotten memories coursed through me. I took off my glasses and wiped my face. Wiping hers, she asked after my journey, my parents, my husband, my sons.

"Mamadou's namesake is here with me," I managed.

"Good. I will meet him," she responded with emotion.

Unable to speak more, I said we'd talk later. She nodded, and shading my red eyes, I exited the patio's shadows and entered the bright muggy sunlight.

As I did, a loud cry went up.

"It's true!" A stout, matronly looking but still handsome Djeinaba stood staring with an exaggerated look of disbelief. With both hands covering her mouth, she jogged over, then hugged me. While holding my hand, she told everyone within earshot her tale. "I was in the fields and my cousin called saying Keyti had just arrived," she began in a loud voice, addressing a growing crowd.

"Keyti? But no," she continued, her voice rising. "I knew she had to be mistaken. Keyti was in Mozambique."

She was referring to Keyti, my namesake, a child born to a leader of the Woman's Cooperative while I was in Civé. A decade or so earlier, Keyti had married Djeinaba's second son, and the two now lived in Mozambique.

"So, I said, 'What do you mean? She can't be here. My son would have told me. And then she said, 'No, it's not Keyti Djigo, it's Keyti Baird.' And I said, 'What? I can't hear you. What did you say???'"

By now Djeinaba's story was drowned out by the chorus of others, few of which I followed, except that all expressed joy over my appearance, followed by wonder over this strange-looking young tubaak with a patchy red beard who was conked out on the dinn-deere, mouth wide open.

Djeinaba let out a hearty laugh and turned to face me. "Why didn't you tell us you were coming?" Before I could respond, a stunned Tall arrived. Soon we were all sitting on a newly made-up seat of honor near my unconscious son, and were sipping delicious, rich tea, the taste of which ushered in a flow of memories. Though I understood little of what was said around me, it almost felt like I'd never left. And the stress of that three-day voyage thankfully melted away.

***

I must have had seven rounds of tea that day while sitting on Mamadou's dinndeere, as each visitor led to yet another. After a lunch of goat and rice, I got a young son of Samba's to guide me around this side of the gully. I visited my old family across the lane and learned that my mother Taanooy had died several years earlier. I admired the large concrete house now located aside my old neem tree and greeted the new residents. I was amazed by the number of houses, both constructed and under construction, in this part of town. I used to jokingly refer to my neighborhood as 'Civé's suburbs.' Now it really had that feel.

Samba's son directed me to the new concrete home of the now-elderly former president of the Women's Cooperative, Sala. I stood a distance away in her courtyard as she, wide-eyed, finished her afternoon prayer.

"It's true," she exclaimed once she'd completed her recitations. With effort she arose, and we embraced, then fell to exchanging news.

"This neighborhood big now. Every person move here, why?" I asked.

"Everyone wants to live out here now," she told me. "The village is too crowded and hot; no breeze enters it."

I recalled that that was why Mamadou had spent Koorka on my veranda three decades earlier. The slightly elevated and more spacious real estate promised more frequent breezes than the compact village ever could. Space here was plentiful, and people were now taking advantage of that. And in addition to building large, plush concrete compounds, I noticed that nearly everyone had a well within. And several compounds, like Mamadou's, were topped with solar panels that at least intermittently provided electricity to charge phones, run refrigerators, and play videos on flat screen TVs.

Where did all this money come from? I wondered in astonishment. Later, my host Samba explained.

"Everyone who has built out here has a family member in France, Nouadhibou, Nouakchott, Columbus, or Mozambique. If they don't, they want one so they can build out here. This compound," he continued, with a proud sweep of his hand, "was built by Abou and me." My country, which during my stay was famous for the foul-tasting kinidi cooking oil it sent, now provided Civé with employment, the results of which surrounded me. That, I was sure, was much better than rancid oil.

Not only did dozens of compounds now have their own well, but those without used centrally located spigots which dispensed water originating from solar-powered storage tanks near the foothills of Dow Hayre. No doubt this was a huge boon to Civé's women and the overall health of its residents. Yet it also changed village life. It was hard to imagine people no longer gathering daily at the river's edge to clean dishes, bathe, wash clothes, and gossip.

Within an hour of arriving, I noticed another remarkable change: everyone had cell phones. Having skipped landlines and gone directly to cellular technology, these devices now substituted for the children who for centuries had served to relay messages. And they also brought the world to Civé, as villagers talked daily to family in Nouakchott, Ohio, France, Mozambique, and South Africa. In these small ways—the technology, the knowledge, the villagers' increasing self-reliance—Civé had taken on features that as a westerner, I found more familiar.

Yet amid such remarkable signs of change, I soon discovered that much in Civé remained the same. Cóndi Hiraande still limped along with broken motor pumps, sparsely attended meetings, and campaigns consisting of a mishmash of crops planted whenever. While the now ninety-something-year-old Doro was no longer its president, it looked like he was.

Early one morning I woke Ben up to accompany me to Becce. After a slow hour walk, we arrived. I was surprised to find so few in the fields. It was, after all, the start of the rainy season. In my era, nearly everyone would have been present; if they weren't, Kebe would have marked them for a 100-ougiya pawgol.

Leaving Ben in the spotty shade of a thorny namari bush, I headed toward a distant, lone man in the fields swinging a jalo. Shortly before reaching him, I recognized his torn T-shirt, broad shoulders, and widely wrapped turban. It was my old friend, Mamadou's quiet younger brother, Sadyo.

"My friend! Konaté, Konaté, Konaté," I called out.

My limited Pulaar vocabulary had slowly been coming back to me, and soon the two of us were exchanging news.

"Why no rice here?" I asked after a while, having scanned the fields around me. Indeed, the mixture of crops and the sparsity of people gave Becce the feel of Cóndi Hiraande.

"I'm one of the few to plant rice this year," he remarked, looking down at a plot densely packed with rice seedlings. "And we don't do a nursery anymore. We just throw our seeds to the wind. See?"

He gave a dissatisfied snort, and indeed I saw that his was the only plot around with rice, and it clearly was not a neatly transplanted one.

"Who president now? Who take Mamadou?"

"No one. We have no one. We don't know what to do. So, I just throw my seeds to the wind. In the Fuuta it is just...."

"Pick and shovel," I ended for him.

He looked up surprised, then chuckled. "Or shovel and pick," he finished with a good-hearted laugh, one that had not changed and that briefly filled me with melancholy nostalgia.

"See. That's all it is. I sent all my sons to Nouakchott for education." He put his hands on his back and straightened up with a wince. "I'm too old for this."

Indeed, he was. I remembered the one rice campaign I attempted, the one Sadyo had helped me manage. How lucky I was not to have had the fate of Sadyo. In fact, three years after this meeting, Sadyo took to his bed and despite the interventions of several Marabouts, never arose. That lovely gentleman now rests in a shadowy spot near his older brother Mamadou.

"So, I see wells now. All over Civé. And people drink. Before, people, wells, no like, they like river."

"You know? The old people still prefer the river. I still go there to drink," he confessed with a smile. "But the young people won't drink from the river. They say it makes them sick."

Good! I thought but nodded sympathetically.

Turning around, he pointed to the orchard looming in the distance. "You see the mangos? They are still here. Lots of mangos."

I asked for a tour, and Sadyo happily dropped his jalo to accompany me to those giant trees, each one still towering 100 feet up.

"They still give birth a lot, a whole lot," he remarked with a grin.

After touring the mature orchard, I bid Sadyo farewell, walked over to gaze up into the protective arms of Baaba Njiia, and then returned to retrieve my son. On our way home, we passed through the women's garden. Messur Lamborghini's heart gave out long ago, and the women hadn't the money to replace him. That afternoon I found a few women in the fields and learned they had replaced Messur Lamborghini with daily prayers for rain. And instead of onions, tomatoes, and cabbage, they grew cassava, hot peppers, and eggplant; vegetables less easily killed by droughts.

***

Later that afternoon, Malaaɗo Camara summoned me.

"She wants to see you, but cannot walk out here," Samba's wife Oumou told me after I returned from Becce.

Malaaɗo was one of my favorite women in the village. Long ago, she had been the dynamic leader of the gardening group and had spent many an afternoon with me under my neem tree helping to manage the faltering Women's Cooperative. And it was she who long ago in Matam told me that Madame Diaw 'had thrown dust in their eyes.' After that, Malaaɗo convinced the other women to take Madame Diaw's land. I always felt a special bond with Malaaɗo, as she was filled with common sense, good judgement, and often confided in me. And I too took the unusual step of occasionally confiding in her.

That afternoon, with many kids for company, I headed across the gully to Malaaɗo's. As I approached her entryway, she stood, and in a way I instantly remembered, began blowing kisses my way. "Wane. Wane. Wane. Baird. Baird. Baird." With effort she shuffled over to meet me as I stepped through the same gap in her fence that I had strode over a hundred times before.

Once in Malaaɗo's compound and seeing her hobbled approach, memories of the countless times I had visited her washed over me. Then, tears streaming down her cheeks, Malaaɗo stood before me, and with leathery hands was reaching for my face while still chanting my name. Uncontrollable emotion welled up in me as my eyes met hers and in a quick glance, took in her facial scars, almond eyes, and crooked teeth. Out it all spilled. The two of us hugged each other tightly, both of us now openly weeping. During this swell of bittersweet emotion, I became vaguely aware of kids circling around our joined bodies, commenting on the spectacle before them while guessing whether auntie or the tubaak was crying more.

Malaaɗo and I stood wordlessly hugging for what seemed an eternity, my head on her shoulder and hers on mine. I smelled her hair oil and smoky skin and felt the relief of both sorrow and joy leave my body. Since arriving, uncontrolled memories had been stirring my insides and spinning my head, and I often wondered if I might be dreaming. That afternoon with Malaaɗo, I knew I was not.

Eventually, Malaaɗo and I breathed deeply, separated our bodies, then sat together on the same dinndeere on which I had so often sat with her. She had been one of the village's five boutique owners, and once a month I had passed hours here doing our 'control.'

We exchanged news of our kids, and in her case, her grandkids, some of whom surrounded us. Most of her words floated by me, and probably mine by her. But that day, we communicated without words.

"We miss Mamadou, may Allah bless him. It isn't the same without him," she said after sending someone off for tufam.

"Amin, Amin," I replied. "He was leader, he was leader like no leader. Even in America, I say, 'Mamadou is best leader. What Allah wanted has happened'."

"Civé has never been the same after you and Mamadou," she said, holding my hand and patting it. "You changed us."

"I follow Mamadou. He leads. I follow," I replied, which really was true.

Someone handed me a bowl of tufam. I took the gourd spoon

and drank. Passing the bowl to Malaaɗo, I continued with a small laugh. "You know, I have records of boutique sales. You. I keep still. Reminder your boutique?"

"Ha!" Malaaɗo replied. "Of course, you and Kelly did the controls. You have those notebooks?"

"Yes, all." I said and we both chuckled as I signaled a stack a foot high. "All my Civé stories."

"Koumba Binta," she said laughing. "And Doro Thioubu." Her laughing doubled. She paused, thought, then added, "Maybe now you can write a book. About Mamadou and the good work you two did."

"And the women," I added, committing Malaaɗo's suggestion to a storage spot in my brain.

After the tufam had been passed around, I got up, and greeted all I hadn't already, including Malaaɗo's co-wife Sira, who was also Mamadou Konaté's older sister. We blessed Mamadou's soul along with the soul of Malaaɗo and Sira's recently departed husband Saloum, and his older brother Bocar, both of whose absence in the compound I felt.

Then prayer time arrived, and my visit with Malaaɗo came to an end.

***

One morning, a few days into our stay, I meandered over to the village's police booth located a few dozen yards from my host Samba Konaté's compound. There for the first time I found present the Pulaar police officer posted to the village. Diop was alongside the booth sitting atop a rusty mattress spring, a teapot boiling at his feet. To my delight, the town crier Ballal was sitting aside him.

"Look Keyti, I'm still alive," he said as I approached. "Mamadou died. May Allah forgive him. But your friend Ballal didn't. It's not the same without him, is it?"

"No. And all phones. Phones everywhere. No more town crier,

everyone use phone," I said, commenting on the passage of time which left him, the town crier, without need for a successor.

"Ah. True. But I still cry out! The villagers may not need me anymore. But I still walk the lanes, telling everyone when to rise for Koorka and when to gather for a meeting. The elders, we don't have watches or phones, so they need me." He pulled up his worn tunic to display his swollen legs and misshapen feet.

"Only thing is, it takes me forever to get around the village on these," he said with a gritty laugh joined by that of the officer aside him. The town crier Ballal had always been like baseball's designated hitter, filling whatever role was needed of him. And even though he no longer could do much, each day it seemed, he suited up.

"Crying is hard work. Village now big, many many houses," I said with a sweep of my arm.

"The poor people, those with nothing, we still live in the village. We can't afford it out here," he commented with a grin.

Indeed, Ballal had always been among the poorest of the poor, which was why he always did whatever anyone asked of him, whether it was announcing a meeting, fixing my wayward fence, or slaughtering a goat. In fact, the word ballal, meaning help or assistant in Pulaar, was a humorous moniker assigned to him. I often suspected it was a slightly demeaning one. But no matter. A bit like a court jester, Ballal always played his role, and played it well.

Just then, a thin man came striding our way. The torn boubou, wiry body, weathered skin, dark sunglasses, and lopsided gait told me it was Amadou Demba. He looked almost the same, except his hair was grey, his skin sagged, and once his sunglasses were removed, his eyes were milky. And, as I soon learned, he no longer smoked.

Amadou Demba and I finished our warm greetings, and I learned his news. The poor state of his eyes had made farming impossible and so he hadn't been to Becce in over a year. However, praise be to Allah, a son working in Nouadhibou sent him money. He pulled out a small photo album he'd stashed in the large front pocket of his tattered boubou. Flipping through that precious keepsake of his life, I saw an ID card now four decades old from the Ivory Coast, pictures of his grown kids, a newspaper article about the two of us that had somehow wound up in the *Honolulu Advertiser,* and then a picture of my mom sitting next to an American flag, her annual picture at the elementary school where she had worked.

"Our mom," he said. And then, most poignantly, a final picture. His young daughter Mairam, the one who died on her parents' bed during my first year in Civé. "It's the only picture I have of her. Thanks be to Allah that you took this."

Bidding goodbye to Ballal and officer Diop, Amadou Demba and I walked over to the Union buildings. Slowly and steadily, internal strife over the last few years had caused the Union to fall apart. Just as the tractors stopped working, so too did the organization. Without a steady stream of outside dollars from the European Union, it folded up, leaving a large compound full of abandoned, rusty tractors and agricultural machinery.

I pondered the sad sight of such valuable but now-neglected machinery pelted daily by blowing sand. I imagined that as Mamadou's ability to galvanize energy and assure goodwill faded, so too did the bonds that had held the Union together. Today, the Union's buildings and rice warehouse join the deserted women's center, their presence in the village like some archeological remnants of a distant epoch that predates the memory of most. I wondered what, if anything, the youngsters in the village knew of that past.

On my previous trip back, I had been haunted by the failure of so much of my efforts to outlive me. This time, thankfully, I did not feel personally responsible for all the forsaken projects scattered about.

Yet despite all that was lost, I also stumbled upon surprising evidence that life in Civé was improving. First there was the unambiguous good news of phones, wells, and electricity. Then one day I chanced upon a woman whose husband drove a taxi in New York

City. His income bought her a fancy sewing machine powered by the solar panels atop her roof. One afternoon, she sat cheerfully in a living room cooled by an electric fan, a large pile of expertly sewn clothes on one side, material for more on the other. A steady stream of clients provided her with a reliable flow of income. Wow, I thought, remembering those endless meetings under my neem tree where we tried to accomplish something one-tenth this ambitious.

Several wealthier farmers had broken off from the cooperatives and acquired their own land and pump, similar to what Mamadou had done out beyond Becce when years earlier he bought those ten hectares. Surrounding the men's and woman's cooperative fields, today in Civé you'll find a host of small privately-owned irrigated plots.

I also visited a new project begun by Djeinaba's older brother, now back from years in Mozambique. He had secured some land near the old patouki grove on the village edge. On it he had built a large pen where he now raised tortoises.

"A Fulbe who herds tortoises?" I joked with him.

"Things change," he responded.

"Who eat meat of turtle?" I asked.

He shrugged. "I hear people in Senegal eat it. We don't. But someone will."

He went on to discuss other projects, including a new agro-pastoral one. He talked of plans to buy cattle bred in the Netherlands that could produce three times the milk of the local Zebus.

Seeing these entrepreneurial activities alongside the skeletal remains of the Union, Woman's Center, and rice warehouse, I couldn't help but wonder if the whole notion of 'cooperatives'—the activity I'd promoted for nearly three years—had been misguided from the start. Cooperative enterprises had been challenged by culture, history, illiteracy, and self-interest.

And now "The Event" and subsequent political developments introduced yet another challenge: politics. If you have someone with Martin Luther King's charisma and Abraham Lincoln's political acumen rolled into one, you might get that model to work. But that's not a very sustainable model. Civé today seems a testament to that.

And yet the Mauritanian Government, in collaboration with international organizations, continues to promote irrigated rice, holding these cooperative projects up as the hope for the region. Even though forty years of experience indicates rice is failing its potential— services remain poorly coordinated, cooperatives lack key ingredients for success, and farmers are still left in debt; the land under rice cultivation has grown tenfold since the 1980s. Numerous abandoned perimeters and unsuccessful projects up and down the Fuuta do not seem to dampen visionary statements or pause the flow of international investments.

While rains in the Sahel remain below their historical average, more rain falls than during the devastating decades of the 1960s, 70s and 80s. At the time, experts thought the drought was exacerbated by residents stripping the land bare, which changed wind and convection patterns. But they no longer believe this. Those changes in rainfall patterns were most likely harbingers of long-term climate change.

Meanwhile, despite repeated denials by officials, slavery still exists in Mauritania. I never directly saw it, but volunteers posted in Moor communities always commented on the indentured servitude they witnessed. It's a touchy issue, obviously, and is bound up in cultural practices within a deeply hierarchical society which make slavery *per se* hard to identify. Even in Civé, the remnants of the Bambara population's servitude to Fulbe patrons remains evident, with Ballal being one example of that. With Mauritania's support of the West's anti-terrorism activities, the geopolitics of the region also mean that Westerners are not eager to criticize Mauritania's internal politics. Yet in 2018, the *Economist* magazine reported that the Mauritanian Government regularly tortured and imprisoned the country's numerous anti-slavery activists.

A large majority of girls in Mauritania continue to have part of their genitalia removed. According to a recent UNICEF report, not only does this occur to most girls, but unlike elsewhere, the practice does not appear to be abating. That said, there is guarded good news on some health fronts. Infants are still ten times more likely to die in Mauritania than they are in the U.S., but the infant mortality rate is way below what it was in the 1980s.

As for politics, The Event left the once-neglected Fuuta integrated into a national political system. Matam, Mauritania has become more than some forlorn forgotten government outpost, and regional mayors have some clout. Two decades ago, Tall became Civé's mayor, an office that comes with power and influence. A couple of years earlier, I had seen Tall in France when my family and I had dropped in on the former army official Kalidou Konaté, a cousin of Mamadou's. Kalidou had been tortured by the government during The Event and had found refuge in France.

To my great surprise, I found Tall also visiting Kalidou, as he was in France on official business. As mayor, Tall gets such perks and more, which leave others jealous and suspicious of him. Not surprisingly, some covet his position. Recently an election for his post divided the village between two candidates. Tall won. For some reason, he also became Cóndi Hiraande's president. Now when Tall calls cooperative meetings, villagers equate attendance with political support, and many fail to show. And so Cóndi Hiraande operates as well as can be expected when many members harbor thoughts of sabotage in their hearts.

On the bright side, conflict between Moors and black Mauritanians has waned, even though deep racial and ethnic divides remain. There is a hopeful semblance of democratic institutions and (for the region) a reasonably free press. Mamadou Konaté's younger brother Souleyman, who hosted me during trips to Nouakchott, was even elected mayor of a Nouakchott district. Such changes have helped built trust among Mauritania's diverse communities.

The rest of my visit revealed to me that what I'd seen in Civé was not unique, as all the other villages dotting the river's right bank had wells, water spigots, new concrete buildings, cell phones, cell-phone towers, and the occasional solar panels. These were good signs that the government had used new wealth from recently developed gold mines, to prioritize basic needs over rewards to its clan. The roads were far better, and potable water and cell towers were visible everywhere. I also learned that many more youth, male and female, attended school without traveling prohibitively long distances. And now there is the huge potential for the internet to transform education and provide villagers with the information and communication that until recently was sorely lacking.

***

Departure day from Civé, Samba secured a place for Ben and me in an early-morning pick-up truck to Kaedi. Standing in the sandy lane, we said our goodbyes and were off in luxury. Once in Kaedi I bought two spots in a taxi with comfortable seats, one person to each, and air conditioning that worked. The formerly rutted, washboard-like road leading out of Kaedi was smooth black asphalt. From Kaedi to Nouakchott, no sand piles or large potholes required navigating around, no flat tires needed fixing, no two-hour lunch with tea was taken; there wasn't even a stop in the desert at prayer time. Between Kaedi and Nouakchott, though, we did encounter at least ten 'security' stops requiring us to produce identification and information on our origin and destination. Uniformed officials peered in the taxi, taking a second look at Ben in the front and me in the back. But we attracted only curiosity, and several asked after our welfare.

"Is all, OK?"

"You haven't encountered any problems?"

I found this odd, but smiled and assured them that, thanks be to Allah, all was very well.

Officials did take interest in the young Malian sitting next to me, however. After closely inspecting his passport, one solider asked him to descend to the small roadside "customs" office.

"Is anything wrong?" I leaned forward to ask our driver, wondering if I should be concerned. He shrugged, shut off his engine, then took out his cell phone and began playing a game.

The young man on the other side of me offered-up his bag of biscuits and explained. "He's from Mali."

"Oh," I answered while helping myself to a handful, even though I had no idea what he meant.

Despite these stops, we arrived in Nouakchott in record time, in fact four hours earlier than I had anticipated.

Mamadou's oldest son Mari picked us up at the taxi garage and drove us to his home. That afternoon, Nouakchott's paved streets were clogged with traffic and roundabouts. Numerous streetlights—I still recall the hoopla accompanying the installation of the nation's first one—directed traffic, and cars mounted sidewalks to circumvent jams. Above me countless billboards hovered, advertising electronics, banking services, a Carrefour grocery store, and an anti-corruption campaign. My senses on overload, I was disoriented with the divide between my memories and these surroundings.

Mari, his wife, and their two teenaged daughters were exceptionally gracious hosts over our four-day stay. Old friends came by to visit, including the women Faba, who had taken my dad's picture from me decades earlier; Kebe, who now worked in Nouakchott; Souleyman Konaté; Faba's husband Mamadou N'Diaye, who had been imprisoned some decades earlier; Djigo, the English teacher at the University of Nouakchott; Kadiatou Yero, a leader of the women's cooperative back in the day; and Oumar, the son of our beloved Peace Corps chauffeur Demba. Demba had been chased to Senegal during The Event, and several years earlier had passed away. Yet he lives on as Oumar is the spitting image of that fine man.

During our first night in Nouakchott, Ben and I lay on thick matlas in Mari's spacious family room while a large flat-screen TV broadcast the news. The family housed teenagers from Civé who attended high school in Nouakchott, one of whom was Mamadou's youngest son, Youssef.

Several, including Youssef, joined us that night. They engaged in jovial banter as the newscaster from Dakar reported on the war in Syria and conflict over nuclear power in Japan. When she turned to events in Mali, the boys' chatter stopped. Up went the volume.

The story focused on religious extremists in northern Mali and showed clips of these fanatics, called Salafists, destroying ancient mosques in Timbuktu and Gao, burning sacred texts, and defacing the shrines of Sufi saints, including those built to honor the 19th century political and religious warrior Oumar Tall and the Algerian Saint Ahmed Tidjiane. Having been ousted from Middle East outposts, there jihadists billed themselves as 'religious purists,' and gathered local supporters by stirring up latent ethnic conflict. Now they controlled vast expanses of northern Mali, and were advancing south toward Mali's capital, raining terror on residents through murder, mutilation, and the cutting off of hands. The teenagers shouted insults at the fanatics before us.

Later, Mari explained what we saw on TV. I learned that the 'security stops' Ben and I experienced during our trip were due to fear that this uprising in Mali would spread. Suspicious individuals, or anyone showing the least support for the Salafists, were quickly rounded up. Not only did these terrorists threaten the Mauritanian government, but they appalled Mauritanians, as the majority practiced a Sufi form of Islam that the Salafists abhorred.

The result is a region in deep turmoil, with terrorist activities spreading. A Nouakchott Fulbe friend told me he always keeps his gas tank full so that on a moment's notice, he can bolt should such fanatics invade.

Once home, I read up on the Salafists in Mali, and learned of their spreading influence across the entire Sahel. Now I see it is not just the region's few resources that cause conflict, as was true in my day: it is also the hearts and minds of the region's isolated and vulnerable inhabitants. While domestic politics have calmed, the international ones now threaten. And a history of conflict continues.

Epilogue

I write from my desk in Tacoma during a cheery spring day. Ceeɗu has arrived in the Fuuta. The Islamic calendar has once again come full circle, as it is also Koorka, the month of fasting. I check my phone app. Midnight in Civé and still 100 degrees. Tomorrow will be 117 degrees. May Allah have mercy on them.

***

In many ways small and big, Civé and its people remain with me. I often check the weather in Matam. I message the kids and extended family members of Mamadou, Djeinaba, Amadou Demba, and others. I send gifts and record greetings at Koorka and Tabaski. I occasionally call Samba and Abou in Columbus to get caught up.

I recall a particular day shortly after I first arrived in Civé. The sky was smoky grey, and a steady northwest wind had me shielding my face from sand and dust. I was balancing along Cóndi Hiraande's diggettes, trying to avoid stepping on painful cracks lining the sides of my heels. Looking out across the cooperative's bewildering state of affairs, I listened without comprehending to the conversations swirling about. So much seemed wrong. I thought long and hard about what exactly was amiss, and what I could possibly do to remedy it. Yet all I could come up with was tradeoffs. This is a basic concept in economics. As true everywhere, life in Civé was marked by tradeoffs. But here, the choices people faced were not background noise that slips beyond the filter of conscious thought: they stared me in the face as they ground people down.

Yes, the canals were horribly inefficient, but I couldn't quite tell people to spend weeks of hard labor fixing them. For what? Two dollars off their SONADER bill? I could understand why there were so many young kids swinging a jalo rather than scribbling with a pen. Even to me it wasn't clear what value there was in attending the barren supply-less classroom which often lacked an instructor. The kids' worth in the fields, on the other hand, was present in each day's lunch bowl.

I eventually realized that for the most part, villagers in Civé did the best they could with the resources they had and the incentives they faced. Djeinaba stayed by Tall's side when women's affairs called, Amadou Demba didn't take his dying daughter to the hospital, Sira Sy wouldn't go to see the French doctor about a cure for her blindness, my Rosso parents kept their mad daughter chained to her cell, and members of Cóndi Hiraande chose to skip meetings and leave their canals in shambles. While I often agonized over such choices, I came to understand them, and even sensed that if I were in their shoes, I'd probably make them myself.

That is a key insight of economics, one college planted into my brain, but Civé wove into my heart. Today I trace my identity as a professional economist to that windy day atop those narrow diggettes; amidst the chaos before me, I was beginning to realize that everyone in this village was engaged in the universal endeavor of coping.

Yet I also came to see the tragic decisions that villagers faced. For instance, there weren't good options if you needed credit, and anyone who borrowed did so at great cost. Unfortunately, some lenders used their lopsided bargaining power to extract not just money, but a bit of your soul. You saw that in the village's pecking order.

The logic of "giving up your kids" also became understandable as doing so could make sure they (and you) could eat. Or the choice of going to the fields with a toothache that left your body throbbing and face radiating pain: there was no sick leave in this village and staying home to calm your pain was a costly option, if an option at all. It was just hard for anything to compete with immediate needs; even prioritizing the high cost of a mosquito net, your barrier against the deadly malaria parasite, was hard when any longer-term benefit from the purchase may never come.

I also came to see drawbacks in the interdependence that marked village economics, as it made relationships infinitely more complicated. One thing that puzzled me was the excess amount people paid because of the way they bought their food; for instance, a large daily dollop of tomato paste rather than a weekly can of it. But eventually I came to see that if you bought the whole can, everyone would know it and your name would be mud if you failed to dole out spoonfuls to all who asked. And that would be many. I gradually came to see how this interdependence also fed the village's stifling conformity, as social disapproval comes with high costs, and was accordingly very effective at keeping everyone in line. All in all, the ability to live the independent lives we cherish in the west comes not from our character or culture, but from the institutions and wealth that people like those in Civé lack.

Did my time in Civé make me a better person? More humble, more able to understand others, more cognizant of the ways in which people are both different and similar? Maybe. But looking back, I can see I wasn't all that tolerant of the Peace Corps staff, or government officials who drank tea and toured in air-conditioned vehicles instead of doing their job. In some ways, I think Civé made me even less tolerant. I try to channel Mamadou, who lived by his adage of "work doesn't end but time does."

The personal crises that were a part of my life in Civé, often leaving me distressed, adrift and swimming to Senegal, should have taught me the wisdom of reaching out to others, instead of strengthening my tendency to rely on self.

For sure now I'm more cognizant of my own privilege as a white American, one I felt acutely each time I saw the doors in Nouakchott swing open for me, or while heeding Mamadou's call for my white face to join him in some complicated mission. I try to continue using my privilege to help those in Civé and elsewhere.

With my help, three from Civé came to the U.S. and are now Americans. In addition to Mamadou's two sons Samba and Abou, I sponsored a young man who as a boy had raced on horseback to Matam as Civé's men were being shepherded away from the village. A few months ago, I tried to sponsor a fourth. I was on the phone pleading with a Homeland Security officer for something called an "A number." This number was what I needed to locate Hamidou, the son of my old friend Sadyo Konaté whose body had given out a few years earlier.

"No. That number is private. Your friend must give it to you," the officer said in response to my request.

"But I can't reach him without it," I explained. "And he needs money to call me."

"Sorry." As with my previous calls, the line went dead.

Hamidou was a man in his thirties who had been tortured back home. I didn't know the details of what caused his flight, although I knew he had just completed a dangerous and very expensive backdoor journey from Mauritania to Texas. He surrendered himself at our border and was now in some ICE facility. To locate him, I needed his Alien number—"A" number in detention lingo.

But this wasn't easy as I didn't know Hamidou's exact name. Pulaars can identify themselves in dozens of different ways, depending on the purpose and audience. And then there is the spelling: Djeinaba, Jeneba, Dieneba, or Djeineba? Hamidou, Hamidu, Hamadu, or Hamady?

Finally, I remembered that months earlier Hamidou had texted me his full name. Now I understood why. If I had known this young man, maybe I would have remembered that text. But I had never met him. I recall that afternoon in 2012 out in Becce's fields when I had spied his father, Sadyo Konaté, tending to Becce's lone rice field. After I joined him, I remember Sadyo telling me that he had sent his sons, including this one, to school in the capital.

"They are smart boys," he had said with a crooked smile reminding me of the past. "But," he added, "it is hard. Life is not fair to us black people."

It was Sadyo I knew, not Hamidou. I thought of Sadyo, not Hamidou, as I watched over Hamidou's journey my way until he crossed into my land. The reciprocity of human relationships across the generations, decades, and oceans.

Eventually I found Hamidou. But ICE doesn't make it easy or convenient. Nor cheap. Phone calls were $5 per minute, plus another take from my credit card company even if, as frequently happened, we were disconnected. I hired a lawyer to help with Hamidou's case. She was good at conveying the drama of his situation, but less effective at giving him the legal knowledge he needed to negotiate the complicated legal processes designed to send him home.

And so, Hamidou's application for asylum was denied. My country has since removed him back to the country that tortured him.

Sadyo was right. Life is not fair. An awareness of the deep inequalities that shape our own privileged lives as well as those in places like Civé, is one that my time in Civé left stitched into my heart.

***

One of the first landmarks that someone entering Civé from the west encounters riverside is a surprisingly shady spot covered by neem and gawdi trees spared from the axe. During that last trip to Civé, I visited this spot. It is a sacred piece of land, the village cemetery for Civé's Bambara population, a place where Mamadou now lays beneath an oversized white tombstone bearing his name.

He lies there alongside other descendants of the Bambara, Mande, Wolof, Mandinka and more who once fled their homes to the east for the refuge of Civé. Djeinaba took me there, opening the creaky iron gate so that we could enter.

What first struck me was the location of Mamadou's grave, arising smack in the middle of the cemetery, the other markers seemingly gathered around, slightly leaning his way. Happenstance or design?

I stood above Mamadou's fresh tombstone, quiet while Djeinaba wandered silently among the others. *The people speak your name, Mamadou.* To me this summed up the sentiment guiding his life, his eye always gazing toward the future.

Djeinaba circled back, and the two of us continued some 100 yards uphill to another shady spot where lay the descendants of other, higher-caste Civéans—including Djeinaba's father, her uncle Kalidou, my 'father' Samba Ba, my neene Taanooy, Sira Sy and Awdy Ba, and now Sala and Doro Thioub—those whose ancestors welcomed the Bambara and their kinfolk to the Fuuta over 100 years ago.

Those traditional distinctions appear less important in Civé today. Maybe it is partly to do with the village elders, some alive and many no longer, some Fulbe, some Toorodɓe, some fisherman, and some Bambara, who decades ago banded together to work for the village's future. Those were good times during difficult years, followed by worse. They were years that opened my eyes to the complexity of poverty in places like Civé.

The village and its people survived those difficult times, but no doubt can count on more. Their towering mango trees still dance in the wind, as they too survived. Every year, four months after thick clusters of yellow flowers burst open on trees lining the riverbank, Civé's residents still enjoy the sweet taste and extra cash their mango trees bring. My hope for Civé is that its future generations follow in the footsteps of those men of Becce and their extraordinary leader,

Mamadou Demba Konaté, so that their memory, like his, will remain alive, always.

One blustery afternoon during that visit, I walked past the village's new mosque and listened to the aging Thierno Ly, who at that time still lived, as he led the murmuring men in prayer. Another day I greeted a family, oversized pencil in the hand of one, as they planted millet in distant dieri fields. They asked my name, praised my family members, then gave a blessing for my safe return home.

Each day I drank tea, tea, and more tea, tasted the dusty air, smelled the tang of mud in the river, and picked thorns out of my slippers.

Each night I ate haako, heard the chirping of crickets and croaking of frogs, and marveled at the bright band of stars above.

At Becce I took in the watchful vantage of the large dounoube tree Baaba Njiia, the father who sees.

Before laying down at night, I bathed in the river, and could feel the presence of those river monsters.

If I have learned one thing, it is how the peculiarities of place can become forever entangled in one's soul.

Glossary

Apollo: Nickname for conjunctivitis. Comes from the confluence of a moon landing and a bad outbreak of the disease.

Baaba Njiia: "The father will see." Name of a forested area between Civé and Matam, and also the name given to a large tree at Becce where farmers gather.

Becce: "Chest." Name of one of Civé's two farming cooperatives.

Bidhan: Literal translation is "white" or "white Moor." Ethnic group of Arabic and Berber descent.

Boubou: Long, loose-fitting garment worn by men and women throughout West Africa.

Caangól: "Gully."

Caangól laddéegi: Name of the gully splitting the village of Civé in two.

Caali: Hangar, used to provide shade.

Ceeɗu: The hot season, begins in March and ends when the rains come in June or July.

Charet: French for cart, refers to a horse drawn cart used for transporting goods and people.

Cóndi Hiraande: "Flour for dinner." Name of one of Civé's two farming cooperatives.

Dabunde: The cool season. Begins in November and ends in March.

Dawol: "Obligatory work day."

Dieri: Sandy lands beyond the Senegal River's flood plains, used for grazing animals and growing rain-fed crops.

Dinndeere: An all-purpose raised platform made of trunks and branches or mud bricks. Attached to each dwelling, usually with a caali for shade.

Fartak: Name of the third cup of tea.

Fergo: "Migration."

Fósinaaji: Collective name of youth who study the Koran with a local Imam. Often seek alms and food by circulating about while chanting the Koran.

Fulbe: One of two noble classes in Pulaar society. Historically have been herders, and are the original inhabitants of the Fuuta. Their kin are spread throughout the West African Sahel.

Fuuta: "Country." Name Pulaars use to describe their homeland of the mid-Senegal River basin.

Haako: Dinner meal made with stewed bean leaves and served over couscous.

Hajj: Pilgrimage.

Haɲaabe: "Crazy". Plural of Kangaado.

Haratin: "Black Moor," members of Moor society whose black African ancestors were enslaved by Bidhan Moors. Historically served as servants and laborers for Bidhan masters. Many Haratin in Mauritania remain in servitude relationships with Bidhan.

Jalo: Agricultural tool, similar to a hoe with a short handle.

Jom galle: "Husband," literally "master of the household."

Jom suudu: "Wife," literally "master of the room."

Jom wuro: "Village chief," literally "master of the village."

Juulde Koorka: Day after Ramadan (Koorka) ends.

Kaaw: "Uncle." Used to convey respect for an older male.

Kangaado: "Crazy." Used to denote someone with mental disabilities, or to say someone is temporarily "nuts."

Kinidi: "Kennedy." Food aid, named after President Kennedy.

Koorka: The Islamic month of Ramadan when people fast.

Liwoogu: "Manatee."

Lowwol: The first cup of tea.

Luugal: A very large pencil-shaped instrument used for punching holes in hard clay pan soil.

Marabout: A holy man.

Matla: "Mattress."

N'dungu: The rainy season. Begins in June or July, and lasts until around September.

Neene: "Mother."

Ouguiya: Name of the Mauritanian currency.

Pagne: French for wrap around skirt that goes to the ground.

Pawgol: "A fine."

Préfet: French term for high official in regional government. Governor.

Saani: Second cup of tea.

Sahel: Semi-arid region just below the Sahara Desert, stretching from the Atlantic Ocean to the Red Sea.

Satala: "Kettle." Found in every household, used for holding water for ablutions or the call of nature. Usually made of aluminum.

SONADER: French acronym for The Mauritanian Ministry of Rural Development (Société Nationale pour le Développement Rural). Charged with promoting rice cultivation.

Thierno: "Imam."

Tidjianism: A Sufi order originating in northern Africa in the 1700s, which subsequently spread to West Africa and the Sahel. Known today as the Brotherhood of Tidjiani, with various spellings (Tidiane, Tidjane, Tijānī, Tijaniyyah), it is the largest Sufi order in West Africa.

Toorodɓe: One of two noble classes in Pulaar society. Historically, educators and religious leaders.

Tubaak: Name for white people throughout West Africa.

Tufam: A drink made from soured yogurt-like milk and sugar.

Waalo: The fertile mud flats created by deposits from an overflowing Senegal River, especially valuable because they can support two agricultural seasons.

Yahre: "Scorpion."

Acknowledgements

This book took numerous years to write, and along the way I was fortunate to have the help of many. Some ten years ago, Anne Beaufort, Michael Kula, Justin Wadland, Pat O'Callahan, Margaret Lundberg, David Morris, Dave Corbett, Turan Kayaoglu, and Mary Hanneman read what was then a very rough short draft, and encouraged me on. Several hundred pages later, Amara Holstein worked wonders with a first full draft, sharpening story lines and developing themes from what can only be described as an avalanche of material. The final version benefited from the editorial expertise of Kiele Raymond, Ingrid Emerick, and Gary Smailes. I owe a special shout out to Rachael Herron; after years of producing what seemed to be endless drafts, her keen eye and warm support finally convinced me I was done.

Many others supported this project, not least of whom was my head cheerleader and mom, Mary Ann Knerr; her carefully filing of my letters and photos made this story possible. Mary Hanneman was always available for discussion and advice. James Corbett read a draft, and some lighthearted passages are the result of his pen. Thanks to Dave Corbett for the space needed to write this book. Olivia Snell did a great job with the map in this book. I am especially grateful to Kevin Atticks and Apprentice House Press for choosing to publish my story.

I am deeply sorry that my friend Amadou Mamadou Djigo was not able to read this tale of his childhood village; among other things, I owe him thanks for his own book about Civé, one which revealed to me unknown and helpful parts of its history. After Djigo's untimely death, Adama Gnokane kindly stepped in to discuss Pulaar culture, language and history with me.

I owe many many Mauritanians deep thanks for their hospitality and friendship over the years. My neene the late Taaynoi Ba and her husband the late Samba Ba; my neighbors the late Harouna Sarr and Maimona Diaw, and their son Hamidou Sarr; Djeineba Deh and her husband Yahya Tall; the late Sala Athioy Ba and her daughter Aissata Baidy; Malaaɗo Kamara; Amadou Demba Kamara and his wife Oumou Sy; Mamoudou Kebe; Fadima Diallo; the late Sadyo Konaté; Wourri Kebe; Souleyman Konaté and his wife Aissata Barry; Athia Diaw; Fati Diallo; the late Kadjiatou Demba Diop; the entire Deh family; the late Awdy Ba and Sira Sy, and their son Amadou Ba (called Moussa in this book); Mamoudou Saloum N'Diaye and Faba Barry; the late Demba Ba; Mari Konaté and his wife Boye Keita; and the formidable Moussa Maladel, otherwise known as Ballal. A very special thanks go to Samba Konaté and his wife Oumou Sy for their warm hospitality, and to Samba's younger brother Abou. Both Samba and Abou embody the best features of their father, the late Mamadou Demba Konaté, the person to whom I owe the most thanks.

About the Author

Katie Baird is a Professor of Economics at the University of Washington Tacoma. Author of the book *Trapped in Mediocrity* (Rowman & Littlefield, 2012), she specializes in public economics and public policy. For three years she wrote bi-weekly columns on public affairs for Washington State's second largest newspaper, and also held an elected office in Pierce County. Katie lives in Tacoma with her husband Dave and dog Kea.

Apprentice House Press
Loyola University Maryland

Apprentice House is the country's only campus-based, student-staffed book publishing company. Directed by professors and industry professionals, it is a nonprofit activity of the Communication Department at Loyola University Maryland.

Using state-of-the-art technology and an experiential learning model of education, Apprentice House publishes books in untraditional ways. This dual responsibility as publishers and educators creates an unprecedented collaborative environment among faculty and students, while teaching tomorrow's editors, designers, and marketers.

Outside of class, progress on book projects is carried forth by the AH Book Publishing Club, a co-curricular campus organization supported by Loyola University Maryland's Office of Student Activities.

Eclectic and provocative, Apprentice House titles intend to entertain as well as spark dialogue on a variety of topics. Financial contributions to sustain the press's work are welcomed. Contributions are tax deductible to the fullest extent allowed by the IRS.

To learn more about Apprentice House books or to obtain submission guidelines, please visit www.apprenticehouse.com.

Apprentice House
Communication Department
Loyola University Maryland
4501 N. Charles Street
Baltimore, MD 21210
Ph: 410-617-5265
info@apprenticehouse.com • www.apprenticehouse.com

CPSIA information can be obtained
at www.ICGtesting.com
Printed in the USA
BVHW030813270922
648045BV00007B/158